Giustina Selvelli

The Alphabet of Discord
The Ideologization of Writing Systems on the Balkans since the Breakup of Multiethnic Empires

BALKAN POLITICS AND SOCIETY

Edited by Jelena Dzankic and Soeren Keil

2   *James Riding*
    The Geopolitics of Memory
    A Journey to Bosnia
    ISBN 978-3-8382-1311-8

3   *Ian Bancroft*
    Dragon's Teeth
    Tales from North Kosovo
    ISBN 978-3-8382-1364-4

4   *Viktoria Potapkina*
    Nation Building in Contested States
    Comparative Insights from Kosovo, Transnistria, and Northern Cyprus
    ISBN 978-3-8382-1381-1

5   *Soeren Keil, Bernhard Stahl (eds.)*
    A New Eastern Question? Great Powers and the Post-Yugoslav States
    ISBN 978-3-8382-1375-0

6   *Senada Zatagic*
    A Neglected Right
    Prospects for the Protection of the Right to Be Elected in Bosnia and Herzegovina
    ISBN 978-3-8382-1521-1

7   *Aarif Abraham*
    A Constitution of the People and How to Achieve It
    What Bosnia and Britain Can Learn From Each Other
    ISBN 978-3-8382-1516-7

8   *Giustina Selvelli*
    The Alphabet of Discord
    The Ideologization of Writing Systems on the Balkans since the Breakup of Multiethnic Empires
    ISBN 978-3-8382-1537-2

Giustina Selvelli

THE ALPHABET OF DISCORD

The Ideologization of Writing Systems on the Balkans since the Breakup of Multiethnic Empires

Bibliografische Information der Deutschen Nationalbibliothek
Die Deutsche Nationalbibliothek verzeichnet diese Publikation in der Deutschen Nationalbibliografie; detaillierte bibliografische Daten sind im Internet über http://dnb.d-nb.de abrufbar.

Bibliographic information published by the Deutsche Nationalbibliothek
Die Deutsche Nationalbibliothek lists this publication in the Deutsche Nationalbibliografie; detailed bibliographic data are available in the Internet at http://dnb.d-nb.de.

ISBN-13: 978-3-8382-1537-2
© *ibidem*-Verlag, Stuttgart 2021
Alle Rechte vorbehalten

Das Werk einschließlich aller seiner Teile ist urheberrechtlich geschützt. Jede Verwertung außerhalb der engen Grenzen des Urheberrechtsgesetzes ist ohne Zustimmung des Verlages unzulässig und strafbar. Dies gilt insbesondere für Vervielfältigungen, Übersetzungen, Mikroverfilmungen und elektronische Speicherformen sowie die Einspeicherung und Verarbeitung in elektronischen Systemen.

All rights reserved. No part of this publication may be reproduced, stored in or introduced into a retrieval system, or transmitted, in any form, or by any means (electronic, mechanical, photocopying, recording or otherwise) without the prior written permission of the publisher. Any person who does any unauthorized act in relation to this publication may be liable to criminal prosecution and civil claims for damages.

Printed in the EU

CONTENTS

PREFACE 11
ILLUSTRATIONS 17

1. INTRODUCTION 19
   1.1 The Balkan space between problems of multiplicity and claims of homogeneity 19
   1.2 The role of writing and of the "Other" in the national discourse 22
   1.3 Methodological considerations: sources and approaches 25
   1.4 Semiotic and relational aspects of alphabets and nationalism 28

SECTION I
ALPHABETIC DISPUTES OF THE 1920s AND 1930s IN BULGARIA 31

2. THE RECEPTION OF THE *ABECEDAR* PRIMER (1925) IN BULGARIA 33
   2.1 Issues related to the adoption of new writing systems .. 33
   2.2 Post-imperial national identity dynamics 36
   2.3 The situation in Aegean Macedonia after World War I .. 39
   2.4 The publication of the *Abecedar* (1925) 42
   2.5 Some peculiarities related to the characters of the *Abecedar* 45
   2.6 The "involvement" of Cyril and Methodius 48
   2.7 Conclusions: the fate of the *Abecedar* after 1925 53

3. THE "LATINIZATION" IDEOLOGY AND THE BULGARIAN DEBATES 59
   3.1 Introduction: issues of script change 59
   3.2 The Latinization ideology in the Soviet Union 60

3.3 The Latin alphabet as a "modernizing" tool in the Balkans 65

3.4 The positions in support of Latinization in Bulgaria 69

3.5 The positions in defense of Cyrillic: contextual and internal factors 76

3.6 Defensive and symbolic motivations rejecting Latinization 81

3.7 Technical imperfections of the Latin alphabet 88

3.8 Conclusions: the national character of the alphabet 92

4. **THE CONTRAST BETWEEN ARABIC AND LATIN SCRIPTS AMONG THE BULGARIAN TURKS 95**

4.1 The impact of the Eurasian alphabet reforms on Turkey 95

4.2 The ambivalent status of the Latin alphabet in Bulgaria 97

4.3 Language and script restrictions for the Turks of Bulgaria 101

4.4 Conclusions: the disruption of writing practices 105

SECTION II
SCRIPT ISSUES IN THE "SERBO-CROATIAN TERRITORIES" IN THE INTERWAR PERIOD 109

5. **SERBO-CROATIAN IN TWO SCRIPTS: DIGRAPHIA, "ALPHABET SYNTHESIS" AND BILITERACY 111**

5.1 Linguistic and historical introduction 111

5.2 Post-war alphabet ideologies: four parallel trends 114

5.3 The influence of the "pro-Latinization" factors 116

5.4 The first proposals of "alphabet synthesis" appearing in *Život i rad* 122

5.5 The "Yugoslav alphabet" by Pavle Ž. Radivojević 127

5.6 Reactions to the "mixed alphabet" proposals 130

5.7 Živaljević's rejection of the Yugoslav alphabet and Trivunac's defense of Cyrillic.. 134

5.8 Conclusions: the developments of the alphabet question in Yugoslavia 139

6. **CYRILLIC AT WAR: SCRIPT IDEOLOGIES IN THE INDEPENDENT STATE OF CROATIA, 1941-1945 .... 141**

6.1 From unitarian ideologies to assertions of difference in the language field 141

6.2 The development of the language situation before the NDH 144

6.3 "Cyrillicide" in the Independent State of Croatia 147

6.4 Writing ideologies between purism and denialism 151

6.5 The "Orientality" of the Serbs and the role of the Glagolitic alphabet 154

SECTION III
FROM THE GLAGOLITIC REVIVAL TO THE NEW DISCRIMINATIONS AGAINST CYRILLIC IN CROATIA 159

7. **THE REDISCOVERY OF GLAGOLITIC: FROM REGIONAL TO NATIONAL PHENOMENON 161**

7.1 The new signification context of the Glagolitic alphabet... 161

7.2 The alphabet issue during the period of socialist Yugoslavia 162

7.3 The creation of the *Aleja Glagoljaša* in Istria and the role of Zvane Črnja 164

7.4 The rebellious and democratic character of Glagolitic . 166

7.5 The universal value of regional Istrian culture 170

7.6 The Glagolitic as a marker of continuity and prestige after the end of Yugoslavia 172

7.7 The institutionalization of the Glagolitic alphabet by the Croatian state 175

7.8 Glagolitic as a national symbol in an "exclusivist" sense 178

8. **THE MODIFIED STATUS OF CYRILLIC IN POST-SOCIALIST CROATIA AND SERBIA.................................. 185**

   8.1 Introduction: Issues of biscriptality................................ 185

   8.2 The first changes in the status of the Cyrillic alphabet 186

   8.3 The Serbian case: will bialphabetism survive? 190

   8.4 The destruction of allographic traditions 194

   8.5 Croatian reactions to the bialphabetic plaques in Vukovar 196

   8.6 The Serb minority in Croatia as the "Other" 201

   8.7 The relevance of the public writing context 204

   8.8 The multigraphic character of the Croatian writing tradition 206

   8.9 Conclusions: patterns of symmetrical differentiation... 209

SECTION IV
THE NEW CHALLENGES OF CYRILLIC IN BULGARIA IN THE NEW MILLENNIUM 215

9. **BULGARIAN CYRILLIC BETWEEN TRADITION AND MODERNITY: THE "KRONSTEINER AFFAIR".... 217**

   9.1 Introduction: the post-socialist ideological context in Bulgaria 217

   9.2 The first debates on writing issues in the late 1990s 220

   9.3 The origins of the "Kronsteiner affair" 223

   9.4 Bulgarian Cyrillic between "Europhilia" and "Russophilia" 226

   9.5 The issue of alphabetic coexistence in the European context of pluralism 229

   9.6 Cyrillic as a "communist" alphabet 232

   9.7 Bulgarian institutions against Kronsteiner 233

- 9.8 Further reactions in the periodical and scientific press 237
- 9.9 Moderate positions on opening to the Latin alphabet .. 242
- 9.10 Conclusions: open issues of transliteration 246

10. THE POPULAR DIMENSION OF THE CYRILLIC ALPHABET AND THE REDISCOVERY OF GLAGOLITIC 249
- 10. The "Kronsteiner effect" 249
- 10.2 Cyrillic and modern technologies 251
- 10.3 The link between Cyrillic and capitalism and the Bulgarian typefaces 253
- 10.4 The popularization of Cyrillic and the May 24 celebration 256
- 10.5 Conclusions: the revitalization of Glagolitic and "ethnogenetic" questions 260

11. FINAL NOTES 265
- 11.1 The relevance of the post-imperial and post-socialist factors 265
- 11.2 The symbolic dimension of the alphabet in the Balkans 268

12. LIST OF REFERENCES 273
- Primary Sources 273
- Official Legislative Sources 277
- Secondary Sources 278

PREFACE

This book examines a series of issues related to the use of alphabets in the construction of national identity in the Balkan region, with a special focus on Bulgaria and Croatia. It does so by following the spread of different ideologies related to writing systems over a period of about a hundred years (1918-2017). Through the comparative and diachronic study of the symbolism of the alphabet in its modern variants, this work aims to help shed light on relevant questions related to processes of nation building in the Balkans and the linguistic ("alphabetic") rights of ethno-linguistic minorities, focusing on the important relationships linking writing systems, culture and society. The analysis opts for a large time span in order to register the recurrence of significant elements in different socio-political contexts in both countries, mainly after moments of political crisis or powerful socio-cultural change.[1] The aim is not to endorse or discredit the truthfulness or legitimacy of particular cultural traditions or identity discourses, but to problematize the value of the alphabet as a cultural element on a symbolic level and, within the "national historical imagination," for the collective consciousness of a country (cf. Marinov 2011: 9-10).

The book starts with an introductory section (chapter 1) that explains the peculiarities of the post-imperial and post-socialist context in the Balkan Peninsula in terms of nation-building processes and the position of ethno-linguistic minorities. I then illustrate the importance of writing systems' symbolic dimension and describe the methodology for considering different "textualities." Finally, I comment on the disciplinary approaches I have applied to the investigation of this topic, referring to the anthropology of writing, cultural memory studies and semiotic approaches.

---

1   Although some of the controversies covered had precedents in nineteenth-century debates in which writing systems played an important role, this book will focus almost exclusively on the period 1918-2017. Moreover, it is important to note that this book is concerned with the topic of writing systems and thus approaches the question of language in a very restricted way.

Chapter 2 analyzes the debates that arose in Greece in the second half of the 1920s over the adoption of a Latin-based alphabet in place of Cyrillic for the language of the Slavophone communities in Aegean Macedonia. The issue is contextualized within the complicated Balkan and European scenario after the end of the First World War, when the issue of protecting the linguistic rights of ethnic minorities first appeared in international law. I then illustrate the specificity of the school primer *Abecedar*, which was produced for these communities in Aegean Macedonia in the local Slavic language but using a Latin alphabet, something contrary to the Slavic Orthodox beliefs of the population, and I analyze the reactions of various Bulgarian intellectuals such as Ivan Shishmanov and Lyubomir Miletich.

Chapter 3 examines the debates about the advisability of replacing the Cyrillic alphabet for the Bulgarian language with a new, Latin script that took place in Bulgaria in the early 1930s. I emphasize the importance of the Soviet context of Latinization, linked to the theories formulated by the Russian linguist Yakovlev about the substitution of all non-Latin scripts by the so-called *alphabet of the revolution*. The debate is reconstructed through the analysis of some texts from this period, in particular the report "Cyrillic or Latin: The Bulgarian Character," published in the journal *Bulgarian Book* in March 1930, which presents the opinions of representatives of the intellectual, graphic and political spheres on this issue.

Chapter 4 explores the issue of the problematic introduction of the Latin alphabet for the Turkish minority in Bulgaria following its adoption in neighboring Turkey in 1928. I explain why this event triggered anxieties in both the Bulgarian state and the more conservative strata of the local Turkish community, which affected the community's "writing" and linguistic rights. In this context, I analyze the attitudes towards the Arabic and Latin alphabets that led to the prohibition of the Latin alphabet for this minority in the Balkan country in the interwar period, in an unprecedented constellation of interests between the Bulgarian authorities and Islamic religious powers.

Chapter 5 describes the "alphabet context" in the Kingdom of Serbs, Croats and Slovenes, later the Kingdom of Yugoslavia, in the

1920s and 1930s. In particular, I consider the issue of "biscriptality" as the official language policy and connect it to debates about the possibility of making the Latin alphabet the sole writing system in the country. I then consider the texts of three authors who see a possible solution to the situation of parallel use of Latin and Cyrillic in the creation of a new *Yugoslav alphabet*, an artificial and mixed writing system containing the characters of both alphabets in equal proportion. Although these proposals were not taken into account by official policy, they resonated in the debates of intellectuals of the time, a fact I demonstrate by looking at the reactions of intellectuals, such as those of the eminent philologist Aleksandar Belić.

Chapter 6 addresses the issue of the so-called "cyrillophobia" towards the alphabet used by the Serbian population, by considering the pre-war context and illustrative cases of the laws prohibiting its use enacted during the years of the independent Croatian state, the Nazi puppet state during Second World War. This issue is inscribed in the context of the growing rejection by a part of the Croatian cultural and intellectual world of any idea of linguistic and orthographic union with its Serbian counterpart. I refer to several texts that downplay the value of the Serbian script tradition and, in contrast, glorify the uninterrupted history of Croatian writing. Finally, I briefly analyze the parallel rediscovery of Glagolitic, including the 1944 case of the Glagolitic inscription in Zagreb Cathedral.

Chapter 7 focuses on the role of the Glagolitic alphabet in Croatia from the 1970s onwards, when the monumental project of the *Glagolitic Alley* was built in the Istrian hinterland. The motif of Glagolitic as a "democratic" writing system is analyzed in depth through the texts of the writer Zvane Črnja, who worked to promote local Istrian heritage and territory. I then address the examples of the institutionalization of Glagolitic as an autochthonous symbol at the state level in the post-socialist period, when this script became a fully national one in the official discourse of the independent country.

Chapter 8 addresses the question of the changes in the status of the Cyrillic alphabet in Croatia and Serbia in the post-socialist moment. I show that, if on the Croatian side this script was subjected to various forms of "marginalization" in the public sphere, in Serbia it became the core of some official and nationalist discourses. To this end, besides the first signs of discontent towards the Serbian Cyrillic heritage in the country, I consider the episode of "anti-Cyrillic" protests in the city of Vukovar in 2013/2014 and contextualize it in the process of Croatian nation-building. I also focus on the legacy of biscriptality in Serbia and briefly mention the debates on the status of the Cyrillic alphabet led by some nationalist actors.

Chapter 9 analyzes the debates that took place in Bulgaria at the turn of the century, triggered by the so-called *Kronsteiner case*, and trace the latter's stages from the initial proposal of the Austrian Bulgarianist to introduce a Latin alphabet parallel to the Cyrillic one in the country. I interpret the polemic by looking at important issues of modernization and European integration that go hand in hand with conservative narratives about national identity in a sometimes contradictory way. In addition to the texts written by Professor Otto Kronsteiner, I present the reactions of representatives of the Bulgarian scholarly and intellectual world to the issue, as well as texts drawn from the wider public debate.

Chapter 10 illustrates a number of initiatives for safeguarding the Cyrillic alphabet in Bulgaria since the country's accession to the European Union (EU), initiated and supported by politicians, intellectuals and even ordinary citizens. I refer to important technical and practical matters related to the use of this script in the context of the Internet, and I examine the theme of the May 24 National Day celebrations and the contemporary ideological value of the Cyrillo-Methodian work (the creation of the alphabet) in the national discourse. In addition, I briefly mention the recent rediscovery of the Glagolitic alphabet in Bulgaria and its use for the purpose of "ethnogenic" affirmation by the right-wing political party *Ataka*.

All of these case studies share similar structural features, a fact that supports my hypothesis regarding the relevance of the alphabet in legitimating certain kinds of identity rhetoric in the context of sociopolitical turning points. At the same time, they substantiate the idea that alphabets represent an element of particular importance in the

Balkan world, intertwined with some "ethnosymbolist" (Smith 2009) identity dynamics active in the post-imperial and then post-socialist period of the affirmation of new political entities.

By looking at the rhetoric and ideologies of different countries in a longer-term perspective, this work does not aim to reduce the topic to a "unitary" or "monovalent" point, such as through simple oppositions and equations. Instead, by virtue of a broad comparative approach, I attempt to reconstruct the ideological background of individual historical-cultural contexts in which specific discourses and practices related to alphabets find their legitimacy. Based on a "relational" logic, such considerations uncover crucial contextual principles that need to be taken into account in order to obtain a more complete vision of the intricate Balkan space at two critical moments in the history of the last century.

ILLUSTRATIONS

1. The *Abecedar* (1925) primer in Latin characters for the Slavic population of Aegean Macedonia, Greece.

2. Biliteracy practices in the Kingdom of Serbs, Croats and Slovenes: the 1924 book by T.K. Pogoreljski Peregud published in Zemun.

3. The monument to Saint Cyril and Methodius in Sofia, Bulgaria (source: author).

4. One of the few surviving examples of Ottoman Arabic public writing in Bulgaria, here in Plovdiv (source: author).

5. Commemorative marble plaque in Latin and Glagolitic in the town of Vrbnik, on the Croatian island of Krk (source: author).

6. Graffiti appeared in Zagreb against the erection of official plaques in Cyrillic in the city of Vukovar (source: Wikimedia Commons. Licensed under CC BY-SA 3.0, https://creativecommons.org/licenses/by-sa/3.0/deed.en).

7. Cyrillic Coca Cola label in Bulgaria during communism (source: socbg.com).

8. Official celebrations of the May 24 Day of Bulgarian Alphabet, Bulgarian Enlightenment and Culture festivity in Bulgaria, at Plovdiv University, 2013 (source: author).

1. INTRODUCTION

1.1 The Balkan space between problems of multiplicity and claims of homogeneity

Both the end of imperial rule in the Balkan Peninsula (Ottoman and Habsburg Empires) and that of socialism triggered complex cultural processes and political mechanisms, ushering in an era marked by the search for an "exclusive" national identity and by the clashes between the various nationalities that emerged from the ruins of the empires. During this period of upheaval, many cultural symbols and mythographies were deployed to meet the needs of modern nation-building processes, in order to create a more homogenous identity for the new nation-states, while many other elements were excluded from the prevailing rhetoric. Political and cultural elites undertook multiple operations of "rewriting" national history with the aim of restoring supposedly "pure" and "original" identities.

The implication was (and still is) that the true identity of the groups somehow lay in a past that had to be recovered: depending on the phase, this was a pre-imperial, medieval or pre-socialist past. In any case, it resided in an ethnically individual past characterized by glorious moments and precise, circumscribed markers of identity. The potential embodied by certain cultural traits was thus also evident at the ideological level: each successor state became much more national and homogeneous than it had been in the imperial period. The builders of the new nation-states in the Balkans continued to refer to the imperial past as a negative term of comparison, used "homogenizing" ideological tools, and often pursued discriminatory policies towards minorities.

More than a century after 1918, it is still useful and appropriate to study the politics of nation-building in the Balkan countries by taking into account the post-imperial context of their history at the political, cultural and ethnic levels, as this is an important aspect in the development of specific discourses of identity. In relation to their dynamics of "self-representation," many countries in Southeast Europe (including Turkey) still seem to be applying a perspective that minimizes internal ethnic differences and the history of diversity that has shaped them for centuries. They prefer to affirm instead a unified and homogeneous vision of the nation that ideally makes them more similar to the countries of the West to which they aspire to belong and towards which they harbor a kind of inferiority complex that could never be fully appeased. Such notions of homogeneity, on the other hand, favor greater control of the state and national discourse over the population, whose potential diversity could endanger the ideal stability and historical mythography constructed in a largely mono-ethnic sense.

On the path of nation-building and identity reconstruction, the countries of the region availed themselves of various rhetorical strategies in public discourse, strategies which concealed the various existing identity ambiguities (mainly in the form of minorities) that could sound a discordant note in the idea of a direct correspondence between ethnic, linguistic and religious identities (Ivanov 2007). Hence, even after a number of years, there was still resentment within the Balkan majority groups against certain minorities (and their cultural elements, including language and alphabet), to whom the characteristics of "enemy" and "foreigner" were attributed. Not surprisingly, this phenomenon also characterized the post-socialist period, when countries had to resort to a new rhetoric of identity based on discourses of the "distinction" and "continuity" of their historical and cultural existence, in which elements such as the alphabet played and continue to play a crucial role.

In Croatia, the problematic history in question corresponds to that associated with the presence of the Serb minority, which is a "disturbing" reality that re-actualizes a part of the past associated with the figure of the enemy. In Bulgaria, on the other hand, the unwanted history is perfectly embodied by the Turkish minority, which brings back into the present the Ottoman, Islamic and foreign past from which the national narrative still tries to distance itself. In both cases, the minority group in question is the majority in a neighboring country, one which has enjoyed greater power in the past and was feared precisely because of this, having been accused of engaging in underhanded collaboration with the independent nation's ethnic minority, as well as threatening renewed oppression and making territorial claims (Kymlicka 2002: 19-20).

These minority communities constitute a kind of Significant Other (Triandafyllidou 2003: 34-38), but in the negative sense, i.e. tabooed, troublesome, although indispensably part of an identity construction that uses the "Other" to affirm what one is not, to achieve a stronger affirmation of the nation and its values. As stated in the preface to *Entangled History of the Balkans. Volume 3*, a work that moves in a critical direction by attempting to deconstruct the individual historiographies (and mythographies) of the Balkan states:

> they tell more or less the same story with different actors — a long and illustrious history with remarkable continuity starting from ancient times; the deeds of a unique people who demonstrated an immense capacity to survive in difficult circumstances and in endless struggles with enemies; a people who, even after falling under brutal domination and suffering horrible losses in lives and territories, managed to resurrect themselves again and again. (Daskalov Vezenkov 2015: 1)

This description, then, could apply to any country in the region that suffers from a kind of "victim complex," whereby it experiences a conflicted and unresolved relationship with its past and carries the seeds of conflict into its present and potential future. These emotional aspects, which are at the same time subjectively experienced and collectively represented, have the power to trigger animosities and rigidities in large segments of the population, bringing to the surface traits of the past that people are still struggling to come to terms with.

Nationalism feeds on national myths (Đerić 2005), on ideas about a supposed historical continuity of identity that has remained unchanged in its essence over the centuries despite foreign domination and the multiple influences to which it has been exposed. The Balkan countries have invested a great deal in the (re)construction of specific narratives of their national history: no country in the region is an exception. National myths are largely tied to historical figures of great "mythopoetic" importance and to cultural elements of the greatest possible prestige, often claimed by several nations, in an exclusivist logic that is a fundamental feature of nationalism itself. In this context, it easily follows that the very idea of minority is problematic, as it can jeopardize the history and image of the nation as it has been propagated and conveyed since the beginning of the country's new post-imperial (or post-socialist) history.[2]

In this context, the decline of the Ottoman and Habsburg Empires can be put in relation with the development of the ideal of the nation-state in Western Europe, compared to which these state entities appeared anachronistic. Indeed, the "heterogeneous" legacy of the post-imperial states was largely incompatible with the ethnolinguistic model of the nation-state, as they were multiethnic, multilinguistic and often even multi-confessional territories (Dogo 1999: 10-15). The only type of identity that took its place was instead a nationalism based on the centralizing model of national unification of the eighteenth or nineteenth century, in which the diversity of identities found no room for legitimization (Hobsbawm 1997: 16).

1.2 The role of writing and of the "Other" in the national discourse

In the process of "positive identification" taking place in the countries of the region, consisting in selecting and highlighting all those cultural features that are perceived as prestigious and characteristic of the national community, the alphabet has proved to be a fundamental element. This is by virtue of the prestige it embodies in the eyes of an internal public that recognizes in it a history of continuity and distinction. Identification, however, is not possible without its negative aspect: the process of national self-definition has always been a process of differentiation from other nations, especially neighboring ones. In this respect, it is particularly relevant to analyze the attitudes propagated by national rhetoric towards the writing systems of the "Others." Indeed, in order to create its own

---

2   In relation to this, it is interesting to note the following: "In fact, minority nationalism in the Balkans is perceived solely as exclusive majority nationalism in an embryonic stage" (Ivanov 2007).

identity, each nation had to create its "antitype" from which to distinguish itself, since it is not enough to affirm who one is; it is equally important to define who one is not (Bugarski, 2009b: 106).

The relevance of the self-representational dynamics goes far beyond individual, social or cultural practices and acquires power at the political level, as these practices influence decision-making processes, the formation of public opinion, and hence the orientation of political parties themselves. Since nationalism presents itself as a "relational" ideology (Ivanov 2007: 2), it must be understood through the analysis of its context in the broadest sense, externally and internally, synchronically and diachronically. Discourses of identity in the region are still shaped by a specific notion of "foreignness" and, consequently, national rhetoric about the autochthonous writing systems has an impact on the construction of the image of the Other and on the role attributed to it as a possible obstacle in achieving a homogeneous vision of the nation. This factor also explains the interest in focusing on the search for origins, i.e. the ethnogenesis of the national people (Todorova 1996: 71), exploring the national past and distinguishing it as much as possible from that of the Other by insisting on certain features of symbolic differentiation.

The national writing tradition is sometimes used as genealogical "proof" when affirming the antiquity and continuity of the nation: historical facts that might undermine these ideals are thus downplayed or made part of a precise rhetoric of salvation, in a kind of teleological vision according to which the nation continued to fortify itself under the foreign yoke. Unsurprisingly, in the Balkan context, the countries that tend to glorify their linguistic and writing heritage are the same ones that somehow try to hide their contradictory relationship with part of their history, especially their minority communities. In the post-socialist context, EU candidate countries such as Croatia and Bulgaria were strongly pressured to adopt "Western" standards of multiculturalism and minority rights (Kymlicka 2002: 2-3). The interesting fact is that the history of these countries was permeated by conditions of multilingualism, multigraphism and the coexistence of different ethnicities and religions:

certainly, the historical interreligious and intercultural experience of Balkan countries like Bulgaria and Croatia is much more remarkable than that of more "mono-ethnic" and religiously homogeneous states like France or others in Western Europe.

Nationalism is certainly a phenomenon determined and shaped by political, economic and social factors, but it would be naive to overlook another fundamental factor, namely its social psychological component (Druckman 1994: 44): in fact, it is also experienced concretely and reiterated metaphorically on many occasions. This means that the individual is also involved in practices of weaving the symbolic imagery associated with collective identity. The nation is hence shaped by the interaction between different levels of power, in a kind of continuous negotiation between the discourses of elites and the responses of the majority, as well as the possible reappropriations of the former by a minority (see Smith 2009: 19). Individuals in a given national community carry and maintain feelings, beliefs and attitudes towards their own nation: these subjective factors in turn influence the value they ascribe to other nations, which may be seen as more or less related and close to their own, or even as threatening actors, or as enemies.

The emotional, social psychological aspects of nationalism largely explain the emergence of stereotypes, which are understood as widespread and shared representations of self and other, and are functional for the maintenance of a certain identitarian "status quo" (Druckman 1994: 50). Often, the group perceived as different from the majority remains trapped in a fixed, even anachronistic representational category; in the Balkans, we find many examples of the use of labels referring to the prejudices and conceptual categories of the past: the adjective "Turkish" as pejorative (cf. Jezernik 2010), "Chetnik" or "Ustasha," etc. This process is linked to continuous practices of "re-actualization" of specific values from a more or less distant past, which are functional to the construction and maintenance of the national image. With regard to understanding this phenomenon, it is particularly relevant to analyze the experience of a nation on a diachronic level and to look for analogies or differences in relation to situations from another, more or less distant, temporal context.

1.3 Methodological considerations: sources and approaches

Since this book focuses on issues of ideology and writing systems in the context of national identity construction, I intend to treat a number of different and heterogeneous textualities as objects of analysis. Although most of the examples I refer to are texts published by scholars and intellectuals who exercised some authority in the cultural discourse of their time, excerpts from literary works, as well as more widely disseminated media in the form of journalistic articles, are also considered. In addition, important official legal documents, state decrees, constitutional laws, and, albeit in a minimal way, the public space of "inscription," in the form of the "linguistic landscape" of official public signage, are taken into account.

My assumption is that the circulation of discourses relating to writing systems takes place at three quite distinct levels of operativity. The first is embodied by the primary source, that is, the official and bureaucratic structure that produces laws and public declarations on matters of writing, and is therefore the most original level and the one closest to the source of ideology, that is, power. At the second level, that of cultural dissemination, to which most of this book is devoted, we find the texts and monuments produced by exponents of the cultural intelligentsia and by public and cultural institutions: academies of science and language, eminent writers and artists, and to some extent the media. It is extremely useful to examine the role of these actors in proposing a particular image of the nation that is consistent (or not) with that of the official rhetoric. Finally, the third level coincides with the socio-anthropological dimension, which refers to the attitudes cultivated by the wider public towards the national discourse, implying a possibility of re-appropriation that is to some extent subjective.

In this book there are only very brief references to the properly subjective aspect of the question, while much more space is devoted to examining the role of popular culture in propagating certain identity messages associated with the alphabet, that is, the question of the transformation of discourse from official to popular. This component of the analysis is considered fundamental in demonstrating how the so-called "operative level" (Malešević 2002: 74-75) of ideology is propagated through a much more effective and direct discourse and language than the primary, official one. Therefore, the level of ordinary and (seemingly) spontaneous practice, a context that might seem detached from the first two, actually represents the most obvious and evident reflection of the penetration of official discourse into the daily life of large segments of the population (Malešević 2013: 120-154).

The main inspiration for the development of this research was provided by the illuminating insights offered by the field of the *anthropology of writing* as practiced by its most eminent representative, Giorgio Raimondo Cardona (1943-1988).[3] This branch of anthropology is the one that has so far paid more attention than any other to the symbolic, cultural and ideological aspect of writing systems (especially in: Cardona 1982, 1986, 2009 [1981], 2009a). It assumes that writing systems represent much more than a simple representation of sounds, bearing a fundamental symbolic dimension that is often underestimated, and which enables them to "emancipate themselves" from their linguistic context.[4]

Writing is understood as both a cultural and a social practice: written texts are central to culture conceived in the broad sense, which in turn is closely linked to society (Cardona 2009a: 64ff). The alphabet also proves to be a privileged site of symbolic production, becoming an effective means of reminding people who they are at the national collective level: in the Bulgarian and Croatian cases, as we shall see, this is fully expressed and linked to modern ideologies of state legitimacy. In the dissemination of identitarian rhetoric, the symbolic aspect of the alphabet plays an important role, stimulating

---

3 He also developed the fields of sociolinguistics and ethnolinguistics in Italy.
4 There is also the field of the so-called "ethnography of writing," which is closely related to the anthropology of writing. See, for example, Mancini & Turchetta 2014.

national consciousness and internal cohesion through the use of elements such as writing, which is conceived as an "identity and symbolic marker" (cf. Malešević 2004: 26). Intellectuals, legitimized by the political sphere (cf. Smith 2009: 84-86), can indeed make certain textualities and messages decisive in propagating certain forms of ideologies: in the cases analyzed in this book, they correspond to "script ideologies."

To understand how writing and written texts are produced and used by different actors in different contexts, we need to examine the values, beliefs and behaviors associated with different forms of writing (Barton & Papen 2010: 9).[5] For this reason, an important focus is placed on those who hold power over writing culture and on the ways in which they engage in broader identity practices by perpetuating specific national ideological discourses and visions about the nature of writing in a certain alphabet. Writing is linked to the ethnic question in a variety of ways and represents a space through which particular symbols are spread. Often, the "autochthonous" writing system represents one of these symbols and hence becomes doubly crucial in the so-called process of the "symbolic cultivation" of identity (Smith 2009: 48-49). The written word also determines the awareness of past times and is thus seen as equivalent to history, to the collective memory of society (cf. Assman 2011).

Writing has been skillfully selected and brought into the collective consciousness through a narrative in which the motifs of historical memory are often transformed into ideological elements aimed at legitimizing the existence of a specific national identity as

---

5   Certainly, even in countries using the Latin alphabet, there can be cases of disputes involving the spelling of the language. An important case is the opposition to the proposals in the 1990s concerning the modification of certain letters of the German alphabet (cf. Johnson 2005: 1-6). Furthermore, as far as Turkey is concerned, we can recall the value assumed by the three forbidden letters of the Kurdish alphabet in recent years in conjunction with the struggle for recognition of the Kurdish cultural identity in the country. Basically, it can be seen that, in a way similar to alphabetical changes, spelling reforms are not easily accepted, especially in the context of communities using highly standardized languages (cf. Gundersen 1977). However, spelling debates are generally quite different from script debates, where much more is at stake, with far more significant implications.

well as a kind of "political imagination" (see again Assman 2011: 111 ff.). Memory itself is exercised on a collective level through a process of symbolic cultivation; in the cases we will analyze, this corresponds to a "rhetoric of the alphabet" that feeds the collective consciousness and promotes the internal cohesion of the national community. In fact, the Bulgarians, but often also the Croats, claim to have become historically a nation only after the creation or adoption of their alphabet. The national historiographies of the countries of the region have thus contributed to revive a particular version of their history, focusing on very ancient times and making them the metaphor of a kind of exemplary "golden age" to be invoked in the era of national "rebirth" (Mishkova 2015: 271).

When dealing with issues related to writing systems, it is not possible to disentangle the latter from their most natural context, that of the language they convey. However, as has been pointed out (Sebba 2009: 35), sociolinguistics has not paid special attention to writing systems so far,[6] even though "writing systems have obvious connections with subjects of great sociolinguistic interest, like identity and ethnicity" (ibid.). As far as the sociolinguistic aspect of alphabets in the Balkans is concerned, scholars such as Ranko Bugarski (1997) and Robert D. Greenberg (2004) are important exceptions; they have shown the importance of issues of language and the alphabet in collective representations in the years before the collapse of Yugoslavia, during the conflict, and, later, in the process of the affirmation of the new nation-states that emerged from the war.

1.4 Semiotic and relational aspects of alphabets and nationalism

If we intend to consider writing systems as symbols of ethnic (and/or national) identity, we must necessarily note that symbols do not exist in themselves: rather, they represent "meanings" according to specific needs and intentions and for a particular

---

[6] One of the most important exceptions is Fishman 1977, a collection of studies devoted to various cases of alphabetical and orthographic reforms in languages from different parts of the world.

audience. Culture, conceived in the form of "webs of significance" (Geertz 1988: 11 [1973]), reveals itself in its essentially semiotic nature. Consequently, it can only be understood through an interpretive analysis that searches for the meanings it expresses for those who "inhabit" it. By applying this theory of a semiotic nature to the phenomena of the ideologization of alphabets, I attempt to understand the meaning that the various writing systems embody for their respective societies. Ideology itself, conceived according to the Geertzian theory, is but one cultural system with its own specific language to analyze.

Hence, in order to reconstruct a "framework of meaning" (in the semiotic sense; see Lotman 1985) for the societies in question, I insist on the need to take into account a plurality of contexts: national, socio-cultural, political (and geopolitical), international, as well as minority and even individual ones. The meaning of a given phenomenon can be deduced from the way it is positioned "systemically" (cf. Bateson 1977 [1972]) in relation to other semiotic objects: the (symbolic) meaning of certain events, phenomena and cultural elements thus corresponds to the position they occupy in the structure of their societies.

In this process, it should be noted how the historiographies of the Balkans turn out to be "still predominantly traditionalist and nationalist" (Daskalov & Vezenkov 2015: 1), perpetuating narratives that tend to overlook the contribution and role of neighboring countries in their history and cultural development, in a perspective we might define as "anti-contextual." For this reason, I have attempted to take a completely opposite perspective in this work, trying to combine as many elements as possible in an overall view to define the complex historical and cultural context of interest.

Indeed, I believe that on a methodological level it is essential to approach the history of Southeast Europe from a relational point of view, since much of this territory has followed a common historical pattern of development. It would be unnatural and counterproductive to isolate particular countries, nations or ethnic groups in the process of analysis: what is needed, therefore, is a contextual or "ecological" approach (cf. Barth 1969: 19), which can also bring advantages when applied at the linguistic level.[7] As has been remarked: "[i]t is only possible to understand the South Slav lands by paying attention to the context within which they are situated. The trajectory of their development needs to be explained in relation to wider processes, involving neighbouring states, the Mediterranean region, the continent of Europe as a whole and indeed the world" (Allcock 2000: 13).

---

[7] For example, in the consideration of the so-called "Balkan Sprachbund."

SECTION I

ALPHABETIC DISPUTES OF THE 1920s AND 1930s IN BULGARIA

2. THE RECEPTION OF THE *ABECEDAR* PRIMER (1925) IN BULGARIA

2.1 Issues related to the adoption of new writing systems

In the aftermath of the First World War and of the dissolution of the Ottoman and Habsburg Empires, the Balkans still stood out as a region characterized by high levels of cultural, ethnic, linguistic and "graphic" diversity. If we consider the number of scripts present in the peninsula at that time, we find almost ten different writing systems in use: Serbian and Bulgarian Cyrillic, Greek, Latin, *bosančica*, Arabic characters modified to write the Turkish, Bosnian, Albanian and Greek languages, traces of the Glagolitic alphabet, Hebrew characters to write the Judeo-Spanish language and Yiddish, and Armenian characters used by the Armenian minorities (cf. Zakhos-Papazahariou 1972: 146, Parmeggiani Dri 2004: 12). This phenomenon was not to be found in any region of Western Europe but was comparable to the situation in some parts of Central and Eastern Europe and must therefore be viewed as a feature of a highly diverse post-imperial world, for whose comprehension the conceptual tools derived from the history of the Western world reveal themselves often insufficient (Barkery 1997: 100).

The composite cultural and linguistic character of the region has been considered by some as an obstacle to harmonious development and progress (May 2013: 24). The nineteenth-century liberal John Stuart Mill, for example, stated in 1861 that "[f]ree institutions are next to impossible in a country made up of different nationalities (...) especially if they read and speak different languages (...) The boundaries of governments should coincide in the main with those of nationalities" (cit. in Edwards 2009: 189). Mill's opinion appears to have been largely undermined by a Western Eurocentric vision, based on a concept of the nation-state that has become more and more dominant since the 19th century. It could also be interpreted as the symptom of a sort of "orientophobia"[8] which applies reductionist criteria to the idea of civilization and to a certain extent fulfills the interests of domination. In fact, it is much easier to exercise political or even just "conceptual" control over a part of the world when it presents itself as linguistically, ethnically and confessionally homogeneous, and not jeopardized, as in the Balkans, by "[s]cores of tongues, dialects and religions," which determined a kind of "handicap of heterogeneity," as one observer affirmed (Roucek cit. in Bardos 2013: 27).

Unfortunately, the influence exerted on the socio-political development of the Balkan countries by this view of heterogeneity as an unwelcome "imperial remnant," capable of hindering the implementation of modern state structures, was immense (see, for example, Todorova 1996: 45-77). The peoples of the region, in fact, "internalized not only the geopolitical split between Western and Eastern Europe, but also the split between Europe and the Orient" (Bjelić 2011: 12). Becoming Westerners implied adopting both the values of the West and the stereotypes it nurtures of the East (ibid., 14). Predictably, this attitude produced various phenomena of "identity short-circuiting," characterized by persistent internal negations, suppressions and conflicts.

In this respect, it is interesting to note the influence of these Western-influenced concepts of identity on the development of alphabet ideologies. A paradigmatic case is that of Romania and its transition to the Latin alphabet after centuries of using the Cyrillic alphabet in the second half of the nineteenth century (cf. Lörinzci 1982). This was indeed a deliberate act of "rapprochement" with the European and Western world, probably also dictated by the hope of gaining important cultural advantages, and a more favorable recognition on the part of the "Significant Others"[9] of the West.

---

8   See on this topic the works *Orientalism*, by Edward Said (1978) and *Imagining the Balkans*, by Maria Todorova (1997).
9   The term "Significant Others" is used in social psychology to refer to those persons who are of sufficient importance in an individual's life to influence his or her emotions, behavior, and sense of self. The first definition of Significant Others dates back to the American psychiatrist Harry Sullivan in 1940. This term

In this context, consideration of the proposals to adopt alternative writing systems is an essential part of the analysis of alphabet ideologies. With regard to the languages of Southeast Europe, between the end of the 19th and the beginning of the 20th century, the adoption of new writing systems played a major role in the history and development of many states in the region, such as Romania (in the 1860s), Albania (1909) and Turkey (1928). The affirmation of a certain relationship of independence between writing and language (Wellish 1978: 41-44) set an important and momentous precedent: a language that had appeared in a particular alphabet could begin to be written at any time using another writing system, one that definitively replaced the previous one.

Against this background, the publication in 1925 of the so-called *Abecedar*, a didactic text intended for the Slavic-speaking population of Aegean Macedonia, led to a lively dispute involving Bulgarians, Serbs and Greeks, as well as members of the League of Nations. At the heart of the controversy was the fact that the text had been written in Latin rather than Cyrillic characters. The dispute over the *Abecedar* was the first opportunity in independent Bulgaria to discuss the question of whether or not to accept an alternative writing system for the national language. In this country, the condemnation of the Latin alphabet was accompanied by a passionate defense of Cyrillic. The testimonies of authoritative Bulgarian scholars of the time, such as Ivan Shishmanov and Lyubomir Miletich, who actively participated in the debate on the *Abecedar*, prove that the Cyrillic alphabet was seen by Bulgarian society as an indispensable element of the national identity, playing a pre-eminent role in the collective self-representation practices of the post-war and post-imperial (Ottoman) period. The traditional writing system, which joined the delicate political debate related to the "Macedonian question," was explicitly made part of a discourse about the country's national and historical identity, imbued with strong symbolic cultural contents and values.

---

can be used at the "macro level" in the study of ethnopsychology or "national psychology".

2.2 Post-imperial national identity dynamics

The collapse of the old multiethnic empires and the emergence of nation-states based on ethno-linguistic criteria, according to the principles of the model proposed by Woodrow Wilson, certainly did not exhaust the identity and ethnicity issues in the new successor countries (Keyder 1997: 41). Among the most important questions that arose after the First World War and the collapse of three multinational and centuries-old empires was certainly that of the status of ethno-linguistic and religious minorities in the new countries. After the First World War, a new legal entity, that of "national minority," emerged for the first time at the level of international law. It was not by chance that this delicate question became the subject of numerous publications during the period, dealing with it from a juridical and political point of view. One of the most significant is *The Protection of Racial, Linguistic and Racial Minorities* (*La protection de minorités de race, langue et religion*) by the French diplomat Jacques Fouques-Duparc, which appeared in Paris in 1922.[10] The concept of the new legal subject was difficult to integrate into the ideas of the nation-state that emerged during the independence struggles in the Balkans, and met opposition by the majority population in some countries, who believed that minorities living on their territory were subject only to national laws and should not enjoy concessions at the international level (Andreev Georgov 1926: 132).

In the new legal framework that recognized and established measures for the protection of minorities, special importance was attributed to the role of so-called "cultural rights," aimed at preserving the cultural features (including language and traditions) of a given minority community, acknowledging the natural instinct of people to pass on to their children the tradition in which they themselves were brought up (cf. Fouques-Duparc 1922: 31-34). In

---

10 Other publications of the period dealing with these issues are *La protection des droits des minorités dans les traités internationaux de 1919-1920* by M. V. Vishniak (1920), *Le problème des minorités devant le droit international*, by Jean Lucien-Brun (1923), *Les minorités, l'État et la communauté internationale* by Dragolioub Krstitch (1924).

connection with these rights, states had the obligation to fulfill three criteria: guaranteeing minorities the possibility of establishing and maintaining private associations and educational institutions; respecting the use of the minority language in the public schools; and, finally, providing the means of support for the education, ecclesiastical institutions, and charity work of the communities concerned.

A key role in managing the delicate process of transition in the post-war period was played by the League of Nations, the predecessor of today's United Nations, which was committed to taking effective measures to ensure real protection for minorities in various European countries. This condition was considered necessary and fundamental for the preservation of peace on the old continent (Shishmanov 1926: 3). The League of Nations judged that it would prove extremely problematic to control possible irredentism, which could prove dangerous to the stability of Europe itself, if national minorities were not granted the rights they sought.

In the post-war Balkan states, a problematic process of coming to terms with the Ottoman and Habsburg heritage was underway, requiring a necessary reckoning with the legacy of a multiethnic and multilingual society. However, this process mostly took the form of a denialist attitude, which in a sense embodied the negative counterpart to the positive relationship with modernity identified with the countries of Western Europe. The Balkan countries thus inherited the task of ridding themselves of what they perceived as a kind of "historical plague," an undertaking that proved extremely difficult (Bjelić 2011: 12). There was an obvious contradiction in this, as Europe itself imposed respect for minorities through its principles, justifying and legitimizing the presence of marginal and heterogeneous identities.

The new forces triggered by the emergence of national movements and nationalism had played a decisive role in the struggle for autonomy within the imperial multiethnic structure. These very often also determined important consequences at the level of religious organization, i.e. in the process of nationalization of the churches of the various states (see Palmieri 1913). Indeed, in the cases in question, the script controversies of the post-imperial period reveal the extent of the disintegration of the old Ottoman Christian Orthodox *millet*, the *Rum millet*. As a religious entity in control of ritual and practice, the *millet* had been in operation during Ottoman rule; later, the development of the Serbian and Greek national movements at the beginning of the nineteenth century encouraged a series of struggles to establish independent ecclesiastical organizations. These gave rise a few decades later to the autocephaly of the Greek Orthodox Church (1850), of the Bulgarian Orthodox Church (1870) and of the Serbian Orthodox Church (1879), which were gradually instrumentalized by their respective communities for political and national purposes (cf. Roudometof 2002: 84-85). Consequently, the idea of a commonality between members of Orthodox Christianity was gradually undermined by the emergence of particularist national interests of the new states.[11]

In this context, it is important to recall the close bond between writing systems and religion that was active in this part of Europe for centuries: more than the language itself, it was the alphabet that was associated with ecclesiastical culture, a fact that in turn led to its being perceived as particularly prestigious and authoritative. Thus, in the Bulgarian context, the Cyrillic alphabet represented a stable and visible element of its culture under foreign rule, expressed according to "ethno-religious" identity criteria. Nevertheless, in the Balkans, after the end of the Ottoman Empire, religion ceased to enjoy sole dominion over local cultures, being replaced by nationalist ideologies and new forms of collective identity construction inspired by the modern principles of the Western nation-state (see Garzaniti 2009). In most cases, the "nationalizing" forces drew their strength precisely from a revaluation and glorification of the (main) national language, which was elevated to the official standard and symbol of national unity (Todorova 2009: 178-179).

---

11 See Roudometof: "the Bulgarian crusade for a national church entailed a direct challenge to the whole Ottoman concept of administration, which identified nationality with religious confession. This was because the Bulgarians did not possess a state of their own (at least until 1878), and therefore there was no territorial political unit that could be directly linked to a Bulgarian church" (2002: 85).

Since the second half of the 19th century, numerous script and orthographic reforms had taken place, which often gained strong political significance: the linguistic element hence exercised, for the first time in modern times, a "secular" force and function within a national political program. However, as a consequence of a historical narrative shaped by "mythographic" intentions, both language and its writing system, having assumed this character, were in a sense transformed into "sacralized" elements, i.e. the cornerstone of the new national identity belief. Religious faith thus became political faith (Stantchev 2015: 130-131) and script choices consequently entailed new identity choices, in a process of nation-building that significantly weakened the original religious component of the writing systems in question.

2.3 The situation in Aegean Macedonia after World War I

In Bulgaria, the so-called "Macedonian question" was a source of bitterness since the Berlin Congress (1878) (cf. Miletich 1926), where a decisive blow was delivered to the country's national vision and imagination. Only a few months earlier, Bulgaria had seen its political unity with Macedonia acknowledged by the Treaty of St. Stephen, in line with the already existing cultural union under the aegis of the Bulgarian Church. After the ratification of this treaty, the conviction remained alive that the Bulgarian Church, together with the Bulgarian language, would remain the only safeguard for the nation, whose unity was threatened by the fragmentation imposed by external powers. The situation continued to develop to the disadvantage of the country with the Second Balkan War (1913) and then the First World War, when almost half of the greater region of Macedonia came under Greek control, to be followed by Western Thrace with the Treaty of Neuilly 1919 (Rossos 2008: 131).

Thereafter, a process of rapid Hellenization began in the region under Greek control, called Aegean Macedonia, determined by two conventions for the exchange of alloglottic populations: the Greek-Bulgarian in 1919 and, especially, the Greek-Turkish in 1923 (Rallo 2004: 17). Through the Treaty of Neuilly, signed at the end of the First World War, Greece and Bulgaria agreed to a voluntary population exchange: about 46,000 Greeks left Bulgaria, while 92,000 Bulgarians left the Hellenic state (Pentzopoulos 2002: 60). Subsequently, under pressure from the League of Nations and in accordance with the new Treaty of Sèvres (the peace treaty signed in 1920 between the Allied powers of the First World War and the Ottoman Empire), Greece was obliged to protect the ethno-linguistic minorities on its territory by providing an adequate education system in their mother tongue (Andonovski 1985: 2).

The Treaty of Sèvres guaranteed ethnic minorities in Greece the free use of their mother tongue in all spheres, and therefore the Greek state had to ensure the establishment of a budget for the development and operation of special schools for minorities. Article 7 of the same treaty also stipulated that all citizens on Greek territory, regardless of their ethnicity, language or religion, enjoyed the same civil and political rights as well as the free use of their language in private communication, in commerce, in religion, in the press and at public meetings (Article 7, Treaty of Sèvres). Article 9 clarified that in villages and districts populated by a majority of non-Greek-speaking citizens, the Greek government was obliged to provide adequate facilities to allow primary education in the minority's mother tongue (Article 9, Treaty of Sèvres).

Despite these stipulations, the educational question remained unresolved for a long time, since Greece was then struggling with serious demographic problems, during the war with Turkey, which caused the Asia Minor Catastrophe and the population exchange of 1923, bringing some 1.3 million people into Greek territory (see Pentzopoulos 2002). The Lausanne Convention of July 1923 ended the bloody Greek-Turkish conflict and established the borders between Greece, Bulgaria and Turkey (Kuševski 1983: 179). The arrival of a huge Greek population from neighboring Turkey led to the deterioration of conditions for the other minorities on Greek territory, including the Bulgarian minority in the region of Thrace and the so-called "Slavophone"[12] minority in Aegean Macedonia. This

---

12   I employ this term in a neutral way to identify the Slavic-speaking communities present in Greek territories in that period.

provoked a reaction from Bulgaria, which had already turned to the League of Nations in March 1923 with a request to intervene to protect the Bulgarian population in West Thrace, denouncing, among other things, the closure of Bulgarian schools and churches by the Greek authorities (Kuševski 1983: 181).

As a result of the negotiations conducted with the League of Nations and in the spirit of the Sèvres Agreement, the Politis-Kalfov Protocol for the protection of the Greek minority in Bulgaria and the Bulgarian minority in Greece was signed in Geneva on 29 September 1924 by the Greek and Bulgarian Foreign Ministers, in the presence of a representative of the League of Nations. Contrary to expectations, however, the Greek Parliament later refused to ratify the Protocol, and tried to disrupt visits by League of Nations officials to the areas of interest in Aegean Macedonia (Michailidis 2005: 95). Indeed, the Greek government feared that the Slavophone population, which, despite the assumptions of the Protocol, was not considered as belonging to the Bulgarian ethnic group, might "pretend" to be such in order to profit from this position and embolden Sofia to strengthen its claims and influence in the region. This about-face by the Greek government was the subject of another meeting of the League of Nations, which called on Greece to implement the agreements reached earlier (Kuševski 1983: 184).

In its letter of reply, the Greek government contested the right of the Bulgarian government to interfere in its internal affairs, claiming that the participation of Bulgarian representatives in the Mixed Greco-Bulgarian Emigration Commission did not confer on the Bulgarian government any rights over the Slavic population living in Greek Macedonia (ibid., 185).[13] The Greeks explained in a memorandum that they were confronted with the presence of various Slavic-speaking minorities rather than a single Bulgarian minority. It should be noted, however, that public opinion in the country was strongly against the recognition of any "Slavic" minority in Aegean Macedonia.

---

13   Cit. in Kuševski 1983: 187.

The League of Nations called upon the Greek government to meet the linguistic and educational needs of its minorities: as a consequence, Greece undertook to prepare textbooks and to appoint teachers for the education of the population concerned in its territories (cit. in Miletich 1925: 230). The next step, therefore, was to prepare a manual to serve as a reference for instruction. The *Abecedar* was printed in Athens in the summer of 1925, based on a hybrid dialect, a sort of mixture of the Florina and Prilep-Bitola varieties. The most important fact, however, is that it was written in Latin rather than Cyrillic letters: the alphabet used was based on Croatian *latinica*, to which some graphemes were added. This fact can be interpreted as a manifestation of Greek willingness to block further claims by Bulgaria and Serbia on the population in question, and thus to alienate their cultural influence through the highly symbolic use of an alternative writing system.

2.4 The publication of the *Abecedar* (1925)

The publication of the *Abecedar* by the Department for the Education of Foreign-Speakers in the Greek Ministry of Education in the autumn of 1925 was widely reported in the Greek press. Nikolas Zafiris, a publicist and specialist on Balkan issues, judged it an "extraordinary event" (cit. in Andonovski 1985: 4) in the life of minorities in Greece. In the daily *Free Tribune* (*Eleftero Vima*) of 19 October 1925, Zafiris wrote:

> We have prepared the *Abecedar* for the Slavophones, which was compiled with care and good intention by the Greek specialists Papazahariou, Sagiaksis and Lazarou [...] The primer is intended for use in the schools that will soon be opened in Greek Macedonia and Western Thrace for the Slavic-speaking population. This primer will be used to teach the Slavophones in Greece. The *Abecedar* is printed in the Latin alphabet [...]. (cit. in Andonovski 1985: 4; my translation)

As expected, news of the publication of the *Abecedar* caused quite a stir in Bulgaria, sparking outrage over what was perceived as an affront to the country's national identity and a new attack aimed at undermining the cultural unity between Bulgarians and Macedonians. With regard to the above-mentioned cultural rights, it can be said that, since in the Bulgarian national vision the authoritative cultural tradition was perceived as linked to the linguistic and written heritage (cf. Dečev 2014: 11), these rights were to some extent "alphabetic rights." In this sense we can understand the Bulgarian desire to protect Cyrillic in the communities of Greek Macedonia, as well as later (as we shall see in the next chapter) in the country itself.

There were many Bulgarian expressions of indignation. The pro-government newspaper *Word* (*Slovo*) called the appearance of this primer "a triumphalist cynicism" (Shishmanov 1926: 4). In an article published on 10 October 1925, the newspaper *Democratic Alliance* (*Demokratičeski Sgovor*) noted that the primer produced by the Greek Ministry of Education was the first act of a "farce full of comic elements," which turned out to be not funny at all, since the whole subject was "infinitely tragic and serious" (ibid., 5). This manual was also described as a provocation to the League of Nations itself, which was called upon to monitor the rights of minorities (ibid.).

Similarly, in an article published 17 October 1925, the Macedonian youth organization, in its newspaper *Impetus* (*Ustrem*), described the *Abecedar* as "a shameless monument to the barbarism and political arrogance of our democratic century, a diabolical and vile invention of Greek Bulgarophobia, the fruit of strong subtle calculations, germinated in a very lucid mind and in one of the murkiest of consciences" (cit. in Shishmanov 1926: 6; my translation). In autumn 1925, the Bulgarian delegate to the League of Nations, Dimitar Mikov, was given permission to report on what he saw as the Greek government's negligence to comply with the needs of the Bulgarian minority, which continued to be denied access to educational institutions in its mother tongue. Mikov drew attention primarily to the primer itself, "a work of dubious respectability which made a very bad impression in Bulgaria" (cit. in Tramontano 1999: 323; my translation).

The publication of this primer in Latin letters irritated not only the Bulgarian government, but also that of Nikola Pašić in the Kingdom of Serbs, Croats and Slovenes. In particular, Pašić reacted by claiming that the Slavic population in Aegean Macedonia consisted of Serbs, a fact which legitimized his defense of the minority rights in this region (Kuševski 1983: 187). The thorny situation in Greece also became an object of interest for the League of Nations, and the petitions of the Kingdom of Serbs, Croats and Slovenes concerning the "Serb minority" in Greece, in the words of Director Erol Colban, added confusion to the complex mosaic of this Balkan region (ibid.).

In this context, it was quite clear that Greece had not acted sincerely towards its Slavic-speaking minority, especially because of the choice of the writing system in which this population was to be taught. A document from the archives of the League of Nations in Geneva[14] illustrates the Greek position in a letter written to Colban on 10 November 1925 by Vasilis Dendramis, representative of the Greek government to the League of Nations (Filipov Voskopoulos 2006: 53-54).[15] In it, Dendramis defended the decision to adopt the Latin alphabet for writing this language, justifying it on the basis of the positions of Slavicists such as Pavel Jozef Šafárik, Kuzman Šapkarev, Stojan Novaković, Vatroslav Jagić and others. In another document we also read that a linguist called O'Mologni, of the Secretariat of the League of Nations, spoke in support of the Cyrillic alphabet, explaining that the decision of the Greek government to adopt the Latin alphabet was connected with national reasons (ibid.). In fact, the motivations for this script choice are to be sought in political dynamics, certainly not in educational or orthographic ones: the adoption of an alternative writing system could serve as a defense against "Slavic" interference, with which the Cyrillic alphabet was associated, i.e., Bulgarian and Serbian propaganda, which, in the Greek view, to some extent threatened its sovereignty over Thessaloniki.

On 18 October 1925, a Greek army detachment crossed the Greek-Bulgarian border at the village of Petrich in Bulgaria. This event, called the Incident at Petrich, gave rise to a revival of the dispute

---

14 Cited in the preface to the third edition of the *Abecedar* in 2006.
15 Cited document: United Nations Library and Archive Geneva, R. 1975, Doc. No. 41/47674/39349.

over the *Abecedar* in the Bulgarian press, which unanimously condemned the appearance of this school manual, describing it as "a document of political hypocrisy and a mockery of the principles of national minorities proclaimed by international treaties and the League of Nations" (Shishmanov 1926: 1). These reactions were joined by those of two eminent scholars: Ivan Shishmanov and Lyubomir Miletich, important representatives of the Bulgarian academic world: the first a renowned philologist and folklorist, the second a distinguished linguist and ethnographer. Both received a copy of the *Abecedar* in the autumn of 1925, studied it carefully, and arrived at their considerations based on the complete original text. The result was a scientific review of the *Abecedar* published by Miletich in *Macedonian Review* (*Makedonski Pregled*), the journal of which he was editor, and a pamphlet published in French by Shishmanov in January 1926 entitled *The Primer for the Use of the Bulgarian Minorities in Greece* (*L'abécédaire a l'usage des minorités bulgares en Grèce*).

2.5 Some peculiarities related to the characters of the *Abecedar*

The *Abecedar* was a text of forty pages: the first part corresponded to the primer proper, in which the letters were illustrated by pictures and examples; in the latter half some parts of speech and eight short reading texts were presented. Since, as mentioned above, the Greek government defended the position that the Slavophones in Greece were neither Bulgarians nor Serbs, but rather a specific nationality, the committee working on the primer opted for a variant of Croatian *latinica*, thus rejecting both the Bulgarian Cyrillic alphabet and the Serbian Cyrillic alphabet reformed by Vuk Stefanović Karadžić. The Latin alphabet used for the manual consisted of 29 letters, two of which were digraphs. Two of the characters devised by the commission were unique and corresponded to phonemes not represented in the modern Macedonian alphabet of 1945: the <î>, for the Bulgarian mid back unrounded vowel <ъ>, and <ü>, which indicated the palatalization of the previous consonant.

Miletich pointed out that the letter <ü> was introduced to indicate the sound corresponding to the Bulgarian Cyrillic letter <ю> (Miletich 1925: 230), as for example in the word *lülka* (люлка in Bulgarian — swing). The scholar rightly remarked that the commission in this case had preferred to adopt the German alphabet letter <ü>, instead of the digraph "ju" coming from Croatian *latinica* (expressed by the Bulgarian Cyrillic grapheme "ю") (Sagiaksis, Lazarou, & Papazahariou 1925: 37).

The authors of the *Abecedar* introduced a further innovation: instead of using the single grapheme <r>, which is characteristic of Croatian *latinica* (as a semivowel or syllabic consonant, as occurs, for example, in the word "drvo" — "tree"), they decided to transliterate into Latin characters the Cyrillic combination <ър> of the two sounds involved. Thus, they represented the correspondent of the Bulgarian Cyrillic letter <ъ> separately, through the use of a letter coming from the Romanian alphabet, <î> (similar to the muted <ı> which would have been adopted shortly afterwards in the new Turkish alphabet). Consequently, in the *Abecedar*, the word for "tree" is "dîrvo." The same <î> designates the Bulgarian character <ъ> in the word *sînceto* (= слънцето in Bulgarian, p. 37). In the texts in the *Abecedar* we can also observe that the authors indicated the specific Macedonian consonant rendered in its contemporary Macedonian Cyrillic version through the character <s> with the digraph <dz>, as well as today's Macedonian Cyrillic letters <ќ> and <ѓ> with the digraphs <kj> and <gj>.

There are many other interesting aspects with reference to the letters in this manual, first of all the fact that the order of the letters is not exactly logical. The letter <b> is followed by <e> and not by <c>, undermining at the very beginning the title *Abecedar* itself; the letter <e> is followed by <v>, a fact which could prompt us to think that the authors were attempting to devise a new alphabetical order. The order of appearance of the 29 letters is in fact as follows:

a	b	e	v	k	i	o	d	m	u	p	t	n	l	s
š	z	ž	r	j	î	c	č	g	f	h	ü	dz	dž	

This is then contradicted by the order on the last page of the first section (p. 34), which follows that of the Latin alphabet:

a	b	c	č	d	e	f	g	h	i	j	k	l	m	n
o	p	r	s	š	t	u	ü	v	z	ž	dz	dž		

If we take a closer look, however, we note that there are 28 letters here, and therefore one is missing: it is the letter <î>. In short, there is a lot of confusion in this text, and the errors do not stop here.

As a general consideration, it is important to remark that, in the process of the creation of a new writing system, all efforts should be aimed at minimizing ambiguity while maintaining maximum simplicity for users (cf. Venezky 1977: 41-42). The work performed by the Greek linguists in designing the alphabet for the Slavophones in Aegean Macedonia was actually quite advanced on the purely technical (and theoretical) level, especially for the modernization of the language's transcription system. This is true especially in comparison to the Bulgarian alphabet of the time, in which some letters that corresponded to mere orthographic archaisms remained (cf. Guentcheva 1999: 359).[16] The latter made this writing system therefore not strictly phonemic, that is, based on the principle of "one letter, one sound."

The combination of two or more letters to represent a single phoneme is generally considered, especially from a Cyrillic perspective, to be one of the major shortcomings of the Latin-based writing system (Wellish 1978: 47); in the case of the *Abecedar*, this element is certainly not the most important problem, as the obstacles to literacy in the Slavic-speaking community emerge in much

---

16 Guentcheva notes: "Though the commission of linguists and writers recommended simplification of the graphic system, the majority of the intelligentsia in Bulgaria insisted on retaining the visual distance between Bulgarian and Serbian through orthography" (ibid.).

more significant imperfections appearing in the text. In his review, Miletich cites a long series of examples from the pages of the primer in which words appear to be spelled incoherently, and notes that these inaccuracies represent a clear act of outrage by the Greeks against the Bulgarian script (Miletich 1925: 232).

It appears that the authors of the *Abecedar* did not pay too much attention to details and neglected the correct use of the writing system they had developed, probably due to a lack of time and attention, but perhaps also, one could assume, due to their own inability to handle a Latin alphabet they had not mastered very well. In this way, they undermined their own linguistic work and jeopardized the possibility of success for the use of the new alphabet by the target population, if that was indeed the goal of their efforts. According to Fishman (1977: xv), the creation of a new script becomes relevant only "insofar as it leads to the acceptance and implementation of the writing systems." In our case, the decisions that taken in the *Abecedar* seem rather to indicate of a lack of will and seriousness in planning alphabet reform.

2.6 The "involvement" of Cyril and Methodius

As mentioned above, the use of the Latin instead of the Cyrillic alphabet provoked strong reactions in the Bulgarian press. In fact, once more precise information about the "character and tendencies of this primer" (Shishmanov 1926: 2) was released, anger seized all social circles, without distinction (ibid.). It is interesting to remark that the Greek authorities, in defending their choice, argued that Latin characters were easier to learn than Cyrillic and better suited to the sounds of the language; they recalled that Latin characters had already been used for writing other Slavic languages such as Croatian, Polish and Czech and that, by using some specific diacritical marks, they were able to make the most of the specific phonology of Slavic languages (Michailidis 1996: 339). It is clear that this comparison is accurate from a purely technical and linguistic point of view, but not from a cultural and historical one, since the Slavic peoples mentioned belong to the Catholic sphere of influence and, for them, unlike for the people of the Orthodox faith, the Cyrillic alphabet had no symbolic meaning.

In discussing the phenomenon of the creation of new writing systems, it is essential to evaluate the importance of some extralinguistic factors (Fishman 1977: xii): the application of a writing system to a language is impossible without the imposition of conventions that are accepted as binding by virtually all those who read and write that language (Wellish 1978: 41). In this case, the will of the people was certainly not taken into account in the choice of a Latin-based alphabet. It was not so much a question of abandoning fidelity to previous writing conventions, since the majority of the population were illiterate, but rather of breaking the bond with the Cyrillic alphabet of the liturgical books and icons in the local churches: that is, with the Orthodox religious tradition.

The Bulgarian and Greek governments, as well as the government of the Kingdom of Serbs, Croats and Slovenes, were all aware of the "power of writing," that is, of the fact that writing, and therefore literacy, would have a great impact on the speakers of a language and their society (Biscaldi, Matera 2016: 91). They also knew that the conventions of writing systems were inherently sacred and that one writing system could only be replaced by another by force (cf. Wellish 1978: 42). In Bulgaria, the concern about alphabet reform in Latin letters for the Slavophone population in Greece was linked to the belief that this would represent a disruption in the cultural and religious tradition inaugurated by Saints Cyril and Methodius, and this would have extremely significant consequences for this minority's identity. This was also the immediate reaction of the local Slavic population to the news of the publication of the primer in Latin characters, who exclaimed: "Are they also going to make us Catholics now?" (Kuševski 1983: 186) — a reaction which shows that use of the Latin alphabet was automatically associated with the Catholic sphere of influence.

In Bulgaria, on the news of the publication of the primer for the Macedonian Bulgarians, the philologist Miletich bitterly commented that it was not written "with their centuries-old Cyrillic alphabet, which they gave to the Slavic world through the Cyrillo-Methodian script, but with a kind of Latin alphabet" (Miletich 1925:

230; my translation). Moreover, Miletich criticized the very definition of *Abecedar*, which was in itself controversial: "The primer is called 'Abecedar,' a name that the Bulgarian population would hardly understand, since it is derived from the first letters of the Latin alphabet." According to Miletich, the Greek government treated its Bulgarian subjects as "a new nation, a recently discovered one, without legitimacy, without its own writing and literacy, without its own literary tradition and standardized literary language" (Miletich 1925: 230; my translation).

In his text, the philologist Shishmanov addressed the Greek Ministry of Education and demanded an explanation for choosing the Latin alphabet for the Slavic people living on Greek territory. Since the Ministry recognized the existence of this minority, he wondered, was it not necessary to retain the Cyrillic script used by this population in all their "many and thriving" schools, whose existence preceded the Greek occupation? Shishmanov also insisted, much like Miletich, on the fact that the Slavic alphabet (referring in his case to the Glagolitic alphabet, not the Cyrillic) was, "as commonly known, created by the brothers Cyril and Methodius on the model of the Greek script." He explained that the Greek authorities' choice in 1925 was provoked by the strong fear on the part of Greek institutions of Bulgarian cultural—and hence political—influence. Consequently, the minority population was deprived of the possibility of reading books and newspapers printed in Cyrillic letters in Bulgaria, and was materially and symbolically isolated from its most "natural" context of reference. Shishmanov also raised a very practical question, wondering what would happen to the Slavic liturgical books if the Greeks were really to force the Slavophone minorities to use the Latin alphabet for education:

> Must these also be translated into the Bitola-Prilep dialect and printed in Latin letters? And from where will "Slavic" priests be taken henceforth who know how to use the Latin alphabet? These disturbing questions have not been answered by the official Greek authorities because they have not thought about these implications at all. They knew very well that in the end it was a simple "bluff." (Shishmanov 1926:14; my translation)

In the Bulgarian national conception of which both Miletich and Shishmanov were representatives, the population of Aegean Macedonia was seen as dependent on the Bulgarian cultural and religious sphere and therefore inseparable from the Cyrillic alphabet (see Tramontano 1999: 323). According to a vision associated with the Slavic Orthodox cultural tradition, indeed, writing exercised a function far beyond the mere graphic representation of phonemes, since alphabet and faith were intimately connected. This is not an exclusive feature of Slavic Orthodox culture, for in other Eastern Christian traditions, as well as in the Islamic world (and also beyond), the value of the written word is also extremely strong (see Cardona 2009b: 133), especially when it occurs in a form perceived as "native." So, in addition to the Glagolitic alphabet for Bulgarians and Croats (as we will see in Chapters 7 and 10), the Cyrillic alphabet for Bulgarians, Serbs, Russians, etc., we also have the examples of the Armenian alphabet for Armenian communities worldwide (associated with the Armenian Apostolic Church; see, for example, Maksoudian 2006, Uluhogian 1996), the Georgian alphabet (see Gamkrelidze 1994) for Georgians, as well as the Ge'ez alphabet for Ethiopians and Eritreans (see Cardona 1986: 151) and their respective Tewahedo Orthodox Churches (see Bekerie 1997).

The value of the Cyrillo-Methodian mission can be understood by its "revolutionary" historical value: at a time when the dogma of the three languages (Biblical Hebrew, Latin, Greek) was in force for the transcription of the Holy Scriptures, a Slavic language was able to assert itself and gain legitimacy thanks to a new work of alphabetic creation. In Shishmanov, the desire to maintain the Orthodox cultural and writing tradition coexisted with a broad international commitment at the European level, as he was one of the founders of the so-called Paneuropean Union, an embryonic version of today's European Union (cf. Koneva 2011). Shishmanov was a great advocate of the idea of a united continent, which included respect for the rights of minorities as a fundamental value. His support for the message of Cyril and Methodius probably also stemmed from his attachment to the deeply European ideals of protecting and promoting cultural and linguistic diversity in every part of the continent.

Cyril and Methodius were "invoked" not only by Miletich and Shishmanov. Reference to their work also appeared in the reaction of an anonymous reporter published in the Bulgarian press in the Macedonian region of the Kingdom of Serbs, Croats and Slovenes, *Macedonian News* (*Nouvelles Macedoniennes*) (Press of the Revolutionary Association VMRO), although the two saints were credited with creating the Cyrillic alphabet and not the Glagolitic one (cit. in Tramontano 1999: 324). The use of the Latin alphabet was also condemned by the pro-Bulgarian organizations of Macedonian refugees in Sofia, who demanded the immediate introduction of the Cyrillic alphabet (cf. Michailidis 1996: 336). In an article published in the daily *Word* on 15 October 1925, the Bulgarian politician and journalist Georgi Kulishev expressed his opinion on the subject, referring to the memory of the Cyrillo-Methodian mission:

> The great work of Saints Cyril and Methodius has been eclipsed [...] three Greek specialists [...] have graced the Bulgarian people of Western Thrace and Macedonia with a new writing and a new manual for education. It is true that this writing is not so new – it is the Latin alphabet adapted to a not very beautiful cause, a semi-barbaric one. (in: Shishmanov 1926: 4; my translation)

In the same article, the author stated that the *Abecedar* represented something completely unheard of and "monstrous." The Greeks had so achieved their goal that the Bulgarians had difficulty in recognizing their own language in the manual, a language subjected to "unheard-of tortures in their martyrology" (ibid.).

Similarly, in a text published in the journal *Macedonian Review* (*Makedonski Pregled*) in Sofia, the historian Georgi Strezov expressed his dissatisfaction with the way the Bulgarians were treated by the Greek authorities in Aegean Macedonia, condemning the violation of their cultural and national rights (Strezov 1926: 146). Strezov affirmed that such actions stemmed from the Greek will to uproot this minority from its land and to appropriate everything that was Bulgarian by every means at their disposal – "imprisonment, exile, pitchforks, primers" – and above all by banning their language: all with the aim of "de-Bulgarianizing" Macedonia. The Greeks hence aimed to eliminate all historical evidence of Bulgarian cultural presence in the area. "But we do not want to leave, we are obedient subjects of the Greek state, and we want only one thing—to pray to God in our mother tongue and to read books in Bulgarian" (Strezov 1926: 148; my translation).

The populations in Aegean Macedonia and Western Thrace that were considered "Bulgarian" by the above-mentioned authors already possessed their own written literary tradition, comprising books, newspapers, writers, printing houses, churches, clergy and schools, one which had reached an enviable level: in short, all the cultural characteristics of an advanced society (see also Rossos 2008: 147). The decision to introduce a different writing system and deprive them of such civilizational elements was incomprehensible to the Bulgarian public and unacceptable from a moral, linguistic, cultural and religious point of view. Referring to the population in question, Shishmanov asked: "What benefit could they derive from this Latin writing system? The result will be their inability to read not only a Bulgarian book, but also a Serbian or Russian book" (Shishmanov 1926: 9; my translation).

Certainly, one can conclude that the Greek commission did not adhere to what, in modern sociolinguistics, is considered to be the basis of linguistic and orthographic planning (cf. Fishman 1977: xv). In any project aimed at introducing a new writing system for educational purposes in a speech community, there are indeed a number of crucial decisions to be made: first of all, the choice between using an existing writing system and one created specifically for that language. The proponents of script reforms cannot decide arbitrarily on this fundamental aspect, but should take into account the reaction of the native-speaking population at all stages of the planning process (Berry 1977: 5).

2.7 Conclusions: the fate of the *Abecedar* after 1925

The function of writing systems as a tool to represent the "distinctiveness" of an ethnic group has been familiar to national movements in the Balkans, and Eastern Europe in general, since the 19th century. In many cases, when an alphabet had already been in use for centuries but no extensive literature existed in the vernacular, it was retained and given a slightly different coloration to distinguish it from the writing system of the dominant power or of a competing ethnic group (Wellish 1978: 43). In the case of the Slavic population of Aegean Macedonia, it was the Greeks themselves who cleverly exploited this element, becoming the protagonists of a "graphopoietic" work, without realizing that they had thus set an important precedent precisely for the "Macedonian cause" that worked against their own interest.

Since one of the main characteristics of the graphic aspect of language, exceeding even the oral aspect, is the fact of its being socially controllable, writing proves to be a strong instrument of power (Cardona 1982: 6). In the Bulgarian case, the alphabet revealed itself to be an essential tool of the "symbolic cultivation" (Smith 2009) of national identity and unity, appearing as an element of continuity in the history of its people: hence, literacy practices themselves became means capable of engaging the public in official debates and rhetoric. After all, literacy itself is based on a system of symbols, since writing is a set of symbolic elements used for communicative purposes that inevitably acquires a strong social meaning (Barton 1994: 43).

At the beginning of his review of the *Abecedar*, Miletich noted that, despite its serious shortcomings, the text at least represented recognition of the wishes of a minority population that boldly demanded its children's right to be taught in their mother tongue. But how closely did this statement correspond to reality? What was the fate of this school manual and what were the reactions of the affected population? Certainly, this school manual did not fulfill its intended role, which was to serve the education of local Slavophones. Rather, it represented an attempt at "imposed literacy" (cf. Barton 1994: 78) by the Greek authorities, as well as a restriction of the Slavophones' possible literacy practices, which were oriented towards different social and religious goals.

A few copies of the controversial *Abecedar* reached the Slavic-speaking villages of Aegean Macedonia in early 1926, several months late due to the Incident at Petrich, the aforementioned invasion of Bulgaria by Greece. However, these copies of the primer encountered an unfortunate fate: in one village, the incomprehensibility of the text to one of the few literate inhabitants (who could read Cyrillic) led the population to throw all copies into a nearby lake (Tramontano 1999: 327). The distribution of the *Abecedar* in the village of Amyntaion, near Florina, proved disastrous: the residents reacted violently and burned all the books, which they considered an insult to their "Greekness" (Michailidis 1996: 341)! The inhabitants of this village, both Slavophones and Hellenophones, protested together for days, finally deciding to send a telegram to the Foreign Minister to express their exasperation at the introduction of an undesirable language into the their children's schools. As if that were not enough, they also sent a message of protest to the League of Nations, which was published in the Greek daily *Newspaper of the Balkans* (*Efimeris ton Valkanion*) on 2 February 1926 (Michailidis, ibid.):

> We pray that our Government will transmit to the League of Nations our and our children's strong protest against the grave insult to our national pride and consciousness.
>
> We confirm our decision to support until death our fathers' institutions and the pure Greek tradition of Alexander the Great.
>
> We declare a bloody war against any violent and illiberal plot against our Greek mother tongue.
>
> We reject the instruction of the Macedono-Slavic dialect in schools, reviving memories of violence, fear, terror, gallows—i.e., the traditional means of Bulgarian practice. […] (in: Michailidis, ibid.)

Undoubtedly, such externalization of Greek identity and rejection of the Bulgarian—or "Slavic"—one can be comprehended on the basis of at least two considerations. Firstly, and rather predictably, by the fact that a population generally prefers to learn and use a writing system that is as close as possible to the prestige language that surrounds it, in order to better integrate into the social context of reference (Berry 1977: 5). Secondly, it should not be forgotten that illiteracy rates were very high at the time, a context that favored the control and manipulation of literacy practices for assimilationist purposes by Greek institutions in various ways.

To conclude, it is clear that the Greek government decided to use Latin characters expecting that the *Abecedar* would be rejected by all actors for this very reason. After various protests from the addressees, almost all copies of this primer were destroyed, and those that remained were withdrawn from circulation. There was no more discussion of education in the mother tongue and in 1927 the Greek government issued a directive aimed at removing all Cyrillic inscriptions from churches, tombstones, icons, and all other monuments in the area: a veritable campaign against this alphabet, revealing an assimilationist and mono-ethnic policy (Rossos 2008: 147). Such destruction of the cultural heritage of minority writing would be repeated on many occasions in the following history of the Balkan region, and not only in Greece.[17] In addition to this, in August 1926, the Greek government and the Kingdom of Serbs, Croats and Slovenes signed a protocol recognizing the Serbian nationality of the Slavic-speaking minority in Greece (Tramontano 1999: 328), a move clearly aimed at keeping Bulgaria out of the matter in every respect.

We can observe two other *a posteriori* elements in relation to the *Abecedar*, which, in a sense, seem to contradict each other. The first is that, at the time of its publication, this primer, which "teemed with errors" (Kočev 1996: 54), certainly did not help create a writing tradition or keep an existing one alive. In fact, as a result of this affair, and especially after a new law passed in 1936 (cf. Tramontano 1999: 328), the local Slavic language spoken by the population in Aegean Macedonia was also banned in its oral form in public places, surviving only in the domestic environment (Kočev,

---

17 Examples of this are the destruction of the written heritage in Arabic characters in Bulgaria, both in the first years of independence and during the assimilationist campaigns in the last years of communism (consisting of gravestones in Arabic or Turkish characters, school registers, documents in Turkish), the destruction of the written heritage in *arebica* in Bosnia during the war by the Bosnian Serbs and the campaigns against the Cyrillic script in Vukovar, as we will see in chapter 8.

1996: 54). In light of this, we can see a further reinforcement of the Greek campaigns of cultural assimilation, confirming that, in the process of creating an independent state after a previous imperial condition, nationalism inevitably coincides with the emergence of forms of "cultural centralism" (Zakhos-Papazahariou 1972: 150).

The second consideration to be made is that, although in practice the primer never reached the school desks of the children of the Slavic-speaking community, it is still considered by Macedonians today[18] as one of the most significant testimonies to the existence of a significant national Macedonian community in Greece, and to its language and thus identity (Andonovski 1985: 8).[19]

---

18   Those in Greece, in the Republic of North Macedonia and in the world diaspora.
19   The *Abecedar* has been reissued two times since 1925, first in 1993 by the Macedonian Information Center in Australia and then in 2006, in Thessaloniki, at the initiative of the Macedonian ethnic (Slavic) political party, Rainbow. In line with the principles of its political platform, the Rainbow Party states that the *Abecedar* constitutes one of a series of official Greek documents that distinguished Macedonian identity from Greek identity well before 1945.

3. THE "LATINIZATION" IDEOLOGY AND THE BULGARIAN DEBATES

3.1 Introduction: issues of script change

The 1920s can be considered the period par excellence in relation to debates on script reform in the wider Eurasian region. Specific political and ideological factors in the post-war period played a fundamental role in the forced introduction of new writing systems for different languages and in the formulation of proposals for more or less effective script reforms. In the development of these issues, one of the most important factors was the idea proposed in the official circles of the USSR for the need to introduce a common Latin-based alphabet in communist Russia.

Discussion of the possibility of replacing the Cyrillic alphabet with the Latin also arose in Bulgaria, especially in the pages of the journal *Bulgarian Book* (*Balgarska Kniga*), through the editorial poll held in 1930 under the title "Cyrillic or Latin: The Bulgarian Character" ("Kirilica ili Latinica. Balgarskijat shrift") that saw the participation of representatives of the intellectual, graphic, typographic and political worlds of the period.

In general, it can be stated that, in the course of the universal history of writing, sudden changes in the graphic form of a language represent a rather rare phenomenon, since linguistic communities tend to stick to a writing system already in use (even in cases where it is a particularly difficult one) for a series of political, cultural and religious or ideological reasons (Cardona 2009b: 141-142). Indeed, the replacement of one writing system by another is perceived not only as a threat to cultural tradition, but also to the power structures with which local intellectual authorities are associated. In this regard, Florian Coulmas has observed that "changes involving the script rather than only the spelling conventions have more weighty consequences for the society, since they entail a much more drastic break with a tradition" (Coulmas 1989: 242). That is, the longer the previous writing system has functioned as a marker of authenticity and specificity (even at the political level), the less likely it is that this script can be entirely replaced without extreme consequences at the level of the organization of power (cf. Fishman 1988: 280, Cardona 2009a: 93-94). For this very reason it is interesting to take a look at the proposals for the adoption of alternative writing systems as well as at their reception, even in those cases where such script reforms did not actually take place.

3.2 The Latinization ideology in the Soviet Union

The case of Soviet Union epitomizes, in some ways, the most striking example of how a government can continually and repeatedly use its power to decide and interfere on script matters. In the seventy-five years of USSR's existence, indeed, Moscow authorities intervened on several occasions in the writing/literacy practices of the country's national communities and minorities, making decisions in this field on the basis of political needs that varied according to the different historical moments and ideological phases the country faced (Collin 2011: 52).

It was only after the Bolshevik Revolution in Russia that the ideology of Latinization, that is, the conversion to the Latin script, began to take concrete shape, thanks to the collaboration of a number of intellectuals, including eminent linguists such as Nikolai F. Yakovlev and Yevgeny D. Polivanov. According to these scholars, Cyrillic was a writing system associated with the religious and ideological values of the Tsarist empire (see, e.g., Yakovlev 1930: 35): consequently, in the modified socio-political context, it had to be replaced by Latin, which appeared to be much better suited to serve the new educational and ideological purposes.

Politically, a Latin-based alphabet represented the most neutral choice, as least influenced by ideological or ethnic identifications: at the time, it was not markedly associated with the West, but rather with the possibility of achieving universal progress and a revolution in the communicative field. For all these reasons, it was decided to support the creation of Latin-based alphabets for all the languages of the nationalities present in the Empire, including those that had been neglected in the past[20] (Alpatov 2002: 117), those which had no written form (see Winner 1952: 134) or those that used writing systems considered unacceptable for cultural and ideological reasons, such as the Arabic alphabet or the ancient Mongolian writing system (Henze 1977: 379).

Before the advent of the ideology of Latinization, the first move in script policy pursued by the central Soviet authorities was the reform of the Arabic writing system. Although this reform was not particularly far-reaching, its main aim was to establish greater coherence between phonemes and graphemes in a writing system regarded as "archaic" (Crisp 1990: 25), and its effects became visible, as in the case of the Tatar communities that adopted the reformed Arabic script with particular vigor (Henze 1977: 414). Among the various examples in this regard, we should also mention the introduction of a reformed and improved Arabic alphabet for the Uzbeks, Kazakhs and Kyrgyzs in 1923.

Nevertheless, after a short time, the central authorities realized that this policy of reforming the Arabic alphabet was by no means the most effective solution for attaining greater unification of the peoples within the USSR. In pursuing the goal of raising literacy levels to the greatest extent possible, the Arabic alphabet was viewed as a major obstacle because of its extreme inadequacy for transcribing languages of non-Semitic origin (cf. Nurmakov 1934: 3-4). From the Soviet authorities' point of view, abandoning this alphabet would lead to the political advantage of disrupting the intergenerational writing tradition, rendering books and other material written in Arabic script unintelligible to new generations (Henze 1977: 375), as well as severing ties with the rest of the Islamic world and the conservative Muslim clergy (cf. Cardona 2009b: 138). Yakovlev maintained on this regard:

> This alphabetic struggle—this was a struggle for a mass, anti-religious and proletarian alphabet [...] which would serve as a weapon for the spread of Soviet culture in the East—a struggle for culture and for the Soviet school and against the alphabet of the caste, sacralized by religion and used almost

---

20 The languages of the Caucasus, Siberia, Central Asia, Central Russia, etc.

exclusively by the Muslim clergy. It was therefore a struggle against the theological schools and against the culture of bourgeois-religious content. (Yakovlev 1930: 33; my translation)

Similarly, in his 1934 text "The Latinization of the Alphabet—A Weapon of the Proletarian Revolution" ("Latinizacija alfavita— orudie proletarskoj revoljucii"), Nurmakov noted that the Arabic alphabet was no longer suitable for modern literacy needs and social, political, and cultural development because of the association with Islam and "Asiatic feudalism" formed by "exploitative groups" (Nurmakov 1934: 3; my translation). From a local perspective, however, there were valid reasons for retaining the Arabic alphabet, which was revered as an element of great cultural significance: it possessed primarily a symbolic meaning, linked to the sphere of Islam, but also a more practical one, relating to the possibility of establishing religious and cultural links with the countries of the Middle East and with the other more advanced Muslim peoples within the Soviet Union (Sebba 2006: 103).

In the second half of the 1920s, the Soviet authorities came to the conclusion that a reform of this writing system, while representing an advance over the previous situation of orthographic chaos, was still not sufficient to solve the specific technical difficulties of the Arabic script, which proved unsuitable for the goal of attaining mass literacy (Crisp 1990: 26). Anatoly Lunacharsky, the commissar responsible for the Ministry of Education, justified the need for script change by pointing to the serious difficulties of learning Turkic languages through the use of Arabic characters and insisting on the greater ease and appropriateness of Latin ones (Lunacharsky 1930: 21-22). In 1925, the Soviets finally decreed that the hitherto Arabic-written languages of the Union would soon be subjected to a process of alphabetic Latinization (Henze 1977: 376).

In the early 1920s, Soviet Azerbaijan was the most developed Turkic nation in terms of industrialization and modernization, and it is no coincidence that the idea of script reform received strong support and reinforcement precisely in this country. In fact, efforts had been made to introduce a Latin alphabet in Azerbaijan already in the 19th century: for instance, Mirza Fatali Akhundov, an eminent writer, had tried to adapt Latin characters to the specificities of the Azerbaijani language, and had published in 1857 a small pamphlet in Persian expressing his positive opinion of such a graphic solution (Caferoğlu 1934: 121).

During a meeting with the head of the Latinization Committee of Azerbaijan, S. Aghamaly-Oghlu, in the early 1920s, Lenin himself became convinced of the advantages of implementing this measure, which in his view would enable a greater penetration of revolutionary ideas (cf. Crisp 1990: 26). Since the Turkic languages possessed phonemes not represented by the Latin alphabet of the time, Soviet linguists developed a new writing system which would have allowed speakers of the closely related Turkic languages to easily communicate with each other through the written form. In 1922, this writing system was proclaimed by Lenin as the "Great Revolution in the East" ("Velikaja revoljucija na Vostoke") (Yakovlev 1930: 34), and in the same year the new Latin-based alphabet was introduced in Azerbaijan by decree under the name of *yeni yol* ("new way"), a fact strongly praised by local intellectuals (Crisp 1990: 26).

In 1926, the first Turcological Congress was held in Baku, where the Latinization of all the Turkic languages of the USSR was officially declared. This event was followed one year later by the adoption of the unified "new Turkic alphabet" (Winner 1952: 136), or *Jaŋalif*, which was almost identical to the one that was soon to be adopted in Turkey (1928). The intention was to create the conditions for facilitating cultural contacts among people of common Turkic origin[21] and for disseminating the ideas of the proletarian revolution more effectively.

The decisions of Turcological Congress, together with the realization of the alphabet reform in Turkey, were major factors supporting the Latinization process in the USSR. Only in the Georgian

---

21 As we shall see, this principle was later undermined by the Soviets themselves. With the introduction of the policy of forced Cyrillization in the late 1930s, there would no longer be even the slightest semblance of alphabetical unity between the peoples of Central Asia; and, indeed, different Cyrillic alphabets were created for each language to discourage any idea of unity between the peoples (cf. Henze 1977: 382).

and Armenian Soviet Republics were the native alphabets tenaciously defended (Alpatov 2001: 15); elsewhere in the Caucasus, as in Vladikavkaz and Nalchik, the idea of Latinization was enthusiastically welcomed already in the early 1920s (Yakovlev 1930: 12). The conviction of the imminent triumph of the world revolution nourished the idea of creating a universal alphabet on a Latin basis (ibid., 31). From 1927 to 1930, the unified Latin alphabet was adapted to all Turkic languages of Soviet Central Asia as well as to other peoples of Turkic origin living in the Altai region: the consequences in terms of culture and literacy were remarkable, especially among the Uzbeks (Henze 1977: 377-8).

In a way similar to the Soviet case, the script change in the Turkish language was part of Atatürk's broader literacy reforms, which aimed to dissolve the political and cultural barriers that had separated the common people from the educated and privileged classes for centuries (Bernal 2007: 182). The success of this reform was in some ways proportional to the previous inadequacy of the Arab-Persian alphabet as a medium for transcribing the Turkish language (Lewis 1999: 27).

From the 1920s to the first half of the 1930s, enormous resources and energies were mobilized in the USSR to create new Latin-based alphabets, which were eventually adopted for some seventy languages of various families and branches, not only Turkic ones. In parallel, in 1930, a group of linguists led by Yakovlev developed a Latin-based alphabet for the Russian language itself in collaboration with the All-State Central Committee of the New Alphabet (Vsesojuznyj Central'nyj Komitet Novogo Alfavita [VCKNA]), active between 1925 and 1937, first in Baku and then in Moscow (Alpatov 2015: 2-3). The Latin alphabet became so popular as an ideological propaganda tool that it was historically renamed the "alphabet of the revolution" or the "October alphabet" (Nurmakov 1934), in a utopian and universalist vision (Hacıoğlu 2020: 20).

In this political and ideological climate, the idea of "Latinizing" the Russian as well as the Ukrainian and Belarusian languages (Duličenko 2001 174-5), which in the meantime continued to be written in their Cyrillic alphabet, also gained popularity. In 1929, a special subcommittee of the People's Commissariat for Public Education (Narodnyj komissariat prosveščenija [NARKOMPROS]) was established under the leadership of Yakovlev himself (Alpatov 2001: 15): the prevailing belief was that the Latin alphabet, by virtue of its revolutionary character and its infinite possibilities of adaptation, could be used for writing any language, even the smallest one (Nurmakov 1934). In parallel, it was felt that by retaining the Russian Cyrillic alphabet, Russia would have distanced itself not only from the West, but also from its own East, as the peoples of the USSR increasingly adopted Latin-based writing systems. The practical realization of the Marxist ideal of world revolution also found expression in a kind of "ideology of letters" (Boneva 2001): the objective was to achieve written unification in order to better control the entire Soviet territory.[22] The introduction of a Latin alphabet for the Russian language appeared hence to be an urgent and timely matter (Lunacharsky 1930).

3.3 The Latin alphabet as a "modernizing" tool in the Balkans

In the Balkan Peninsula, the diversity of languages, dialects and alphabets, also in the form of local particularisms and syncretic practices, considerably diminished in the post-war period. With the collapse of the Ottoman Empire, the Arabic alphabet began to disappear from areas where it had been present for centuries as the writing system of the ruling authorities. Moreover, with the elimination of the Arabic alphabet in the new Turkish Republic, the Kemalists launched a decisive attack on Islam, which also marked the beginning of a new "cultural centralism," aimed at belittling all local peculiarities from Thrace and Anatolia, whose literary traditions were strongly linked to the Arabic alphabet (Zakhos-Papazahariou 1972: 153-4).

---

22 Interestingly, in 1943, guided by anti-Soviet considerations, the Nazi SS chief Heinrich Himmler urged Bulgarian Prime Minister Bogdan Filov to replace the Cyrillic alphabet with the Latin, in order to unite Europe under the rule of Nazi Germany, thereby symbolically severing its cultural ties with Russia: See B. Z. Filov, Дневник. Под редакцията на И. Димитров (1990), 343, cit. in Boneva 2002.

In this connection, it is worth mentioning that only a few decades earlier, in Habsburg-administered Bosnia and Herzegovina, a proposal had been made to adopt Arabic characters for writing the Bosnian language at the official level, by using the so-called *arebica*, a writing system that had developed locally, and was based on Arabic characters (see, e.g., Huković 1986 and Lehfeldt 2001). The arrival of Habsburg rule and the German language had determined the predominance of the Latin alphabet, and it was in this context that a reformed version of the *arebica* was formulated by the intellectual Mehmed Džemaludin Čaušević, which took the name of *matufovica* or *mektebica*. Interestingly, Čaušević implemented his reform on the basis of the Cyrillic alphabet, founding it on the phonemic principle proposed by Vuk Stefanović Karadžić, by assigning to each of Karadžić's graphemes a corresponding character in the Arabic alphabet. Čaušević believed that, in order to prevent the overwhelming of this writing system by the dominant Latin alphabet, it was essential to eliminate the orthographic chaos that had accumulated over time and to simplify the use of the Arabic script to transcribe the local Slavic language (cf. Selvelli 2015a: 215). In the hope of saving the Arabic alphabet from its probable disappearance, Čaušević and several other cultural representatives of similar Islamic background began using this alphabet in the bilingual periodical press (in Turkish and Bosnian) aimed at local Muslims (Huković 1986: 19).

Despite such attempts, the Latin alphabet was becoming increasingly welcome in the Balkans as well as in the Middle East as an indicator of modernization and was actively promoted by the more progressive sections of society. In the years following the First World War, rhetoric spread in Greece, Yugoslavia, Bulgaria and, of course, Turkey, but also in Palestine, Iran, Egypt and many other countries about the value of this writing system in terms of literacy advancement, as evidenced by the text *The Universal Adoption of Latin Characters* (*L'adoption universelle des caractères latins*) (1934), a publication promoted by the International Institute of Intellectual Cooperation, a body of the League of Nations for the promotion of international communication and peace through mutual rapprochement also in the field of writing.

This context at least partly explains the Greek authorities' decision to print the didactic text *Abecedar* in Latin letters (see chapter 2), since the ideologies of Latinization were linked to concrete proposals for a similar reform of the Greek language. Indeed, in the context of the educational reforms implemented by the Venizelos government (1929-1932), influential Greek intellectuals such as Dimitrios Glinos and Menos Philintas held the view that adopting the Latin alphabet would set the country on a path of cultural Westernization and put a definitive end to orthographic chaos by promoting literacy (see Bernal 2007). As stated by Philintas in a 1929 article that contained a practical proposal for the Latinization of the Greek language: "I do not think there is any serious reason (...) why we should not also adopt this reform, since the Turks, the Japanese [sic!] and some other nations have done it before us" (cit. in Bernal 2007: 179; my translation). In a text that appeared in 1931, Glinos similarly observed: "My personal opinion, as I have said before, is that we must adopt the Latin alphabet. I am convinced that this will finally happen ..." (ibid., 180; my translation).

The reasons why a script reform of the Greek language was never carried out are very similar to those which explain its missed adoption in Bulgaria: it would be very interesting to devote a specific study to the comparative analysis of these two cases, highlighting common elements in the national rhetoric and in the factors of resistance to script change. Another important factor, especially for Bulgaria, was the adoption of the Latin alphabet by Romania, which replaced the Cyrillic alphabet previously in use. Yet, although the country's religious identity was bound up with the Orthodox Christian faith, its language did not belong to the Slavic family, but to the Romance one. The proposal to render it through a suitable writing system had been made on several occasions, and it was not surprising that ideological and pragmatic arguments led the country to opt for a Latin-based alphabet (cf. Edroiu 2015: 237). Significantly, Romania's transition from Cyrillic to Latin was accompanied in 1873 by an edict affirming the "Latinizing" (or "Romanizing") and "Christianizing" role of the country in the context of the "pagan" and "Slavic-Muslim" Balkans (Kolarz 1946, cit. in Fishman 1977: xvii). The Latin alphabet, equipped with many diacritical signs, began to be used in the 1860s, but Romanian orthography would not be standardized until 1954 (Wellish 1978: 54).

The last Indo-European language to undergo a process of Latinization in the Balkan area was Albanian (Şimşir, 2008: 38-43). Political emancipation in the country went hand in hand with alphabet reform: when the National Congress gathered in Monastir (now Bitola, North Macedonia) in 1909 decided to fight for autonomy from the Ottoman Empire, of which Albania was still a province, the symbolic choice was the introduction of the Latin alphabet (Elsie 2017). Previously, the Arabic alphabet had been used to write this language, and some local patriots had created original Albanian alphabets by mixing letters of the Greek and Latin alphabets, but without much success (Elsie 2017, Kumnova & Shabani 2010: 70).

Certainly, since the late 19th century, the dynamics of self-representation of ethnic identity in Southeast Europe passed through the choice of the graphic form of the language, which had an extremely significant and legitimizing value for Western eyes. Thus, the Latin alphabet became established in Romania, Albania, and, though not entirely, in the Kingdom of the Serbs, Croats and Slovenes, without Catholicism influencing this in any way: it was also adopted for languages such as Turkish, with which it previously had had no connection (cf. Zakhos-Papazahariou 1972: 149). In this case, its status actually stemmed from the fact that it was perceived as the alphabet of the most "civilized" countries, that is, those of Western Europe.

Nonetheless, there was also strong opposition to various Latinization proposals in the Balkans, and the animated debates in Bulgaria, Greece, and Yugoslavia made the implementation of these projects unfeasible. To some extent, this can be explained by the fact that writing systems in the Balkans were never conceived as a kind of impartial technology that could be adapted and changed to suit the needs of its speakers and writers. Most proposals for the introduction of a new script did not meet with any possibility of adoption, which shows that questions of script in the Balkans (as well as in the Caucasus in Georgia and Armenia, the only other examples of "resistance to script change" in the wider Eastern European space) were deeply rooted in discourses of identity linked to irrepressible ideological, religious and cultural dynamics. I will now illustrate the deep-rooted reasons for such ideological positions in the Bulgarian case.

3.4 The positions in support of Latinization in Bulgaria

In the late 1920s, the *Abecedar* affair (discussed in chapter 2) was still experienced as a fresh and sensitive wound in Bulgaria. In addition, the Turkish alphabet reform most likely came as a surprise: many would not have expected their neighbor and former ruler, seen as culturally "retrograde" and "oriental" (cf. Todorova 1997), to take steps towards the West in such a resounding and symbolic way. Added to this, the defeats suffered since the Balkan wars and the unresolved issues concerning Bulgarian minorities outside the country's borders constituted a factor of deep frustration for Bulgarian public opinion.

As a consequence, one of the main features of post-war Bulgarian nationalism was its "defensive" stance (Todorova 2009: 182). On the one hand, Bulgarians had to prove that they were worthy of being classified and identified as a nation on the basis of the historical/political criteria adopted by Western Europe; but, on the other hand, they were concerned about losing their own identity, both politically (precisely in relation to the Macedonian question) and, as this case will show, in relation to the possible abandonment of a millennial writing tradition. In short, there was a delicate tension between the issues and forces of "tradition" and those of "modernization." It is through this lens that we can interpret the important debate on the retention or reform of the Cyrillic alphabet that arose at the end of the 1920s and materialized, in particular, in the survey carried out by the journal *Bulgarian Book* in 1930, as well as in other texts published in those years.

As for the newly founded journal *Bulgarian Book*, its editors asked a number of experts and professionals for their opinion on the question of switching to the Latin alphabet. On one side were representatives of the graphics, printing and typography sector such as Aleksander Makedonski, Ivan Kadela, Vassil Zahariev, Stefan Kutinchev, T.D. Plochev; and, on the other, intellectuals and academics such as Stefan Mladenov, Elin Pelin, Petko Stajnov, Sirak Skitnik, as well as the politician Stoyan Omarchevski. However, the investigation did not include the representatives of the religious world or the Slavic paleographers, who actually had the closest relationship with the old Bulgarian book. The introductory words of the text reveal to the reader the reasons why the editorial committee decided to undertake the survey:

> The prospect of the possible introduction of the Latin alphabet in Russia [...] brings the question of the alphabet also to our agenda. All the more so since it has recently become known that there is a similar discussion in Yugoslavia about the introduction of the Latin script throughout the country. (Balgarska Kniga 1930: 167; my translation)

The editors of the journal therefore invited a number of competent persons in public life to share their opinion as to whether the adoption of a new writing system was appropriate and opportune. The response of the experts was by no means unanimous, with positions in defense of the Cyrillic script and against the adoption of a Latin-based writing system clearly predominating. In favor of a new Latin script were Aleksander Makedonski, Elin Pelin, Petko Stajnov and Ivan Kadela, who justified their position on the one hand with a number of practical reasons related to the economy and printing, and on the other with cultural and ideological reasons connected with progress and modernity.

As for the reasons belonging to the first category, the most "technical" opinion belonged to the director of the National Printing Office Aleksandar Makedonski, who stated that if such a reform had really taken place in Russia, he would have backed the introduction of the Latin alphabet in Bulgaria (Makedonski 1930: 168). In clarifying this position, perhaps one of the few distinctly "pragmatic" ones among the experts involved, Makedonski noted that the Latin alphabet could be advantageous in the modern printing context, especially by virtue of the much simpler and cleaner forms of its characters. Latin, according to the expert, was not only "more beautiful and readable" but also cheaper in design and print: the same idea, written in Bulgarian, could be expressed by Latin characters, "with an economic advantage of 16 percent over Cyrillic" (ibid.)! In this context, Makedonski also noted that in the general typographic situation at that time, the choice of different Latin fonts seemed limitless, in contrast to that of Cyrillic ones.

It should be noted that Makedonski's pragmatic arguments were to some extent similar to those used by Yakovlev in the USSR to justify his decision to reform the alphabet: the Russian linguist put forward not only arguments of a purely ideological nature, but also scientific and technical ones. Yakovlev himself had shown that printing with Latin instead of Cyrillic letters was much cheaper and resulted in an easier reading process (cf. Alpatov 2001: 2). In this framework, it must be kept in mind that Bulgaria was in a situation of serious underdevelopment as concerned the availability of typefaces, a fact attributed by Makedonski to the cultural disadvantage suffered by Bulgaria, compared with Western European nations: "[w]hile the Western peoples dedicated themselves to their culture, we were oppressed by a spiritual and political yoke. All our ancient literature went up in flames" (Makedonski 1930: 167; my translation).

Unfortunately for Bulgaria, when Russian graphic designers and printers began to work on Cyrillic fonts, the revolution broke out, followed by the rise of Latinization ideas. For this reason, according to Makedonski, if the Latin alphabet were introduced in Russia, the lack of Cyrillic letters would become even more serious and the Bulgarians would not have been able to fill the gap on their own. Bulgarians and Serbs were indeed small and poor nations, with limited need for typefaces. Makedonski explained that for this reason a Cyrillic-printed page resembled a "cobblestone pavement in whose holes we so often stumble, lost in reading" (ibid.; my translation). Moreover, he felt, the Serbs would probably soon follow the Russian example: "Will the Serbs not take the reasonable step of unifying writing and language in Yugoslavia, through the alphabet that the Croats already use?" (ibid., 168; my translation). In short, under such circumstances, the difficulties of printing with Cyrillic characters would become insurmountable for the

Bulgarians, and the country would suffer very serious economic consequences.

In harmony with Makedonski's opinion was that of Ivan Kadela, another exponent of the world of typography. According to Kadela, in order to judge the question of alphabet reform from the practical standpoint of his profession, it was essential to take into account the spread that Cyrillic and Latin characters would undergo. If the introduction of the Latin alphabet were effectively implemented for the Russian language, its adoption would sooner or later become necessary also in Bulgaria, especially since in neighboring Yugoslavia, within the "advanced Croatian culture," the question seemed more topical than ever (Kadela 1930: 169). The development of original matrices from which new typefaces could be obtained was, in the opinion of the printer, an extremely laborious task, and so it appeared clear that the production of Cyrillic typefaces would imply much higher costs. Considering these practical reasons, therefore, any attempt to introduce a special Bulgarian alphabet would be doomed to failure.

The second category of motivations in favor of adopting the Latin alphabet were of a cultural and contextual nature, related to ideas and ideologies associated with the progress and modernization of the country. In this respect, Makedonski himself, supporting his "pro-Latinization" position, warned against the possible cultural isolation of the country, in a context where the whole Eurasian space, with the exception of Bulgaria, used the Latin alphabet. In short, the country would stubbornly maintain its tradition of the Cyrillic script, without having the means to print it in a manner appropriate to modern needs:

> And, in this way, we will remain alone. Our means are not sufficient and will not be able to meet the needs and concerns associated with writing. And foreigners will not care for our culture. All these conditions are stronger than tradition and we will have to sacrifice it and adopt the Latin alphabet. (Makedonski 1930: 168; my translation)

In his text, Makedonski approached the question of the writing tradition in a rather pragmatic way, without delving too much into its emotional implications, perhaps a little naively, not realizing how much the affective component of the alphabet played a fundamental role in the reception of this reform proposal.

In this regard, the position adopted by the writer Elin Pelin is also interesting: on the one hand, he evaluated the issue in purely technical terms and declared himself open to the possibilities of change; on the other, he referred to what could be considered the "sacred value" of a writing system in the consciousness of a nation. His contribution began precisely with a reminder of this fundamental aspect of writing, its function being not only technical but also symbolic:

> The writing system of a people, with its signs and rules, is a tradition that has become sacred, transformed into moral law. And it cannot be so easily overthrown. (Pelin 1930: 178; my translation)

Immediately afterwards, however, he stressed the importance of the modern communication factor, expressing his wide-ranging international vision of the matter:

> But today, when the world has become accessible and common to all, when one can travel the globe in a few days, when the radio simultaneously connects the four corners of the world, it will also be necessary to unify alphabetic characters. People are increasingly looking for innovative and simple means of communication to understand and comprehend each other. And in this desire, we should not be so surprised if traditions that are sacred but have a purely technical meaning collapse. (ibid.; my translation)

Curiously, Pelin's position in favor of the Latin alphabet seems to echo the words used by the linguist Otto Jespersen, creator of the artificial language Novial, in 1928 and, as we shall see, a strong advocate of a universal Latinization campaign:

> In these days of cheap travel, of commercial interchange between all parts of the world, of airplanes and broadcasting, of international science and of world-politics, it seems an urgent need for merchants, technical men, scientists, literary men, politicians, in fact for everybody, to have an easy means of getting into touch with foreigners and of learning more from them than is possible by visiting other countries as tongue-tied tourists [...] nowadays we have come to the point of needing an international language. (Jespersen 2010: 400 [1928])

In Pelin's view, considered strictly as a technical, graphic system that functioned for communication purposes, the Cyrillic alphabet could easily be replaced by another due to historical contingencies. In a sense, this reflected precisely the most representative vision of the "pro-Latinizing" movements of the time, which associated this writing system with principles of modernization and technological advancement. Indeed, in the Soviet Union until the 1930s, attempts to introduce the Latin alphabet were driven by ideals of progress and modernity and by the conviction that it would simplify communication between the various peoples of the Union as well as their literacy practices. It is noteworthy that, in some cases, Soviet linguists also created new Latin-based scripts for the languages of peoples who were not part of the USSR but were ideologically linked to it, such as Mandarin. It was indeed believed that the Marxist revolution was going to triumph in China too, and Chinese characters would be subsequently abandoned, replaced by modern Latin-based literacy practices (Henze 1975: 393, Wellish 1978: 75-77).

Petko Stajnov, an influential intellectual and member of the Bulgarian National Assembly, openly Russophile (cf. Boneva 2001), considered quite rationally the prospect of alphabet reform in Bulgaria, pointing out that his country could not escape the influence of "great Russia," which had "always and in spite of everything" been decisive for Bulgarians (Stajnov 1930: 175; my translation). However, he did not express the enthusiasm of the more "pro-Latinization" positions, and foresaw that script reform would require in any case a long period of time. Commenting on the technical question of writing the Bulgarian language in Latin letters, Stajnov remarked:

> I have never attempted to write in the Latin alphabet, but I suppose it is not impossible for experts to arrange adequate letters or signs from Latin for all the sounds of our language, as has already been done for Romanian and Turkish, though the Slavonic character might be better suited for this purpose. (ibid.; my translation)

In those years, as we have seen, Yakovlev's belief in the Latinization of the Russian language was itself very strong, and seemed destined to become a reality within a short time. In his vision, the Cyrillic alphabet represented an obstacle to the construction of socialism, both because of its association with the country's Tsarist past and as a graphic boundary separating the peoples who were already using the Latin alphabet. In short, it was necessary to create a new writing system that would embody the alphabet of socialism:

> Hence, in the context of the construction of socialism in the USSR, the existence of the Russian alphabet represents an absolute anachronism — a sort of graphic barrier dissociating the largest group of peoples in the Union from both the revolutionary East and the working masses of the proletariat in the West. (Yakovlev 1930: 35; my translation)

In Bulgaria, Stajnov pointed out that the adoption of the Latin alphabet by neighboring Turkey had already had significant consequences, as the Bulgarian Turks themselves "had to abandon the characters bequeathed to their language over the centuries" (Stajnov 1930: 175; my translation), a statement which seems to manifest a sort of regret at the loss of Arabic characters in relation to the Turkish language in Bulgaria. The fate of the Turkish alphabet reform in Bulgaria, however, as we shall soon see, followed a very peculiar course.

Stajnov also mentioned the case of Yugoslavia, which in those years made both alphabets equally obligatory: thus, Latin had prevailed even in Bosnia (Stajnov 1930: 175). We can note that if Soviet linguists often cited Atatürk's successful reform as a positive argument for their proposed script change, in the Bulgarian case the proponents of Latinization did not base their argument on the "Turkish model", since only the Russian one was considered relevant. Rather, this model was used by the opponents to the reform as an example of a different writing context, not comparable to the Bulgarian one.

Like Elin Pelin, Stajnov acknowledged the importance of cultural and more "sentimental" factors in connection with the Bulgarian Cyrillic alphabet, but only to note that, after the adoption of Latin by Russia, the question of the appropriateness of this alphabet reform would arise in the country "in reverse":

> [...] is it appropriate for Bulgaria to persist in remaining a Cyrillic oasis only because of its national originality, because of the tribute to Saints Cyril and Methodius, because of its outward loyalty through the alphabet to the orthodoxy of the motherland? (Stajnov 1930: 175; my translation)

Stajnov commented that, from a personal point of view, he would certainly feel sorry for the loss of the alphabet of his childhood and his ancestors. He conceded, however, that this was a purely personal and above all "emotional" matter, which could not prevail against the dictates of technology, the need for unification and the influence of the surrounding context on his country. For "reasons of rationality," the same rationality that had led the Bulgarians eventually to "accept Arabic numerals instead of Slavic ones, to eliminate a number of letters, to modify the same signs, to adopt the Gregorian calendar" (ibid.; my translation), Bulgarian culture had to follow the universal course of technology and communication. The personal and emotional desire to remain faithful to the hitherto prevailing traditions had to be sacrificed for the collective good. As for the timing, Stajnov expressed his conviction that the alphabet reform would eventually prevail in the country, though perhaps not in his lifetime, if technology did not find "another way of writing and printing or a special shorthand that would save us from Cyrillic as well as from Latin" (ibid.; my translation)!

In this context, the printer Kadela expressed a similar opinion, giving voice to his displeasure at the demise of a writing tradition characteristic of his country and the Slavic world in general: "It is only a pity that with the introduction of the Latin script one of the peculiarities associated with Slavic culture and preserved for centuries will be lost" (Kadela 1930: 169; my translation). Undoubtedly, this question appeared to be a rather sensitive one and, far from being a mere technical controversy, it implied a series of considerations that were not always easy to deal with.

3.5 The positions in defense of Cyrillic: contextual and internal factors

Many of the arguments of those who opposed the introduction of the Latin alphabet in the country were based on considerations of the political and cultural differences between Bulgaria and the countries where this reform had been or was about to be carried out, as well as on its peculiarity within the Slavic world. An example of the former is the position of the President of the Union of Bulgarian Printers, T. D. Plochev, who, in contrast to personalities such as Makedonski and Ivan Kadela, but coming from the same professional field, declared total opposition to the adoption of the Latin alphabet for the Bulgarian language:

> Russia may adopt the Latin alphabet in place of the Cyrillic. Our country, however, cannot solve the tasks that do not belong to us. Do we also need to change our alphabet and replace it with the Latin alphabet? I see no reason to countenance this change. (Plochev 1930: 172)

If Bulgaria were to follow the path of alphabet reform, in Plochev's opinion, this would result in a long interruption in the spiritual life of the country, as well as in enormous material losses.

Former minister Stoyan Omarchevski also spoke out on the issue in the survey organized by the journal. The politician, who headed the Ministry of Education during the Stamboliyski government, had become popular in 1922 for his proposal for spelling reform with the aim of "democratizing the language" (cf. Guentcheva 1999: 362). Despite these premises, which might lead one to consider the politician a convinced "modernizer," Omarchevski seemed to accept script reform only as an "inevitable and painful event" (Omarchevski 1930: 178). His position appeared ambiguous, as the former minister, like Petko Stajnov, referred to the examples of Romania and Turkey, which had adopted the Latin alphabet under the influence of certain strategic commitments.

In addition, Omarchevski mentioned another context of reference, that of the Macedonians. The politician referred in a polemical sense both to the *Abecedar* in Greece and to the process of Latinization underway in Yugoslavia, suggesting that these states wanted "to get rid of the Bulgarian" (Macedonian) element by assimilating it through a foreign writing system (Omarchevski 1930: 178). In a sense, Greece had actually helped to extend the general discussion about the modernization of writing to the Cyrillic alphabet used in its territories, claiming its unsuitability for the writing practices of the population in Aegean Macedonia. In this way, the Hellenic authorities had justified the introduction of a Latin-based writing system, which was much better suited for literacy purposes.

> The Greeks introduced the Abecedar into purely Bulgarian lands, and in a similar way present-day Yugoslavia is contemplating the adoption of the Latin alphabet in order to remove from the language of Cyril and Methodius the most active and lively element, the Bulgarianness. And there, where the principle of the Bulgarian state and the cradle of the Bulgarian script reside, today they want to eradicate Bulgarianness by the introduction of Latin in order to tear apart our spiritual unity. (ibid.; my translation)

In addressing the alphabet controversy, Omarchevski then referred to religious and identity grounds and acknowledged the fundamental importance of the Cyrillic alphabet for the intellectual history of his country and the Bulgarian minorities residing outside its borders. His inclination to accept the Latin alphabet was perhaps dictated by more pragmatic considerations: he recalled how important it was for his country not to remain isolated, as Bulgaria too had to open up to the "general laws of universal development" (ibid.; my translation).

As for the Turkish case, the script reform set a crucial precedent that appeared as a recurring motif in the debate, although in ambivalent terms. For instance, Stefan Kutinchev, publisher and former director of the National Printing Office, expressed a sort of praise for Atatürk's work in the field of literacy. He saw this important event as dictated by the ideal of the Europeanization of the nation in order to place it in the ranks of "civilized" countries and create the conditions for the beginning of modernization. Moreover, the change of the alphabet was aimed not only to facilitate the future generations' approach to European civilization, but also to familiarize Western Europeans with the new cultural values of the Turkish Republic. According to Kutinchev, Turkey's alphabet reform would also benefit Europeans by stimulating their interest in the country's literature and by promoting cultural and economic ties through an accessible and simplified script (Kutinchev 1930: 174).

What Kutinchev did not point out was that this reform in Turkey also served to symbolically distance the country from its political past and its Arab neighbors. Indeed, in Turkey, the alphabet of the national language was Latinized in part to distinguish Turkish nationalism from transnational Islam (Safran 1999: 84).[23] A need for distinction was also expressed to some extent in Bulgaria, but it moved in the opposite direction precisely because many neighbors were considering adopting the Latin alphabet or had already introduced it. We can see that for some of the representatives of Bulgarian culture, the will to preserve the "national" writing system also depended on contextual factors that were perceived as potentially assimilating. Kutinchev himself, acknowledging the diversity of the local context in relation to the countries affected, noted that the reform of the Turkish alphabet had been carried out at the cost of great turbulence and economic sacrifice for the country, something Bulgaria could clearly not afford: "Bulgarians would commit a sin if they dared to play with the reforms of their alphabet today" (Kutinchev 1930: 174; my translation).

The Russian context too was very different from the Bulgarian one: Russia epitomized the land of radical change, where social reforms were being imposed after a decade of political and economic struggles: the introduction of the Latin alphabet hence fit smoothly into this path of great innovations. In a way, this reform, like Turkey's, would benefit not only Russia itself, but also the rest of the world. Soviet Russia intended to make the social and political values of the revolution accessible to the European proletariat and to prepare the ground for a common and universal activity (ibid.).

In truth, although the dominant idea was that Latin characters would soon be introduced for the Russian language, despite the efforts of scholars such as the linguist Yakovlev and the Minister of Education Lunacharsky, this reform was eventually abandoned. Indeed, even the Latinization of Russian itself presented obvious difficulties, since there were millions of Russians who could read and write Cyrillic, far more than the representatives of other nations

---

23   This practice was quite common, and there are numerous examples, such as those of Moldova and Tajikistan, where the Soviet authorities imposed the Cyrillic alphabet on local languages in order to differentiate them from Romanian and Persian respectively.

belonging to the Union, who did not enjoy a long or extensive written tradition, and among whom the illiteracy rate was very high, as in some remote areas of Siberia and Central Asia. Another factor not to be neglected in this case was the very high cost of this project (Alpatov 2001: 24).

The Bulgarian art critic Sirak Skitnik argued that the ideological and political factors that drove the political elites of the Soviet Union towards Latin could not be considered relevant in Bulgaria. Comparing the cultural life and political conditions and ideas in Bulgaria and Russia, he maintained that in the Balkan country not only national interests, but also cultural and purely literary ones urged the retention of the Cyrillic script. The replacement of the Cyrillic alphabet would provoke the distancing of the wider public from the "Bulgarian book" for a long time and the implementation of this reform required, in his opinion, higher literacy rates in the country (Skitnik 1930: 176).

This last assertion appears to be in complete opposition to the predominant opinion among Russian linguists. For them, low literacy rates represented the ideal condition for the successful execution of a script reform. In this context, it is important to keep in mind some remarks about the spread of writing and literacy. Indeed, the reference category in which writing circulates differs from the community of speakers, in the sense that there is no homology between speakers and writers. Those who can write may be a restricted group, a social class, but they will certainly be less numerous than speakers who are merely "users" of writing produced by others (Cardona 2009a: 66). According to the definition of Armando Petrucci, literate people can be defined as those who master without difficulty, both in terms of production and employment of texts, all the graphic typologies in use in the societies to which they belong; they can normally also write texts in one or more languages other than their mother tongue (Petrucci 2002: 20). As regards these definitions, in the aftermath of the First World War, only a limited population was proficient in the writing domain in Bulgaria: only a tiny minority of literate people could thus attempt to read in two different alphabets.

Within the Latin/Cyrillic debate, questions of literacy revealed themselves as crucial. In the Soviet Union, the various manifestations of "script politicization," first with Latinization and then with enforced Cyrillization, could occur precisely thanks to the high degree of illiteracy of the populations concerned and the absence or scarcity of written literature. Significantly, however, two cases indicate that this factor was necessary but not sufficient. In China, where attempts at Latinization were introduced by a dictatorial regime and where illiteracy was as widespread as in Turkey, the reform failed; nor was it adopted in Japan (Wellish 1978: 89-93).

It is obvious that, the moment a writing system is radically changed, a large part of the population becomes illiterate for a certain period of time. In the case of Bulgaria, in 1920 the literacy rate among the Bulgarian population over ten years of age was 48% among the Bulgarian majority, 7% among the Turkish, Tatar and Roma communities, and 73% among people of Jewish origin. By 1934, the rates had risen to 75%, 18%, and 82%, respectively (UNESCO 1953: 50). This meant that the Bulgarian population presented high literacy rates in comparison to other areas such as Central Asia, Anatolia, etc., where script reforms were relatively easy to push through.

An important factor mentioned in the debate was that the reform would have consequences not only for the population inside the country, but also for that living outside its political borders. Skitnik predicted that Bulgaria would permanently lose the "Bulgarian book's readers" outside its territories, and that this change would promote the denationalization of the Bulgarian minorities that remained under foreign rule, namely those in Greece and in the Kingdom of Yugoslavia.

3.6 Defensive and symbolic motivations rejecting Latinization

In considering the symbolic and identitarian motivations put forward by some exponents of the Bulgarian cultural intelligentsia in defense of their "anti-Latinization" positions, it is appropriate to ask whether the type of writing system a society uses is influenced by the culture of the society itself, and to what extent a writing system can in turn exert an influence on that culture and society. In the Soviet Union, Yakovlev stated that the alphabet was not a simple writing technique, but reflected ideology itself, and associated the Cyrillic alphabet with the exploitation of the people in the Tsarist era:[24]

> It would be ridiculous, however, to claim that the question of the ideology of the alphabet [...] is an empty question, it would be ridiculous to claim that it has nothing to do with our success on the fronts of production and culture, that any alphabet, whatever the form of its graphics, can be used with equal success on such fronts, it would be ridiculous to understand the alphabet as mere technical signs. Every writing system reveals itself not so much through its technical signs as through the reflection of its ideology. (Yakovlev 1930: 36; my translation)

With this statement, Yakovlev justified the idea that the Russian Cyrillic should be replaced by "the alphabet of socialism," to allow the creation of an international graphic system entirely consistent with the essence of socialist culture: form and content would thus coincide. As we have seen, this link between alphabet and ideology in the Soviet context was also widely acknowledged by some Bulgarian representatives, who noted that the reasons why Soviet Russia considered introducing Latin characters were related to the changing social worldview. However, the situation was quite different in the Balkans, where certain identity dynamics and writing ideologies were very deeply rooted, and functional for the assertion of a certain continuity and distinction in the history of the country. Here, the coincidence between form and content manifested itself in a very different way, as the ideological content of the national identity structure on which the country built and founded its history was not at all linked to the desire to "negate" the past. The only past to reject was the Ottoman one, but this was certainly not a problem for Bulgaria at the alphabet level, although, as we shall see, even this principle would have been partly overridden in the script policy implemented towards the Turkish minority in the country.

---

24 In a way similar to Nurmakov's definition of the Arabic alphabet (see Nurmakov 1934: 3).

When the idea of a "sacred" connection between tradition, script and culture is emphasized in a country's national rhetoric, then ideologies related to writing can be expected to spread effectively among large segments of the population. Cardona (2009: 154) argues that, although the sphere of writing is more circumscribed than that of language, "it is also likely that, because of the prestige it enjoys even among those who do not possess it, the ideologies that accompany it will radiate into wider spheres" (ibid.; my translation). For this reason, the stances supporting the safeguarding of Cyrillic appear entirely in line with the dominant cultural discourse in Bulgaria, as well as with its "mythographized" history. Hence, the centuries-old habits and traditions of some millions of Bulgarian speakers were extremely relevant factors that appeared to be in opposition to any idea of a transition to a new alphabet.

In this regard, the aforementioned President of the Union of Bulgarian Printers T. D. Plochev observed that, in the event of alphabet reform, the consequences for the country would be not only practical but also moral, "since to the present Cyrillic we owe our awakening as a people"; thus, the introduction of Latin characters would hinder Bulgaria's natural spiritual development (Plochev 1930: 173; my translation). Similarly, Skitnik noted that in the country "not only national interests, but also cultural and purely literary interests" required the retention of the Cyrillic alphabet (Skitnik 1930: 176).

In Bulgarian history, there were certainly painful issues and wounds that hindered the implementation of this reform. Indeed, the Bulgarians were not yet able to stabilize themselves within what Skitnik defined as their "ethnographic borders": "We are still discussing the origin of the creators of our alphabet, the boundaries and places where the Bulgarian word is pronounced and understood" (Skitnik 1930: 174; my translation). It was feared, therefore, that the abandonment of the Bulgarian alphabet would cause historical and national ideals to fall into oblivion, encouraging the assimilation of Bulgarian identity: "With the new influence that would come with the new alphabet, we would dissolve our national traits and get lost among our usurpers" (ibid.; my translation).

The opposing views on the Latinization of the Bulgarian alphabet expressed by experts in the debate in *Bulgarian Book* were joined a few months later (still 1930) by an article by the ecclesiastic and scholar Ivan Goshev entitled "Latin or Cyrillic" ("Latinica ili Kirilica").[25] In this text, the author downplayed the arguments used by the "pro-Latinization" advocates expressed in the journal, since Yugoslavia, Turkey and Russia could not provide a model for Bulgarians to imitate. In particular, the situation in the Kingdom of Yugoslavia differed significantly, since part of the population, especially the Croats and Slovenes, had long used the Latin alphabet, which proved to be an attested tradition of writing for many (Goshev 1985 [1930]: 153).

According to Goshev, the boundaries of the Bulgarian nation at that time were not marked out by political borders, but by two indissoluble barriers, consisting of the vernacular and the alphabet. Removing the Cyrillic script therefore meant endangering the country's survival: "[o]ur ъ, our ь, our ѣ and our ѫ have been the guardians of our borders until today" (ibid.; my translation). By adopting a new writing system, Bulgarians would expose their newly acquired national borders to a "foreign invasion," threatening their spiritual identity and severing ties with their cultural past, which unfortunately represented "a thorn in the eye of many." But perhaps the most salient element in Goshev's vision, as in Skitnik's and Kutinchev's, was the risk that the links between generations would be broken:

> Our grandchildren and great-grandchildren will look at the dusty old Bulgarian manuscripts with superficial interest, they will wonder at their letters and ornaments, and when some scholar will read something to them or will ask them to try to read it, they will shrug their shoulders as if they were looking at some Chinese characters or Egyptian hieroglyphics. (ibid.; my translation)

---

25 "Latin or Cyrillic". This contribution was included in a collection of texts related to the celebration of the Cyrillo-Methodian tradition, in the form of a small volume entitled *И на вси словене книга да четат. Сборник материали за Кирил и Методий*, published in 1985 by Sinodalno Izdatelstvo in Sofia. Goshev's text bears the date 1930, but it is not known in which press organ it was published.

The adoption of this script reform would have implied, again according to Goshev, the loss of the immeasurable work of Cyril and Methodius, as well as a threat to the literary, scientific, artistic, national and political wealth for which the Bulgarians had fought so tirelessly through the centuries. According to this view, script reform would have invalidated the entire history and the very reason for the existence of Bulgarian culture, condemning the entire past to a kind of "collective oblivion": Bulgarian books, from all historical periods, would end up "in museums and archives, to be read only by scholars and eaten by bookworms" (ibid., 154; my translation).

The concerns of Skitnik, Goshev, Kutinchev, and all those who insisted on the importance of maintaining the link between generations through writing may seem exaggerated, but they correspond to a very real situation of which the cultural development in Turkey provides a significant example. Atatürk's alphabet reform certainly contributed to bringing Turkey closer to Europe, and perhaps Europe's acceptance of Turkey grew after the country adopted Latin characters. However, one not insignificant consequence is that Turks today are unable to read significant works written in their own language[26] from a period that covers most of their history.

The effects of the disruption in the writing tradition are felt for a long time, and its consequences on society have been enormous. In the case of the Arabic alphabet in the post-imperial territories, its disappearance in Bosnia and Turkey, although seemingly not exerting any visible impact for many decades, has only recently begun to influence some of the socio-cultural and religious dynamics of the countries concerned, where this writing system is undergoing a form of rediscovery and "revival." For example, whereas, during the socialist period in Bosnia, the *arebica* fell into disuse, surviving only in the private practice of some families, a number of contemporary examples indicate the renewed status of this writing system in the post-socialist country, which also involve its use in writing in

---

26 More precisely, an earlier version of their language, containing more Arabicisms and Persianisms.

modern domains such as comic books for children (Gažáková 2014: 464).

In recent years, debates on the status of Ottoman Turkish started taking place in Turkey, involving interesting ideological factors. The country has a great need for people trained in reading the Ottoman script, given the millions of documents waiting to be deciphered and used by researchers in archives and libraries. Indeed, the representatives of the generation that could read the old Ottoman alphabet gradually disappeared, and this writing system was transformed into a sort of "tabooed" element on a social and cultural level, a fact that made the entire tradition of calligraphy, reading and writing inaccessible to the ordinary citizen.[27] The situation has taken an interesting turn since 2015, when the ruling AKP (Justice and Development) Party put forward a proposal to reintroduce Turkish Ottoman alphabet teaching in schools after almost 90 years, but the outcome is still uncertain.[28] It follows that the interruption of a writing tradition certainly entails severing a link with part of one's past, and although some countries have inclined to do this, the "writing past" can resurface generations later as an unresolved issue that demands attention, especially in times of identity crisis or political transition.

To return to Bulgaria: when intellectuals argued about the possible consequences of alphabet reform, the question was raised as to the possible impact of this script change on the external representation of the country, along with the loss of an element of the legitimacy of Bulgarian identity and distinctiveness in the eyes of the Great Powers. Was it really possible for the Bulgarians to choose the path of "pan-Europeanism," discarding what was their own and adapting to foreign influence, the very people who had "given the alphabet to the Slavs?" (Goshev 1985 [1930]: 155; my translation).

27　On this subject, see the novel *The Calligraphers Night* by Yasmine Ghata (Hespereus Press, 2006), based on the true story of the female calligrapher Rikkat Kunt (1903-1986): "God is not interested in the Latin alphabet. His dense breath cannot skim across those squat, separate letters."

28　This was actually a much more political than culturally motivated move on the part of Erdoğan's AKP party.

The emergence of the symbolic dimension within positions defending the Cyrillic alphabet contrasted with the prevailing discourse (cf. Bernal 2007: 188), which favored writing systems based on phonemic principles, i.e. evaluating the alphabet according to its suitability for the phonology it represents and the extent to which it provides a two-way correspondence between signs and sounds. In Bulgaria, and in the Balkans in general, this aspect is not in the foreground;[29] rather, it is the ideological discourse that imposes itself as the strongest, as an "extralinguistic" factor. Indeed, the alphabet has always maintained a strong connection to religion and literacy practices, a reason why any discourse on the preservation or reform of an alphabet also concerns the role that this part of the cultural heritage plays, involving issues of tradition and identity. Thus, the alphabet associated with a particular religious affiliation has the power to both divide and unite, as it represents not only a spiritual but also a national community (cf. Sebba 2006: 124n).

One of the most salient "mythographic" elements from Bulgarian history is certainly the memory of the Cyrillo-Methodian mission: by claiming that the Bulgarian alphabet was the first Slavic alphabet, Bulgarians affirm their historical primacy in the context of the development of Slavic culture in general. This emphasis on their past civilizing mission could be interpreted as an attempt to guarantee Bulgaria a central function in Slavic culture and literature (cf. Sygkelos 2011: 189). In this regard, graphic artist Vasil Zahariev commented in his contribution to *Bulgarian Book*: "Our alphabetic character was and will remain the symbol of Bulgarianness. We, who gave the alphabet to the Slavic peoples, must not renounce the Cyrillic script and replace it with the Latin script" (Zahariev 1930: 169; my translation).

The prevalent rhetoric maintained that the Bulgarian nation had been created in the 9th century and affirmed by faith and script, and that these two pillars of the nation would be irreparably damaged by script reform. In particular, the Bulgarian Church would be placed in a very difficult situation, deprived at length of its

---

29 Although, as we shall see, a substantial part of the positions defending Cyrillic also leverages the question of its technical superiority.

liturgical and theological books. Furthermore, in this regard, Goshev asked whether reprinting the Sacred Texts in the Latin alphabet would not constitute "the most sacrilegious mockery" from a national point of view (Goshev 1985: 155; my translation)

The defense of the spiritual heritage epitomized in the tradition of writing suggests that in the Orthodox Christian world (but not in it alone) religion and the alphabet played a paramount role in the processes of ethnic identification and group demarcation. As a religious symbol, the alphabet was an integral part of the dominant national imagination and thus helped to trace and affirm ethnic boundaries as well. The invention of Bulgarian writing occupied a central position in the construction of a national past, and this explains the constant reference to Cyril and Methodius, which persists unaltered to this day.

3.7 Technical imperfections of the Latin alphabet

In the responses of the experts to the survey conducted by *Bulgarian Book*, the technical positions supporting the maintenance of the Cyrillic alphabet referred mainly to the imperfect applicability of the Arabic alphabet as a legitimizing element of the Turkish alphabet reform and, at the same time, to the phonemic inferiority of the Latin alphabet in comparison to the Cyrillic for the transcription of the Bulgarian language.

As already mentioned, in Turkey the situation was quite different from Bulgaria, as the Arabic script was phonemically defective and appeared less functional compared to the Cyrillic or Latin scripts in terms of clarity and legibility: therefore, script reform there proved extremely helpful and effective. According again to the President of the Union of Bulgarian Printers, T. D. Plochev, the Turks were tired of the "difficulties and oddities" of the Arabic alphabet, which was "a serious obstacle to their education" and allowed few people to read and write in their own language. The Bulgarians were certainly not in the same situation, since they had been using modern Cyrillic characters "for more than a hundred years," and all their scientific and literary works were printed in this alphabet (Plochev 1930: 172-173; my translation).

As we have seen, especially in the 1920s, negative ideologies regarding Arabic script intensified, both in the countries where it was used (such as Turkey or Azerbaijan) and outside. In both cases, it was identified as an anachronistic writing system that was not suitable for modern literacy needs. Arabic script was indeed characterized by a great variety of forms: the same sound could be represented in different ways depending on its position within a word, and it also lacked specific graphemes for marking vowels. It was therefore certainly unfit for transcribing Turkic languages, especially those that had retained the principle of vowel harmony, such as Turkish, Azerbaijani, Kyrgyz and Kazakh. In Bosnia, the *arebica* reformed by Čaušević had in a sense attempted to integrate the writing needs associated with both tradition and modernity, as it was reformed phonemically to meet these criteria (cf. Selvelli 2015a: 214-215).

In the debates of the 1920s, however, Arabic script became one of the first "victims" of modernization. It is a fact that some writing systems are certainly more difficult to learn than others, and sometimes literacy difficulties can be interpreted as deriving from the complexity of the writing system itself and to certain socio-cultural contextual elements. For example, low literacy rates in the Arab world may be associated with the difficulty of learning to write in this writing system, in contrast to high literacy rates in the Western world, where Latin-based alphabets are much easier to learn (Suleiman 2004: 43).[30]

In dealing with the question of alphabet reform from a contextual point of view, the philologist Stefan Mladenov recalled in his contribution to *Bulgarian Book* that the same fate of script change might soon befall not only Cyrillic but also its original model, the Greek alphabet. Indeed, in those years, as we have seen, intellectuals such as Philintas and Glinos engaged in debates similar to the Bulgarian ones about the modernization of the Greek alphabet. In their opinion, the phonetic simplification of Greek orthography and the adoption of the Latin alphabet were realistic reforms, as

---

30 Collin (2011: 40) notes that the Japanese case represents the limit of this argument, but there are many cultural factors of prestige and context involved.

testified by the case of the Greek communities in the Soviet Union, which used Latin-based transcription systems in their publications (Bernal 2007: 181).

Nevertheless, Mladenov noted that there was a great difference between the Arabic alphabet on the one hand and the peculiarities of the Cyrillic and Greek alphabets on the other. If the use of the Arabic alphabet for the contemporary Turkic, Tatar, Persian and Indian languages was accompanied by "extraordinary difficulties" (Mladenov 1930: 177; my translation), the Slavic languages were efficiently and easily written with the Cyrillic alphabet, as well as Greek with its alphabet. Stefan Mladenov was particularly active at this time in the journal he founded, *Native Speech* (*Rodna Rech*), which published several of his articles on the need to preserve the richness and purity of the Bulgarian language. In his opinion, the idea of replacing the Cyrillic alphabet with the Latin one was unfeasible, and one of the main reasons was the imperfection of the latter: "[w]ith respect to this, Cyrillic, which is adapted to one of the richest sounding languages—Old Bulgarian—occupies an incomparably higher place than the Latin alphabet" (ibid.; my translation). Indeed, the character set of the various Latin alphabets used in Europe and beyond differed considerably, with the result that there was an enormous variety of orthographies among the Western European peoples, the Slavs, and all others who had adopted the Latin alphabet. Mladenov provided some examples of such orthographic confusion:

> Just one example: the sound č, represented in Cyrillic by the letter ч exclusively, is indicated in English and Spanish with two Latin letters—ch in French with three—tch, in German with four Latin letters—tsch (and even 5: tzsch!). (Mladenov 1930: 177; my translation)

In some countries, the linguist noted, the Latin alphabet was enriched with diacritical marks, but even in this case difficulties remained, because of the arbitrariness of their application. The same examples were brought by Mladenov a couple of years later, before the International Institute of Intellectual Cooperation, the body of the League of Nations which elaborated the Latinization project *L'adoption universelle des caractères latins*. The book bearing the

French title contains an excerpt from a letter written by Mladenov on 28 April 1932, in which he expressed his opinion on the subject of Latinization:

> We would be willing to introduce Latin characters into our writing, but some difficulties prevent us from carrying out this reform at the moment. This is mainly due to the lack of Latin characters that can adequately represent a series of specific phonemes. [...] (Mladenov 1934: 178-179; my translation)

The Latin alphabet used by the European peoples represented in the eyes of Mladenov a "Tower of Babel" (Mladenov 1930: 177), and the attempts of some Slavic nations to achieve uniformity in this writing system added to the confusion. In this context, it is interesting to remark that Yakovlev had also commented on the diversity of Latin scripts in Western Europe, and praised the endeavor of script unification carried out in the Eastern Soviet territories: "It should be noted that in Western Europe we still have not reached any unification of the Latin alphabet. A unified Latin alphabet does not exist anywhere except in the Soviet East" (Yakovlev 1930: 34; my translation).

Mladenov summed up his opinion by stating that, if faced with an alphabet switch from Cyrillic to Latin, every educated Bulgarian should respond with "four emphatic no's," adding that, "[a]s long as the civilized Western Europeans stubbornly cling to the tradition of their meaningless Latin alphabet, the introduction of Latin in Bulgaria would be neither desirable nor timely" (Mladenov 1930: 177-178; my translation). This philologist was surely not the only one to attach special importance to certain characters of the Cyrillic alphabet in Bulgaria. For instance, Goshev also reflected on the possible consequences of replacing the Cyrillic script with the Latin one, noting that the Bulgarian language would thereby encounter the same difficulties noted by the ancient Bulgarian writers when they were confronted with the Greek alphabet. Here, reference is made to Chernorizets Hrabar, a monk and scholar active in the period between the 9th and 10th centuries, and significantly, both Goshev and Mladenov appear to draw on his arguments in the crucial work *On Letters* (*Za bukvite*) in their expressions of guardianship and affirmation of the superiority of the Cyrillic alphabet over the Latin (see also Mladenov 1931: 3-6). Despite the almost exclusively technical character of Mladenov's argumentation, his extensive scientific intervention supporting the retention of the Cyrillic alphabet, aimed primarily at exposing the limits of the Latin alphabet, can in fact be inscribed in the well-established "polemical tradition" in Bulgaria, part of an unaltered "ideology of letters" whose origins can be traced back to the Cyrillo-Methodian work itself.

3.8 Conclusions: the national character of the alphabet

In the post-imperial context of political and socio-cultural change in the Balkans and elsewhere, including the Soviet Union, it was clearly not the alphabets themselves that embodied the preferred target of attack or discussion, but what stood behind them, namely the political, ideological, cultural and religious values attributed to them (cf. Unseth 2005: 22). In general terms, during crucial historical turning points, societies are able to shift the public's attention and tension towards certain elements that are indicators of something else, on a level of discourse that is purely metaphorical but no less powerful for that. This fact substantiates the importance of symbols as representational markers in the national discourse on identity and "alterity" (Bugarski 2009b: 114).

Writing undoubtedly conveys linguistic content, but it is above all "a primary symbolic system that directly cyphers cultural meanings" (Cardona 1982: 4; my translation). In the case here considered, the opinions of scholars from different professions help to provide an integral picture of the alphabet question, which includes factors that are simultaneously symbolic, political, and pragmatic. It would therefore be wrong to reduce the complexity of the issue to merely "national propaganda discourse," partly because, as we have seen, some participants in the debate also spoke out in favor of script reform, although to a lesser extent. These included a highly influential writer such as Elin Pelin, whose clear and rational motive for adopting the Latin characters could also exert an influence on the community's self-perception, on its national self-identification and on the symbols that constituted it (see Smith 2009: 31).

The Bulgarian case demonstrates that the long-established writing practices of a linguistic community can prove to be, in a sense, intolerant of any scope for change, in this way joining other conventions related to the religious, moral, artistic and cultural spheres. The rules that underlie a writing system can thus in certain cases crystallize in a "monolithic" whole that resists any prospect of changing its graphic repertoire, even the possibility for certain signs to be removed or added in order to improve the alphabet's suitability to the needs of a language (Wellish 1978: 41). As concerns the Bulgarian case, in fact, a few years before the debate on Cyrillic, in 1923, a spelling reform proposed by the Minister of Education Omarchevski for modernization purposes had been discarded.

Many other discussions of the issue took place, in particular during a meeting of the Bulgarian National Assembly in 1928, in which Omarchevski insisted on the necessity of applying rules to simplify the spelling of the language, albeit in vain (cf. Stenografski dnevnici 1928). On this occasion, politicians who took sides against Omarchevski defended the "indicted" letters and pronounced statements such as the following:

> You do politics with the ъ. The operation to remove the ъ was undertaken by the Serbs. The ъ is a national symbol and cannot be eliminated. (Stenografski dnevnici 1928: 874; my translation)

> Spelling is a matter of centuries, and not only of your heads. Я and ь — these represent Bulgarianness, the history of Bulgaria! [...] [T]hey mean Cyril and Methodius, they mean Paisij.[31] (Stenografski dnevnici 1928: 883-884; my translation)

The positions of the proponents of this spelling reform were based on the idea that a new orthography would facilitate the literacy process, making writing itself more accessible to the people, and thus

---

31 The reference here is to Paisij Hilendarski (Saint Paisius of Hilendar), a central figure of the Bulgarian National Revival in the 18th century. Konstantinov accused Omarchevski of creating a situation of "spelling chaos" in the country with his 1922 reform, and also claimed that if the threatened letters had not existed, Macedonia would not have existed either (Stenografski dnevnici 1928: 884).

free from the "monopoly" of the "cultural castes": "The present orthography is more an orthography for the aristocrats of writing — if one can put it this way — for writers and professors" (Stenografski dnevnici 1928: 875; my translation). In the final analysis, the struggle was also in this case between the defenders of tradition and those of modernity.

From the Bulgarian debates on script reform, we understand how ideologies about literacy and alphabets could be linked to specific questions of identity and modernity at key moments of political transition. To some extent, we can speak of common elements that characterize the post-Ottoman period in the various successor states: in the process of asserting a new national identity, new modernizing perspectives opened up, in which cultural history played a fundamental role, and whose narratives often incorporated the traditions of the writing systems. Essential in this process was the kind of bond the nation maintained with its past: if Turkey and Bosnia undertook the removal of their Arabic writing heritage for very different reasons, it was because the political ideologies of the newly established states were incompatible with the values of the past. Thus, instead of trying to attain some form of compromise, they preferred to make a clean break with tradition. For other states, such as Bulgaria and Greece, the relationship with the past proved to be crucial in the process of post-Ottoman identity construction and remains so to a very high degree. A real spelling reform of the Bulgarian language was not to take place until 1945. Alphabet reform did not arise as a topic of discussion again until the post-communist era, an issue that will be addressed in chapter 9.

4. THE CONTRAST BETWEEN ARABIC AND LATIN SCRIPTS AMONG THE BULGARIAN TURKS

4.1 The impact of the Eurasian alphabet reforms on Turkey

As seen in the previous chapter, the adoption of the Latin alphabet for the transcription of the Bulgarian language met with rather strong opposition in the Balkan country and the project was completely abandoned in the 1930s, in part due to the modified script ideologies in the Soviet Union. Nevertheless, the controversy related to the introduction of a Latin-based writing system in the country did not end there. These debates can indeed be interestingly connected to the topic of the writing practices of the Turkish minority living in Bulgarian territories, which faced significant socio-cultural changes after the end of the Ottoman Empire and the proclamation of the Turkish Republic in 1923. The fate of the Turkish language in Bulgaria epitomizes an almost "paradoxical" situation of coexistence and clash between the different writing ideologies and identity/power dynamics active in this delicate post-imperial and post-war period, affecting both Bulgarians and Turks.

As mentioned above, the establishment of the Turkish Republic was followed a few years later (1928) by the alphabet reform of the Turkish language, i.e. the abandonment of the Arabic writing system for a Latin-based alphabet. This graphic revolution acquired paramount significance for the history of the country: it was a decision that sprang from a nationalist program that viewed the previous writing system as a symbol of spiritual oppression and backwardness. Not only in Turkey, but also elsewhere, the adoption of the Latin alphabet coincided with a desire for modernization, and marked a clear break with earlier political and/or religious elites. For example, this is what happened in Albania, where Latinization was introduced by official decree after the Congress at Monastir (now Bitola) in 1908, and to some extent this was also the case for Malaysia and Indonesia (Wellish 1978: 44).

As early as the beginning of the 20th century, similar proposals to adopt the Latin alphabet had been made by several writers associated with the Young Turks movement, but without success.[32] The issue was raised again starting from 1922 in the political context of the new republic, triggering a public debate that lasted for several years (Lewis 1999). The most conservative and religious factions rejected the idea of alphabet Latinization, fearing the possible separation of the Turkish Republic from the wider Islamic world. Furthermore, in their view, the traditional sacred religious community would be endangered, and its supra-national values substituted with an "alien" (i.e. Western European) concept of national identity. Others opposed Latinization on practical grounds, expressing doubts about the suitability of a Latin-based writing system for the graphic representation of Turkish phonemes.

In this context, some suggested that a better alternative might be to modify the Arabic alphabet and introduce additional characters to represent the Turkish vowels more effectively, as had been done to some extent before, for example in Čaušević's reformed Bosnian *arebica* (Caferoğlu 1934: 122). In 1926, however, the Turkic republics of the Soviet Union adopted the Latin alphabet, setting an important precedent for reform advocates in Turkey. In the same year, the issue was raised at the government level in the country through a proclamation of the Ministry of Public Education, which generated a positive response in the press (ibid.).

In Atatürk's vision of cultural reform, the new 29-letter Latin alphabet was seen as a fundamental step for the progress and modernization of the country. After the establishment of a one-party

---

32 Clayer (2004) points out that there is a further relevant case of the practice of transcribing the Turkish language with other alphabets, namely that of some Balkan printers who realized the convenience of using the Latin alphabet to transcribe the Turkish language long before it became the sole norm for this language. In fact, a few years before the First World War, a number of Turkish-language newspapers printed in modified Latin characters appeared in the Balkan provinces of the Empire. An example of this is the newspaper *Esas* published in Monastir, in today's North Macedonia, in 1911: two pages in Arabic characters and two in modified Latin characters for the Turkish language.

state ruled by the People's Republican Party (Cumhuriyet Halk Partisi [CHP]), the Turkish leader managed to dissolve opposition to the radical reform of the alphabet by establishing his own Linguistic Commission (Dil Encümeni) in July 1928, which was responsible for adapting the Latin script to the phonetic needs of the Turkish language. The resulting Latin alphabet was intended to reflect the actual sounds of the Turkish language. Atatürk himself was personally involved in these decisions and called a sort of "alphabetic mobilization" to promote the change in script usage. He visited far and wide the areas of the country to illustrate the new Latin letters and to encourage their rapid adoption.

The reform was formalized by the Turkish Republic through Law No. 1353 (Kanun 1928), which was adopted on 3 November 1928. In the first article of this law, the new characters of this alphabet were defined as exclusively "Turkish": "Instead of the Arabic characters hitherto used for writing the Turkish language, it has been decided to accept, under the name of Turkish characters, the use of the characters given in the list annexed hereto and derived from the Latin alphabet" (Kanun 1928; my translation). The following article stated that the use of this alphabet was to be compulsorily extended not only to documents written in Turkish in ministries, companies, insurance companies and public institutions, but also in private institutions. The law came into force on 1 January 1929 and made the use of the new alphabet obligatory in all areas of public communication.

4.2 The ambivalent status of the Latin alphabet in Bulgaria

In the Bulgarian Turkish community, which numbered 750,000 at the time, the Turkish alphabet reform was not received with favor by all. The reactions of the elites and the more conservative factions, such as the Islamic authorities and the stricter believers, were in line with those expressed by their counterparts in Turkey (cf. Galanti

1995 [1927]).³³ Unsurprisingly, they sharply criticized the script change, judging the Latin alphabet as harmful to the integrity of the Islamic community and, above all, to the historical continuity of a writing tradition inscribed in the context of the Ottoman cultural and intellectual world. In contrast, the Association of the Turkish Teachers of Bulgaria emerged as a great supporter of this alphabet reform for the Turkish language.

In the early years of the Turkish Republic, when there was still great strife in Turkey between Kemalist and Islamic ideas, the Turks of Bulgaria founded an organization called *Turan*,³⁴ dedicated to the propagation of Kemalist ideology. It also published a newspaper of the same name, which, together with the magazine *Deliorman*,³⁵ constituted the main press organ supporting the Turkish republican government. In opposition to this, the most religious part of the Bulgarian Turks published a newspaper called *Civilization* (*Medeniet*), which disseminated elements of "counter-propaganda" against Atatürk's reformist and modernizing thought.

In the immediate post-war period, the Turks of Bulgaria were mostly viewed by Bulgarian authorities as a powerful instrument in the hands of Ankara; nevertheless, until 1923, this community experienced a relatively easy period in its history: about ten Turkish deputies enjoyed representation in the Bulgarian Parliament, and the minority benefited from relative press and educational freedoms. However, after the coup d'état of 9 June 1923, which overthrew the Aleksandar Stamboliyski government, and the subsequent seizure of power by Aleksandar Tsankov, the number of Turkish deputies fell from ten to five and later to four (Nahapetyan 2007: 34).

In those years, the pro-Kemalist newspaper *Deliorman* often pointed out that the Turkish minority in Bulgaria constituted a "national minority" and not a "religious minority." In their view, in times of great modernization and especially in the context of the

---

33 "Arabic letters do not hinder our progress" is the title of a book published by Avram Galanti, an author of Sephardic Jewish origins, in 1927 in Istanbul.
34 A reference to the name of the original Central Asian homeland of the Turkic people.
35 The Turkish name for the Ludogorie region of Bulgaria.

discussion of the national minorities question with the League of Nations, characterizing this community on a religious basis as a "Muslim minority" instead of a "Turkish minority in Bulgaria" represented an outrage to the new Turkish republican identity and to minority rights (cit. in Şimşir 1988: 57-58). In fact, Bulgaria had signed the 1925 Treaty of Friendship with Turkey, in which the Turkish communities in Bulgaria were defined as "Muslim minorities" (see Protocol B in: Treaty of Friendship 1925).

Undoubtedly, Atatürk's alphabet reform had a direct impact on the development of the religious, cultural and educational fate of the Turkish minority in Bulgaria, which depended to a large extent on the ideological choices of the neighboring country. Of particular interest is the fact that the Turks in Bulgaria were actually the first to adopt the new Turkish alphabet outside Turkey (Şimşir 1992: 302), with the Yambol newspaper, *Innovation* (*Yenilik*), which began printing entirely in the new Turkish alphabet on 13 October 1928, thus even before the alphabet reform officially took effect in Turkey (Şimşir 1988: 103).

The most reform-minded members of the community considered it appropriate to adapt to what was happening in the neighboring country, where the new writing system was about to be officially adopted in the school curriculum. They took care of the creation of suitable textbooks for Turkish pupils in Bulgarian schools (Dayıoğlu 2005: 238), as it was forbidden to receive them directly from Turkey. In the late summer of 1928, some of these teachers were sent on a mission to Edirne, the first Turkish city after the border, to learn the new alphabet that would be taught to the Turkish population in Bulgaria (Haksöz 2007: 29). After their return, they undertook to prepare the reference text for the instruction of the pupils in Bulgarian Turkish schools, and it so happened that in a publishing house in Haskovo, thanks to the work of Ahmet Sükrü, one of the teachers of the Turkish school in Plovdiv, a primer called *Turkish Alphabet* (*Türk alfabesi*) was published (Mutlu & Kavanoz 2010: 373). During the creation of this alphabet manual, some technical difficulties were encountered in relation to the graphic rendering of the two Turkish letters <ş> and <ğ>, which were not available to Bulgarian printers. This problem was solved through a "creative strategy," by placing a comma or (upside down) question mark below the letter *s* and a comma above the letter *g* (cf. Starshenov 1933 and Şimşir 1988: 97).

The opposition between the reactionary and the reformist factions within the community concerning the alphabetic innovations developed unexpectedly. The Bulgarian government, in fact, decided to endorse the Turkish conservative and religious elite, decreeing a ban on the use of the Latin alphabet in schools, and delivering a decisive blow to the educational destiny of the community (Mutlu & Kavanoz 2010: 369). In this way, Bulgaria stood on the side of the defenders of Islam, against the modernizing ideological line that Turkey was pursuing through its many cultural, economic and social reforms.

We can interpret the Bulgarian government position as reflecting its desire to isolate the Turkish population in Bulgaria from the latest political and ideological developments in Turkey, and also against the *turanic* ideology that glorified a connection between all peoples of Turkic origin living in the Caucasus, Russia, Central Asia and beyond (see Karpat 2004: 737). The idea of an unbroken chain of Turkic peoples from Europe to Asia employing the same Latin alphabet evidently frightened the Bulgarians, even before the Russians, who in the late 1930s decided to substitute their policy of Latinization with Cyrillization, precisely because of this concern. Moreover, the role of the anti-Kemalist political refugees from Turkey, whose asylum applications were accepted by Bulgaria at the time, should also be highlighted: they were active promoters of forms of resistance to Atatürk's innovations and, paradoxically, felt fully legitimized to pursue their goals in Bulgaria. The new events that marked the beginning of an era of great change and reform in Turkey were therefore often received with suspicion and fear in Bulgaria, due to the sensitivity to possible threats of expansionism and even assimilationism (cf. Muyhtar 2003: 30).[36]

---

36 In the Bulgarian press, however, there were also expressions of enthusiasm for Atatürk's reforms.

In order to analyze the scope of the "Latinophobic" ideology in Bulgaria, it is therefore necessary to consider not only the context of Latinization on a Eurasian scale, with its effects on the Bulgarian debates, and the case of the *Abecedar* in the Latin alphabet for the language of the "external" Slavic-speaking minority in Aegean Macedonia, but also this seemingly marginal, but in fact quite relevant historical case, which concerned the Turkish internal minority (cf. Vjolgi 2012).

The reaction to the decision of the Bulgarian Ministry of Education to ban the use of Latin characters, made in mid-November 1928, a week after the introduction of the new alphabet in Turkey, provoked positive reactions from the main conservative factions among the minority in Bulgaria, who considered the Arabic alphabet a sacred writing system linked to the Holy Scripture of the Koran. In response, the Turkish Ministry of Public Education and the Turkish Ambassador in Bulgaria tried to put pressure on the government in Sofia by denouncing the violation of the Turkish community's rights, and by pointing out that the Bulgarians themselves would benefit from the adoption of this alphabet by the community in question, as this script was associated with the Western world and its values (Şimşir 1988: 99).

The Bulgarian Ministry of Education finally decided to comply with the demands of the most reform-minded local Turkish community by issuing a circular on 14 January 1929, granting permission to receive instruction in Turkish schools in the country in the new Turkish alphabet (Mutlu & Kavanoz 2010: 369). The Turkish press in Bulgaria therefore soon adopted this script, with the exception of the main organ of the conservatives, *Renaissance (Intibah)*, which continued to publish its articles in Arabic characters.

4.3 Language and script restrictions for the Turks of Bulgaria

As far as the alphabet question was concerned, the Turkish minority in Bulgaria found itself in a complex situation: albeit in different ways and to different intensities, many students had indeed to learn three different writing systems. These were the Arabic alphabet in the context of religious education, the new Latin-based Turkish alphabet, and the Cyrillic alphabet for the Bulgarian language. The conviction of the religious representatives was that, of the three, the Arabic alphabet was the most necessary, as it maintained that the Koran could not be transcribed in the Latin alphabet. This script also served the religious and national affairs of the community and had to be preserved at all costs.

Nonetheless, after the introduction of the Latin alphabet in the country's educational institutions in 1930, the Bulgarian Ministry of Education went so far as to ban the use and teaching of the Arabic script in minority schools. The same happened in Turkey, where, on 1 June 1930, the Arabic alphabet was prohibited, and its use made subject to sanctions (Rossi 1934: 135). It thus appeared that the struggle between the two alphabets had ended with the definitive triumph of the Latin script, after two years of controversy and disputes over the cultural and educational destiny of this community in Bulgaria.

In parallel with this decision, however, a campaign with weighty consequences began in Bulgaria in March of the same year: dozens of schools belonging to the Turkish minority were closed by order of the same Ministry of Education, and many others were "Bulgarianized," i.e. they were forced to teach exclusively in Bulgarian (Mutlu & Kavanoz 2010: 369). In many institutions, the only concession made consisted of a few hours of oral religious instruction in the afternoon, depriving children of the possibility of reading or writing in their mother tongue, in whichever alphabet it was written: Arabic or Latin.

After the coup d'état of 19 May 1934 and the establishment of the military government of Kimon Georgiev, the "alphabetic" situation was again reversed. In a surprising turn of events, the new government restored the teaching of the Arabic alphabet in schools and banned for a second time the new alphabet, on the official grounds that "Muslims should be encouraged to develop links with their religion" (Balım 1996: 104). As an immediate consequence, all Turkish newspapers in the country printed in the new alphabet were prohibited, and Turkish intellectuals who defended the Latin alphabet were persecuted or forced to flee (Şimşir 1988: 104).

The minority press was almost completely suppressed: in the first year alone, ten community newspapers ceased publication, including some of the most influential publications, such as *Deliorman* and *Turan* (Shivarov 2008: 135), accused of spreading Kemalist ideas and Turkish nationalist propaganda that posed a threat to the integrity of the country. Thus, the only periodical publications of the Turkish community that survived the repression were those with an Islamic content, such as *Medeniet* (*Civilization*), published in Arabic characters, and *Hakikat Şahidi* (*Witness of Truth*), the organ of Protestant missionaries in the country, which, curiously, also used Arabic letters (Shivarov 2008: 136). Unsurprisingly, the pro-Kemalist organization *Turan*, which spread secular and liberal ideas, was dissolved and banned outright in 1936.

The Bulgarian government was indeed interested in mobilizing anti-Kemalist forces in the country in order to reduce Ankara's influence on Bulgarian Muslims. For this reason, an ideology opposed to Kemalism and progressivism was favored, even if it involved the promotion and imposition of a Muslim education for the Turkish minority in the country. Following this view, Bulgarian authorities supported the spread of religious publications, conferences and other activities among the Bulgarian anti-Kemalist Muslims. For example, they encouraged the activities of the anti-Kemalist organization *Society for the Protection of the Muslim Religion* (*Obštestvoto za zaštita na mjusljumanskata religija*), founded in 1934.

At this time, teachers and informants visited Muslim schools to monitor and report attempts to spread Kemalist ideas among students (Crampton 1997: 163). Muslim education and religious activities were encouraged, but only with the aim of curbing the diffusion of Kemalist propaganda and serving Bulgarian nationalist goals (Höpken 1997: 62-63). The reason why Kemalist activities were so strongly feared lay in Bulgaria's "paranoia" about the possibility of Turkish agents preparing actions aimed at advancing imperialist ideas of "reconquest." This was in line with worries that Muslim-majority Southern Bulgaria could be turned into a "Turkish territory" which could eventually be annexed by the neighboring country (Muyhtar 2003: 31, Neuburger 2004: 45). Moreover, Kemalism was associated with communist thought and ideology by the various Bulgarian governments, especially between 1923 and 1934.

Hence, the members of the Turkish community in Bulgaria were perceived as representing a value system that was at odds with that of the state, and that is why they were denied the opportunity to use their language (cf. Safran 1999: 85). It was on the basis of these beliefs that, in the interwar period, the Bulgarian government defended on several occasions its decision to isolate the Turkish population from the influences of modernization and secularism that were so active in Atatürk's Turkey—in a clear example of linguistic (and cultural) discrimination. With the reintroduction of the old Arabic alphabet in the school curriculum, the rights of the Turkish minority were increasingly violated, especially their so-called "alphabetic rights," the same rights that had been at stake in the *Abecedar* issue for the Slavophone communities in Aegean Macedonia that had caused such a huge scandal in Bulgaria.

In the following years, through numerous efforts of the most reform-minded members of the Turkish community in the country, the Bulgarian government was finally persuaded to authorize the teaching of the Turkish Latin alphabet, a decision formalized by a circular of 12 April 1938 (Şimşir 1988: 122). The possibility of teaching and learning the new Latin alphabet, however, encountered particularly severe material constraints, as the Bulgarian government's discriminatory policies over the course of the previous two decades had reduced the number of Turkish-language schools by about three-quarters. Where, according to official Bulgarian statistics, about 1,700 schools for the Turkish minority were active in 1921-1922, by 1936 there were only 540 left (Muyhtar 2003: 28). The Turkish population, however, was stable, or rather, according to census data, had actually grown between 1920 and 1934, from 520,339 to 591,193 (data from the 1926 Bulgarian Census).

We can conclude that such a discriminatory policy against the Latin alphabet by the Bulgarian government was a clear expression of the desire for "ethnic exclusion," which can manifest itself in various forms or levels of intolerance towards national minorities

(Latcheva 2010: 202). According to the international law in force at the time when the issue of the Slavophones of Aegean Macedonia was debated, minorities living in Europe had to be granted a number of cultural, linguistic and religious as well as political rights. Examples of these were the right to establish their own associations and organizations for the promotion of the culture of the minority community, the right to publish books and magazines in their own language, the right to have newspapers and radio broadcasts in their own language, and the right to participate in education in their mother tongue (cf. Latcheva 2010, Rechel 2009).

The case of the conservative and anti-Kemalist publications in Bulgaria, which continued to use Arabic characters until 1943, is of great historical significance. This is probably a unique example in the former Ottoman Empire, surpassing the case of the Sanjak of Alexandretta (present-day Turkish Hatay province, on the border with Syria), which was under French dominion at the time of Ankara's alphabet reform, and where local Turkish-language newspapers did not adopt the Latin alphabet until as late as 1934.[37] In a way, Bulgaria remained a kind of "oasis" for the Arabic alphabet in the Balkans, since the new Latin alphabet had been adopted by the Turkish populations in Greece, Romania, and Yugoslavia (cf. Rossi 1934: 137).

4.4 Conclusions: the disruption of writing practices

In the period between the late 1920s and 1930s, the Arabic alphabet continued to occupy a dominant position in the scriptural and educational culture of Turkish minorities in Bulgaria. This fact was accompanied by a strengthening of the power of Islamic representatives, a clear paradox if we consider the secularist changes that had been taking place in Turkey for many years. In a sense, by favoring the Arabic alphabet over the Latin one, the Bulgarian government fostered partitions among members of the Turkish community in the country and isolated it from Turkey, encouraging tensions that

---

37   In the Turkish context, it is not surprising that the older generations continued to use the Arabic alphabet in their private correspondence and diaries until the 1960s (see Zürcher 2004: 189).

obstructed progress in the writing domain. Illiteracy was viewed as a useful instrument for impeding relations with Turkey, while Kemalism and intellectual advancement took on the opposite value, since they furthered relations with Turkey and threatened Bulgarian national integrity.

It could be maintained that the Ottoman post-imperial factor and the international modernization scenario were two equally significant elements in defining the Bulgarian official policy on writing issues in the country. The so-called "imperial legacy" (Köksal 2010) played a crucial part in the early years of Bulgarian nation-building, one which determined the options and constraints within the framework of a minority policy; in this sense, the government's policy towards the Turkish minority in Bulgaria evolved at different stages according to criteria of "denial," "tolerance," and, later, attempts at assimilation.

These tendencies were part of Bulgaria's path to modernity, marked by a painful relationship with its Ottoman past, in an attempt to "emancipate" itself culturally by developing a national identity within the benchmarks of East and West, respectively corresponding to "backwardness" and "progress" (Latcheva 2010). This process of rewriting the nation faced a number of cultural groups that represented a kind of "disturbing" hybridity, as they challenged the supposed homogeneity of the Bulgarian people as well as of their Christian tradition: i.e. Turks, Tatars, Pomaks and Muslim Roma (Neuburger 2004). The widespread dissemination of nationalist ideas in the 19th century had enforced the idea that the establishment of the nation-state and of ethnic homogeneity were two crucial factors for a country's progress. But the ethnic composition of Bulgaria was far from homogeneous: after the liberation from Ottoman rule, large Armenian, Jewish and Greek communities lived in Bulgaria's major cities alongside the Bulgarian population, while some regions of the country were populated mainly by Vlachs (Aromanians), Pomaks, Roma and, of course, Turks, who were the second largest ethnic group in the country after the Bulgarians.

The dynamics of "suppression" of the part of the past marked by foreign domination was also evident in the destruction of some symbols of cultural heritage. In fact, the policy supporting the teaching of Arabic script to the Turkish minority did not match its defense on the historical or cultural level: on the contrary, the prevailing rhetoric asserted that the oldest traces of the rulers' imperial culture had to be destroyed. As a result, elaborate and artistically valuable public inscriptions on mosques and the tombs of Islamic spiritual masters were erased (Bernard Lory 1985). Furthermore, old gravestones in areas with a significant Turkish presence, still inscribed in Ottoman Turkish with Arabic characters, were vandalized and desecrated on different occasions over the course of the twentieth century. Others with Turkish or Arabic names were simply replaced (Marushiakova & Popov 2004: 23). The destruction of Turkish cemeteries, carried out in parallel with other discriminatory measures, epitomized the desire to erase as many traces as possible of a Turkish and Muslim presence in the country. Unsurprisingly, very few Ottoman newspapers published on the territory of the Bulgarian principality and Eastern Rumelia in the last decades of the 19th century have survived: some series of issues have been completely lost (cf. Shivarov 2008: 135).

The problem of minority rights and integration was certainly not solved after the Second World War: with regard to language and script questions, it is important to remember that during the communist regime, for instance, the Koran itself was for a time no longer available in Arabic, but only in Bulgarian translation, and the minority's periodical press could appear only in the language of the majority (see Cultural Survival Report 1995). In the most critical period before the collapse of the communist regime, in addition to removing any traces of the written Turkish language from Muslim cemeteries, municipalities even went so far as to change the names of the deceased and ancestors of the Turkish population (Dermendžieva 2015).

The restrictions on the Turkish language had a very significant impact on the writing practices of this community, especially those of the younger generations. In one of his articles, anthropologist Ali Eminov describes the case of a young relative of his who used to write the Turkish language in Bulgarian Cyrillic during the most intense years of the assimilation policy towards the Turkish minority. Since Turkish children at that time knew the Turkish language only orally and mastered only the Cyrillic alphabet for writing, it is not surprising that such cases could occur frequently, despite the probable efforts of the family to teach the children to write in the Turkish Latin alphabet (Eminov 1997: 156-7). The same happened to the population belonging to other minority groups in the country, whose educational institutions suffered a similar fate, as in the case of the Armenian community in Plovdiv, which still remembers the dark times when its Tiutiundjian school was closed (1976) and the teaching of the Armenian alphabet was interrupted. The effects of this break in the continuity of the transmission of the written language can still be seen today, almost 50 years later (cf. Selvelli 2015b: 168).

SECTION II

SCRIPT ISSUES IN THE "SERBO-CROATIAN TERRITORIES" IN THE INTERWAR PERIOD

5. SERBO-CROATIAN IN TWO SCRIPTS: DIGRAPHIA, "ALPHABET SYNTHESIS" AND BILITERACY

5.1 Linguistic and historical introduction

From a sociolinguistic point of view, the Serbo-Croatian language and contemporary Serbian represent an almost unique example, since they challenge the principle that a language is transcribed with only one writing system at a time (cf. Gelb 1963: 227).[38] In fact, we are dealing with the peculiar situation of two writing systems being used simultaneously for the same language, an interesting case of "digraphia" (cf. Baglioni & Tribulato 2015: 14), or rather "synchronic digraphia" (Dale 1980: 5). Linguist Petr Zima was one of the first to coin the English term *digraphia* in a 1974 article describing the state of the Hausa language, written in two different writing systems: the Boko alphabet, based on Latin characters, and the Ajami one, based on Arabic. Zima defined this condition as one in which "[t]wo types of written form of one language co-exist, based upon the usage of two distinct graphical systems (scripts) by the respective language community" (Zima 1974: 58). In recent times, in addition to the term "digraphia," the English terms "biscriptality" (Bunčić 2016) and "biscriptalism" (cf. Greenberg 2004: 41, Feldman & Barac-Cikoja 1996) have emerged to describe the same phenomenon, and are much more used today.

The condition of "digraphia" or "biscriptalism" generally occurs when a linguistic community appears to be divided between two different religious identities or between two conflicting national identities (cf. Collin 2011: 40): it is therefore a phenomenon that can be symptomatic and a harbinger of profound political consequences. As stated by Robert D. King (2001: 44), "digraphia is

---

[38] The author adds: "While it is true that in general a language chooses only one writing as its means of expression, there are no limitations as to the use of one writing for any number of languages" (228).

regularly an outer and visible sign of ethnic or religious hatred. Script tolerance, alas, is no more common than tolerance itself."

Most historical examples of digraphia in the Slavic linguistic and cultural sphere can be traced back to the different levels of competing influences of Western and Eastern religious cultures. In the case of Yugoslavia, the Latin and Cyrillic alphabets were used side by side in what was the borderland par excellence where the so-called *Slavia Latina* and *Slavia Orthodoxa* (cf. Picchio 1991, Garzaniti 2007) met. This juxtaposition of writing systems has produced, in Serbo-Croatian, a series of conditions of digraphia through which, to some degree, the Latin alphabet gradually extended its presence by penetrating eastward.[39] Nevertheless, the most appropriate term to describe the graphic situation in these areas would be "multigraphism" or "graphic polycentrism," since, as already mentioned, there were also other writing systems in use, such as the Arabic characters to transcribe the local Bosnian language, and the Glagolitic alphabet.

As for the Serbo-Croatian language, the parallel existence of the Latin and Cyrillic alphabets became an issue of debate for Serbian and Croatian scholars from the 19th century onwards. In parallel with the orthographic modernization of their respective writing systems, scholars were indeed concerned with the question of the optimal transcription from one alphabet to another. Inspired by the principle of perfect correspondence between phoneme and grapheme, Serbian Vuk Stefanović Karadžić had carried out a spelling revolution in the first half of the 19th century, developing a reformed and simplified Serbian Cyrillic script through the removal of many superfluous characters from the previous alphabet.[40] Karadžić wanted to get closer to the "brothers of the Catholic

---

39 See also Cardona 2009b [1987]: 137 on Serbo-Croatian: the languages "spoken in the 'Slavia Orthodoxa,' i.e. in the area of the Byzantine Orthodox religion [...] use Cyrillic scripts (a script derived from Greek); the languages of 'Slavia Latina,' on the other hand, use Latin scripts; and we can observe the border between the two regions in Serbo-Croatian, which is written today in both scripts, symmetrically" (my translation).

40 In doing so, he had struggled for the liberation of the written language from its dependence on the Slavic-ecclesiastical writing linked to the authority of the

faith" (cit. in Bojić 1977: 100; my translation), that is, the Croats under Habsburg rule, in order to reach literary unification, which could be facilitated by a consistent system of transliteration between the two alphabets:

> We should all strive to ensure [...] that every book can be transcribed letter by letter from Latin to Slavonic characters, and from Slavonic to Latin characters, and so (and only then) will we be one people and will we have a single literature. (cit. in: Bojić, 1977: 100; my translation)

In parallel to this, the Croats living in the Habsburg Empire founded the so-called Illyrian movement, whose aim was to achieve the unification of the South Slavic peoples and the attainment of a common literary language. One of its greatest exponents was the linguist and writer Ljudevit Gaj, who in the same years carried out the spelling reform of the Latin alphabet for the Croats on the model of the Czech script. In his *A Short Foundation of Slavic-Croatian Orthography* (*Kratka osnova horvatsko-slavenskoga pravopisaña*), published in Budapest in 1830, he stated that, similarly to the principle applied by Karadžić, each phoneme in the oral language should correspond to a single grapheme in the written language (cf. Cubberley 2003: 45).

The efforts of both Karadžić and Gaj contributed to bringing Serbs and Croats closer in terms of a literary language: the *ijekavian* variant of the language chosen by Karadžić in his works was acceptable to the Croats, in contrast to the *ekavian* one used by the literati of Vojvodina. This step therefore facilitated the language agreement concluded by the Habsburg authorities in 1850 to simplify the translation procedures of the language of their Serbo-Croatian subjects in the administration.

A real program of "alphabet unification" based on the exclusive adoption of the Latin alphabet was theorized around 1914[41] when Jovan Skerlić, an eminent Serbian literary critic, expressed his

---

Serbian and Russian Orthodox Churches, and also to develop autonomously in the new context of liberation from Ottoman rule.

41 Although there had been earlier attempts to achieve unification of writing, such as Ignjat Alojz Brlić's proposal that Croats adopt Cyrillic, expressed in his *Grammar of the Illyrian Language* (Buda, 1833). See Naumow 2015: 247.

willingness to find a compromise, triggering a famous debate that involved a number of intellectuals (cf. Banac 1984: 211). According to Skerlić, the Serbs had to abandon the Cyrillic alphabet in the context of public usage, while the Croats had to adopt the *ekavian* variant of pronunciation instead of *ijekavian*: in this way, Serbo-Croatian would become a properly unified language. However, both Skerlic's early death in 1914 and the outbreak of the First World War shortly afterwards interrupted the debate, which resumed only after the end of the war.

5.2 Post-war alphabet ideologies: four parallel trends

In the sociopolitical context following the creation of the Kingdom of Serbs, Croats and Slovenes at the end of 1918, the alphabet question began to arise for the first time at the institutional level in the new state entity. This led to the formalization of a condition of "synchronic digraphia" or "biscriptality", which had already been defined in the 1917 Corfu Declaration. As a first official step towards the establishment of the common state, the Declaration indeed stated that the Cyrillic and Latin alphabets were equal before the law[42] (cf. Krfska Deklaracija 1917).

However, the controversy over script issues did not end there; in particular, there was much discussion about the situation of digraphia, called "dvoazbučnost" (Bugarski 1997: 38, 91) in Serbo-Croatian, and also about "biliteracy" (Bunčić 2016: 68). This last term refers to the situation in which, unlike digraphia, both alphabets are used interchangeably by one or more parties. This was indeed the situation originally envisaged in the new Kingdom, which later persisted to some extent in the Second Yugoslavia, and which is still current in Serbia today.

In 1929, the regime of King Aleksandar (the so-called "6 January Dictatorship" ["Šestojanuarska diktatura"], established that year) confirmed by law the equal use of both alphabets through the

---

42 Cf. the 6th principle: "Both alphabets, Cyrillic and Latin, are also completely equal and everyone is free to use either throughout the Kingdom. All state and self-governing authorities are obliged and have the right to use both alphabets, in accordance with the wishes of the citizens."

publication of the *Spelling Instructions for all Primary, Secondary and Vocational Schools in the Kingdom of Serbs, Croats and Slovenes* (*Pravopisno uputstvo za sve osnovne, srednje i stručne škole u kraljevini SHS*), which stipulated the obligation to learn both alphabets from the third grade of elementary school (cf. Pravopisno upustvo 1929), thus supporting the practice of "biliteracy." Nevertheless, not everyone was in favor of making both alphabets compulsory in the country. Indeed, in addition to the idea of biscriptality, three main lines of "script ideologies" were taking shape in those years.

The first was advocated by those who saw Cyrillic as an obstacle to the achievement of genuine national unification (in agreement with the principle already affirmed by Skerlić just before the war), in line with the ideological trends of modernization active in the other Balkan states, as well as in the wider Eurasian space. Apparently, Cyrillic was also considered a problem by the same King Aleksandar who had envisaged the abolition of this writing system in the interests of "Yugoslavism"[43] (in: Stefanović 2015: 112), a program that was, however, never carried out.

The second script ideology corresponded to the opinion held by scholars (of Serbian origin) to introduce the Cyrillic alphabet as the exclusive writing system for the entire Kingdom of Yugoslavia, emphasizing its value for the collective Slavic cultural history, especially through the work of Vuk Stefanović Karadžić.

In addition, there was another very singular, though marginal ideology, advocated by those who affirmed the need to develop a new "Yugoslav alphabet" consisting of a combination of characters from the Cyrillic and Latin alphabets, which developed between the end of the 1920s and the beginning of the 1930s. We will now analyze these currents in more detail, devoting special space to the last ideological strand, the one supporting the "Yugoslav alphabet."

---

43 Apparently, the opinion of the eminent linguist Aleksandar Belić had discouraged the king from pursuing his intention (in: Stefanović 2015: 5).

5.3 The influence of the "pro-Latinization" factors

In the context of the socio-political changes initiated in the immediate post-war period, the "pro-Latinization" movements continued to refer to the proposal made a few years earlier by Serbian literary critic Jovan Skerlić to introduce the Latin alphabet in place of the Cyrillic alphabet among the Serbs, in exchange for Croatian acceptance of the Eastern dialect.[44] It thus constituted an important and legitimizing precedent for those working for Serbo-Croatian language union. Towards the end of 1913, Skerlić published an article, "Eastern or Southern Dialect" ("Istočno ili južno narečje"), in the journal he edited, the *Serbian Literary Gazette* (*Srpski Književni Glasnik*), in which he also dealt with the alphabet question:

> But sooner or later the Eastern dialect will become the general Serbo-Croatian dialect, for it is known that in thirty, forty, or fifty years, when the Serbo-Croatian people will be nationally secure, as was the case with the Orthodox Romanians, Latin will become the common literary alphabet. (Skerlić 1913: 872; my translation)

In a survey[45] conducted by Skerlić in the *Serbian Literary Gazette* in 1914, different scholars (both Serbian and Croatian), some of whom even addressed the question of the alphabet, presented various opinions on the subject of language unification. Among these there were some who openly advocated for the Latin script, such as Serbian writer and literary critic Marko Car: "As far as the graphic question is concerned — Cyrillic or Latin — I have been a 'Latinizer' for a long time and, together with the beautiful oriental dialect, I would like the victory of the beautiful worldly Latin" (in: Skerlić 1914: 118; my translation).

Similarly, Croatian politician Josip Smodlaka declared that the *ekavian* variant and the Latin alphabet constituted the elements of a compromise formula and, at the same time, the most practical way "to achieve complete literary union between Serbs and Croats" (in: Skerlić 1914: 123; my translation). Yet, of the approximately thirty

---

44   The *ekavian* variant of Šumadija and Vojvodina.
45   Entitled "Anketa o južnom ili istočnom narečju u srpskohrvatskoj književnosti": "Survey on the Southern or Eastern Dialect in Serbo-Croatian Literature".

responses to Skerlić's survey (which also appeared in further issues of the journal), only six in total favored the use of the Latin alphabet; however, this was simply because no one else commented on the alphabet question,[46] focusing instead on the issue of the dialectal variant, which Skerlić had actually put forward as the main concern. In this respect, the majority of scholars declared themselves in favor of the Eastern variant. In any case, this investigation set a crucial precedent for the national intelligentsia.

After the war, the Latinization context of the 1920s also began to exert a significant influence on the discussions about script choice in the new Kingdom of Serbs, Croats and Slovenes. An important contribution in this direction was the article which appeared in December 1930 in the journal of the Novi Sad Institution Matica Srpska, by writer and museographer Franjo Malin. Malin downplayed the national value of the Cyrillic and Latin scripts by considering them in a neutral and not "nationalized" way: "[t]he Cyrillic alphabet is not by origin and use Serbian, nor is the Latin one a Croatian alphabet"; he thus recommended the adoption of a single writing system for the "single Yugoslav nation." The writing system favored was Latin, in line with the prevailing ideals of modernization and unification at the international level. Although Malin's proposal was to make Latin the official public alphabet, he nonetheless envisaged the survival of the Cyrillic script in certain domains, including the ecclesiastical sphere and the press, while providing that it should be taught in schools: "[t]he school and the church would cultivate Cyrillic by keeping the link with our past alive" (Malin 1930: 187; my translation).

Malin's article marked the beginning of the debate on Latinization in the Kingdom of Yugoslavia, and in the following issue (January/February 1931), the journal *Letopis Matice Srpske* decided to organize a survey on the subject, similar to what had happened in Bulgaria a few months earlier with the initiative in the pages of *Bulgarian Book*. Two reactions were published in the journal, both

---

[46] With the exception of Ivo Vojnović from Dubrovnik, who declared himself in favor of the equality of both alphabets.

of which were against the policy of Latinization. One was the article entitled "Two Slavic Characters" ("Dve slovenske bukvice"), written by Mita Đorđević, in which he argued for the need to preserve both the Cyrillic and Latin scripts in the Kingdom of Yugoslavia (Đorđević 1931: 150-153).

The second was the text by Poleksija Stošić entitled "Some Words on the Need for a Single Alphabet" ("Nekoliko reči o potrebi jednog pisma"), in which this literary scholar argued for the introduction of Cyrillic as the only writing system in the country: "Cyrillic should be adopted for the reason that most of our literature, from its beginning until today, is written in Cyrillic, and that the masterpieces of our literature, our folk songs, in all their editions, are printed in Cyrillic" (Stošić 1931: 157; my translation). Later, in the spring 1931 issue of *Letopis Matice Srpske*, another article appeared, "For a Single Alphabet" ("Za jedno pismo"), using the title of Malin's own article, in which Dr. V. Isaković[47] explained the need to introduce the Latin alphabet exclusively, basing his arguments on the "people's desire" to use this script, which he had directly observed during his professional activity[48] all over the country.

Further echoes of the debate on Latinization can be detected in the statements made in an article published by the Croatian senator Frano Ivanišević[49] on the periodical *National Defense* (*Narodna odbrana*) in the summer of 1933, entitled "For *latinica* and *ekavian*" ("Za latinicu i ekavštinu") (in: Živaljević 1935: 11). In particular, Ivanišević affirmed his belief in the necessity of adopting the Latin alphabet as the sole writing system, in line with the Eurasian trend of Latinization:

> It is well known in the civilized world that among the Russians, as the largest Slavic branch, and also among the Asiatic peoples of China and Japan, there is a general tendency to introduce the Latin alphabet as soon as possible in order to facilitate communication with the whole developed world. In principle, the matter is accepted; one has only to wait for its implementation.

---

47 It was not possible to determine the first name of the author.
48 In relation to cinema, and thus indicating movie subtitles.
49 He was a senator between 1933 and 1939 and, interestingly, also the author of a book on Glagolitic: Ivanišević, F., *Pobjeda glagoljice kroz tisućuljetnu borbu* (Split: Jugoslovenska Matica, 1929).

> Among the Asiatic peoples, the acceptance of the Latin letters is much more difficult than among us, both from a technical and linguistic point of view. The reformer of the Turkish Republic, Kemal Pasha, who had great opponents in the more conservative Muslim elements, was not deterred by these obstacles and so he banished the Arabic script and introduced the Latin script. (cit. in: Živaljević 1935: 20; my translation)

According to Ivanišević, the Cyrillic script posed also an obstacle for Western Europeans who wanted to learn Serbian: there were many admirers of Serbian literature, especially among the French, who "unfortunately" experienced not only linguistic but also graphic difficulties in dealing with it (in Živaljević 1935: 22).

In France, a Yugoslav diaspora newspaper called *Jougopresse* published on 31 March 1934 a text entitled "Cyrillic – Latin" ("Ćirilica – Latinica"), written by a certain Žurov; while describing Cyrillic as "our Slavic alphabet," he stated that this should nevertheless be replaced by Latin, as the only official alphabet in Yugoslavia, justifying his position with practical arguments and data from national statistics: "For those for whom the proportion of Latin alphabet usage in the world is not enough, we point out that, according to the latest statistics, in Yugoslavia 45% are Orthodox, 40% Catholics, and the rest of other faiths" (in: Živaljević 1935: 35-36; my translation).

It should be noted that in the late 1920s, in addition to those in Bulgaria and Greece (see chapters 2 and 3), discussions about the status of the Cyrillic and Latin alphabets were also taking place in Czechoslovakia, in connection with the writing of the Ruthenian language. Here too there was a contrast between those who enthusiastically supported the adoption of the Latin alphabet and those who rejected the idea altogether. An example of this is the article "Latin or Cyrillic" ("Latinika ili cyrilika"), which criticized the plan to Latinize the writing system for this language and pointed out that it was the Cyrillic alphabet that had protected the Carpatho-Ruthenians from assimilation by the Hungarians and other peoples (in: Duličenko 2001: 179).

As evidence of the importance of the "Latinizing" context of the late 1920s/early 1930s, it is essential to mention once again the important work of the International Institute of Intellectual

Cooperation. Indeed, in 1929, this body of the League of Nations decided to undertake a scientific study of the possibility of promoting the use of Latin characters throughout the world in order to achieve better understanding and communication between the Western countries and the East. The Institute inaugurated its activities at a time when there was widespread optimism in various parts of the world about a possible change in the graphic domain in this direction, encouraged by successful cases of alphabet reforms such as the Turkish one and those that were underway in various areas of the Soviet Union, as well as by the development of transcription schemes into Latin characters for the Chinese and Japanese languages.

Five years later, in 1934, the Institute published the report on the state of Latinization in various countries of the world entitled *L'adoption universelle des caractères latins*, containing examples of reforms that had already been carried out or were considered possible. In the introduction to the book, the Danish linguist Otto Jespersen argued that the Latin alphabet, despite all its imperfections and shortcomings, was the only one whose universal adoption could be recommended, by virtue of its greater clarity and suitability for writing and printing in comparison to other writing systems. The most decisive reason for its "universalization," however, was the fact that the use of such an alphabet was a firmly established practice in the West, in the countries "most important for the whole of world civilization" (Jespersen 1934: 13; my translation), a view that today appears very Eurocentric. Moreover, Jespersen argued in "utopian" terms for such a reform:

> There is no doubt that intellectual cooperation throughout the civilized world would be greatly facilitated if the same writing system were used everywhere; the diversity of alphabets in use is one of the greatest obstacles to reconciliation between nations and races. (Jespersen 1934: 13; my translation)

Jespersen also denounced the forces that opposed such alphabet reform in countries that already possessed a writing system other than Latin: these fed not only on a conservatism "strongly rooted in human nature" but also on a nationalism that refused to adopt an alphabet "borrowed" from another nation (ibid.). In this context, the linguist cited the case of Yugoslavia, where one could observe the "strange spectacle" of a population divided into two religious spheres that used two different writing systems to transcribe what was "actually the same language" (in: ibid.; my translation). Significantly, Jespersen compared the Yugoslav case with the Indian one, where the Hindustani language was divided into its Muslim form, i.e. Urdu, and the Brahmi one, Hindi, which used two completely different alphabets: an Arabic-based one for the former and the Devanagari for the latter.

In the section on country reports in the volume published by the International Institute of Intellectual Cooperation, we also find a short text on Yugoslavia, extracted from a letter by the French linguist and Slavicist André Vaillant, a professor at the *École nationale des langues langues orientales vivantes* in Paris, dated 14 April 1934. Here, Vaillant maintained that "the existence of the two alphabets in Yugoslavia is impractical and everyone suffers the effects, especially since these two alphabets are almost identical in the form of some letters" (Vaillant 1934: 184; my translation). He also recalled the attempts made in Serbia before the war to remedy this situation (referring, though not explicitly, to Skerlić), through the proposal to adopt the Croatian *latinica*. In this regard, however, Vaillant noted that public opinion in Serbia did not seem at all ready to abandon the Cyrillic alphabet. This appears indeed evident from a number of articles published in a number of influential journals during those years, including the aforementioned *Letopis Matice Srpske* in Novi Sad, which testify to the parallel efforts of prominent Serbian intellectuals to defend this script. The question had developed a little "by virtue of the closer contact between Serbs and Yugoslavs in the Western provinces" (ibid.; my translation).

Vaillant also recalled King Aleksandar's inclination to impose a single alphabet, the Latin one: "[a]t one point the dictatorship had announced a project to unify the two alphabets, clearly to the benefit of the Latin alphabet, but it seems he retreated in the face of the difficulties in implementing this radical project" (ibid.; my translation). In short, the problem was political and religious: the issue was certainly complex; but as far as pedagogy was concerned, according to Vaillant, a solution could be found.

5.4 The first proposals of "alphabet synthesis" appearing in *Život i rad*

The situation described by the linguist Otto Jespersen concerning the Serbo-Croatian language was quite representative of the condition of "synchronic digraphia" for which he saw a remedy only in the exclusive adoption of the Latin alphabet. As noted above, the script policy adopted in the Kingdom of Serbs, Croats and Slovenes, and later in the Kingdom of Yugoslavia (with the exception of the short-lived idea of King Aleksandar to eliminate Cyrillic), seemed instead to be aimed at creating a form of state biscriptality and biliteracy, in which all citizens would be able to write and read in both alphabets.[50]

In those years, however, there were those who, in the interests of Yugoslav unity, went even further in conceiving a unifying literacy policy, to the point of elaborating a particular proposal of "alphabet synthesis," a very rare if not unique fact in the history of writing systems. Armando Petrucci has noted that, unlike languages, "the graphic systems in use today seem to be strongly impermeable to one another, often also, if not mainly, for ideological and political reasons of prestige and national identification" (Petrucci 2007: 52). The case of the so-called "Yugoslav alphabet," although never put into practice but only theorized, seems to fundamentally undermine this basic principle of writing systems' functioning in the modern era. It can indeed be seen as a case of "script-mixing" (grapho-hybridization) (Rivlina 2016), or a "hybrid graphic system," a mixed system, obtained "through the transfer of characters not from a single writing system, but from several different systems" (Baglioni & Tribulato 2015: 22; my translation), a

---

[50] A fact also demonstrated by the publication of several texts on learning both writing systems that came out in those years, including: *Način učenje latinice posle ćirilice i ćirilice posle latinice* by Jovan Udicki, published in Novi Sad in 1921, and *Album šrifta: ćirilica i latinica* by T.K. Pogoreljski Peregud, published in Zemun in 1924.

phenomenon associated with scripts presenting a certain degree of artificiality.

Proposals along these lines had already been made in the previous century, as in the case of the Croatian philologist Đuro Augustinović, who in his work *Thoughts on Illyrian Orthography* (*Misli o ilirskom pravopisu*) (Vienna, 1847) had suggested, among other things, introducing the characters <ж>, <ч>, <ш> from Cyrillic into the Latin alphabet and adding new graphemes for the letters <lj>, <nj>, <đ> and <ć>, as well as a specific sign for the semivowel <r>. Moreover, according to him, Cyrillic should have adopted the letters <v>, <n>, <r>, <s>, <u> from Latin, and possibly also <m>, <t>, < d> (Moguš & Vončina 1969: 80).

A major proponent of the "mixed alphabet" solution in the interwar period was the Serbian scholar Božidar Stojanović, who in the autumn of 1934 published an article in the journal *Život i rad* (*Life and Work*) with the telling title of "Yugoslav Alphabet" ("Jugoslovenska azbuka"). The reasons why Stojanović called for the introduction of such an innovative writing system were numerous, all of an obviously ideological and in a sense utopian nature, linked to the facilitation of the unification of Serbs, Croats and Slovenes, who, in his view, constituted a single nation of "blood and language" (Stojanović 1934: 724; my translation). The author noted that the coexistence of two alphabets constituted the greatest obstacle to achieving this goal; however, this situation was surmountable through "acceptable sacrifices." Two alphabets were a "luxury," and contributed to the development of a kind of "tribal antagonism"; they also confused children, and made their education, as well as that of national minorities, much more difficult (ibid., 726).

With regard to the Cyrillic script, the author acknowledged its importance for the Serbian people, noting that it contained both "tribal attributes and religious traditions." The association with confessional sentiments derived from the mission of its creators, Saints Cyril and Methodius: it was therefore an expression of Orthodoxy and could be called "the Serbian Orthodox alphabet." Stojanović argued that it was nevertheless unthinkable to make Cyrillic the only alphabet in Yugoslavia precisely because it was a distinctly Serbian alphabet. The same was true of the Latin alphabet, despite its widespread use throughout the world, since it embodied a "Croatian" and "Catholic" element in Yugoslavia (Stojanović 1934: 727).

Many decades later, in defining the historical factors that separated the peoples of the former Yugoslavia, the linguist Ranko Bugarski similarly recalled how differences in writing reflected underlying religious fractures. Indeed, the alphabet followed the course of religion and was only secondarily linked to the national question: "In our case, Cyrillic is originally an Orthodox alphabet and Latin a Catholic one. The identification of the former as Serbian and the latter as Croatian (...) is a historical derivation" (Bugarski 1997: 90-91; my translation).

Considering that any attempt to introduce only one or the other alphabet would necessarily provoke friction and be doomed to failure, Stojanović recommended the establishment of a new writing system, which he named the "Yugoslav alphabet," to be used for the "Yugoslav language." This was extremely easy to learn and consisted of a mixture of Cyrillic and Latin that "guaranteed the principle of fairness to the point of mathematical precision," so as not to favor one alphabet to the detriment of the other (Stojanović 1934: 730; my translation). Half of the letters were to be taken from Cyrillic and half from Latin, in addition to the characters shared by the two scripts. Stojanović also specified some practical and technical details of the introduction of this new writing system in the country:

> The "Yugoslav alphabet" is to be introduced and special decrees are to be issued immediately for this purpose. It must be ordered that all existing printing presses and typewriters be organized and adapted to the requirements of the Yugoslav alphabet. Books and textbooks, all periodicals, newspapers, state administration publications and in general everything of a public character should be printed and written exclusively in the Yugoslav alphabet. (Stojanović 1934: 732; my translation)

The introduction of the new alphabet would imply many practical advantages in terms of literacy: for example, if the average Yugoslav citizen wanted to access the classic works that had not yet been published in the new Yugoslav alphabet, this would not be too difficult, since he or she would have to learn only the remaining twelve letters of either Cyrillic or Latin, something requiring only a minimal effort. In fact, by learning the Yugoslav alphabet, people would automatically become familiar with "three-fifths" of both writing systems. Stojanović's "Yugoslav alphabet" impeccably fulfilled the phonemic principle, since it presupposed the elimination of all digraphs appearing in the Croatian Latin alphabet. The writing system was constituted by the following letters:

a	б	в	g	d	ђ	e	ž	z	i	j	k	л	љ	m
n	њ	o	п	p	s	t	ћ	u	f	x	c	ч	џ	š

Drawing comparisons with the abandonment of the Arabic alphabet in Turkey, the author explained that Atatürk managed to "hypnotize" the masses and transform the country, which had previously embodied a paradigm of "fanatical conservatism," through "very courageous" reforms aimed at securing the future interests of the entire nation (ibid., 733). Stojanović particularly praised the achievements in terms of literacy, as the new Turkish leader managed to replace the "difficult," "outdated" and "inconvenient" Arabic writing system with a foreign alphabet that was new to the masses but much more suitable. He commented:

> And if these people abandoned everything that stands in the way of progress and a better future, even adopting a completely unknown and foreign alphabet they had to spend months learning to get used to—why should we falter, why should we not replace our two alphabets with a Yugoslav one, which contains no foreign letters, since it is of enormous importance and interest to our whole people, and incomparably simpler and more acceptable? (Stojanović 1934: 733; my translation)

In short, possible objections to such a reform, according to Stojanović, could not invalidate the fundamental advantages that would result from the introduction of the "Yugoslav alphabet" as the latter would lead not only to the assertion of a common language, but also a common culture and "Yugoslavism" in general (ibid., 731). As far as the economic impact was concerned, its introduction would imply the least possible sacrifice for the peoples involved, in contrast to the situation resulting from the simultaneous use of both alphabets, whose damage to the country was enormous:

> The introduction of the Yugoslav alphabet, therefore, would not only bring enormous material savings, but also give a new beginning and a strong impetus to the whole spiritual rebirth of our nation, because it would lead us by the shortest way to total spiritual fusion into one Yugoslav nation. Therefore, the moment of the introduction of the Yugoslav alphabet would be one of the most important for the internal consolidation of our country. (Stojanović 1934: 731; my translation)

Stojanović concluded his text by saying that he was optimistically waiting for a response, confident in the victory of reason and the imminent acceptance of his "Yugoslav alphabet."

In a later issue of *Život i Rad* (118) of the same year, a short text commenting on Stojanović's proposal appeared, written by Dr. Vojislav Kujundžić,[51] entitled "Yugoslav *latinica*" ("Jugoslovenska latinica"), which opened with the following sentence:

> In a nation with a unique national language, in a nation-state with a single sovereign and a common name, as in the case of our nation of three peoples in Yugoslavia, the strong need for a unified script is felt immediately and increasingly every day. (Kujundžić 1934: 862; my translation)

The author first justified this statement on practical grounds, illustrating the enormous simplification in the printing domain that would result from the use of a single alphabet. He then referred to the urgency of script unification in the public debate of the last two decades, citing the Latinization proposals by various representatives of society, including Skerlić, and the 1929 recommendation by the Slovenian jurist and politician Bogumil Vošnjak to adopt the Latin alphabet as the sole writing system for the country (Kujundžić 1934: 863).

Kujundžić's proposal was similar to the one made by Stojanović a few months earlier, although he called this writing system Yugoslav *latinica*. Although this might appear as a form of "discrimination" against Cyrillic, the author justified this definition by

---

51 From the scarce information available, we know that he was a doctor and founder of the Rotary Club of Belgrade in 1927.

observing that the Latin alphabets used by different peoples in the world were all different and possessed their own peculiarities: they could therefore be better distinguished by the use of a national marker (Kujundžić 1934: 864). Kujundžić's alphabet consisted again of a mixture of Latin and Cyrillic, although it appeared quite different from the one devised by Stojanović. Here too, the seven common characters were retained, and all digraphs were removed: <dz>, <lj> and <nj>. In contrast to the "Yugoslav alphabet," all characters with diacritical marks, <ž> <č> <ć> <š>, were eliminated, and replaced with corresponding ones taken from Cyrillic, together with five other Latin letters. Overall, this is what Kujundžić's "Yugoslav *latinica*" looked like:

a	b	v	g	d	ђ	e	ж	z	i	j	k	л	љ	m
н	њ	o	п	p	s	t	ћ	u	f	x	c	ц	ч	ш

5.5 The "Yugoslav alphabet" by Pavle Ž. Radivojević

The third author to propose a mixed alphabetic solution was Pavle Ž. Radivojević in his pamphlet *Cyrillic – Latin? Or Cyrillic in Latin?* (*Ćirilica – Latinica? Ili Ćirilica u Latinici?*), printed in Belgrade in 1934. Basing his affirmations on roughly the same grounds as the other two authors, Radivojević quoted the French philosopher Charles Bernard Renouvier, who stated that "civilization began with writing" (Radivojević 1934: 7; my translation). Since all Latin and Slavic alphabets had a common origin, having both evolved from Greek, which in turn had originated from the Phoenician alphabet, Croatian Latin and Serbian Cyrillic "came from the same source." The Latin alphabet was a "fraternal" alphabet, since the destinies of these two alphabets had always been very close to each other, in particular, during some important moments that influenced their respective destinies in the field of writing since the 9th century.

The first moment, which consisted in their literacy through the use of the Glagolitic alphabet, provided the ideal framework for the proper development of their intellectual and national community.

The forces of history started eroding this "unitary community" in the second half of the Middle Ages. Subsequently, the unity of the Serbian and Croatian spiritual communities had been threatened at the root by the establishment of two distinct spheres of influence which had separated the "two branches of the same people": over the course of time, a kind of intellectual and cultural dualism developed, whose most visible element was precisely that of the alphabet. Constantinople and Rome became two different magnets, the effect of which was that Serbs and Croats encountered each other "with their backs instead of their faces" (ibid., 11; my translation).

Radivojević described the shortcomings of the Latin alphabet and pointed to the inadequacy of the English alphabet, labelling it an "illegible" Latin-based writing system. The author recalled the attempts made as early as 1818 for the achievement of a unified "universal alphabet," referring to a Latin-based one developed by the French historian and orientalist Comte de Volney, founded on the principle of unambiguous correspondence between phoneme and grapheme.[52] Radivojević then expressed more concretely his position on the matter:

> The aim of this work is to contribute to the general use of a single alphabet in everyday life in the territories inhabited by three peoples of the same nation, where centuries-old aspirations have only recently been translated into living reality, after nearly two decades of free life. This question may eventually be resolved by compromise in such a way that Cyrillic and Latin participate equally in the construction of our future alphabet. (Radivojević 1934: 18; my translation)

The possibility of applying the new script solution was realistic, according to its inventor, since several examples attested to the fact that such "mixing" of the two alphabets did already occur in common practice, especially in private use, and sometimes involuntarily (Radivojević 1934: 19). In his view, one had to recognize the

---

[52] On this subject, see also Lepsius, *Standard alphabet for reducing unwritten languages and foreign graphic systems to a uniform orthography in European letters*, London, 1863, 20-22.

potential symbolic, ideological and unifying value of the new "Yugoslav alphabet":

> It is certainly not unknown that there are Serbs who live among the Croats and soon begin to write with the Latin alphabet, and likewise there are Croats and Slovenes who live among the Serbs and begin to use Cyrillic. How can this be explained? By the fact that [...] the alphabet, which until 1918 was a symbol of the nation and religion, has now become in Yugoslavia what a writing system actually is: a social convention. This adaptation is, in a way, an act of sociability and sophistication. (ibid.; my translation)

Nevertheless, Radivojević added, it would be naive to assume that Croats who used Cyrillic among the Serbs would forget their Croatian origins. It was understandable that the Croats were fond of their alphabet and considered it their national writing system, just as the Serbs loved their Cyrillic, rooted in "local, tribal and territorial patriotism" (Radivojević 1934: 22; my translation). Moreover, it was very difficult for the Serbs to abandon an alphabet they considered "more perfect than all other Latin and Slavic alphabets." Here we find an interesting reference to the idea of the Serbian alphabet's "perfection," which appeared to be quite widespread at the time (cf. Živaljević 1935: 3, 10).

The Swedish linguist and Slavicist Johan August Lundell, for example, attempted to rank the world's writing systems in terms of phonological accuracy in his 1930 work *Principles of Writing (Principes d'écriture)*: the Serbian and Finnish scripts were assigned the grade "excellent," the Croatian and Czech alphabets "very good," while English writing was described as "the most absurd" (cit. in Wellish 1978: 32). Even the writer George Bernard Shaw, who was keen on orthographic matters, was aware of the "flawlessness" of this writing system (Stojanović 2020: 203). The myth of the Serbian alphabet's perfection could in a way be viewed as the manifestation of what has been called "alphabetocentrism" (Cardona 1982: 3), i.e. the belief that an alphabet developed on a phonemic basis represents the most advanced, practical and logical writing system that mankind can conceive (see also Bugarski 2009a: 25). According to one definition, "alphabetocentrism can be seen as a local, exacerbated case of graphocentrism. The discourse isn't new (...). European alphabets would be at one end of a scale of perfection opposed to other forms of writing, just as Western monotheism would be at the peak of a supposed universal pyramid of religions" (Peyró 2016 192).

Radivojević presented his concrete proposal for a mixed alphabet by selecting eighteen characters from the Cyrillic alphabet and seventeen from the Latin alphabet. Of these, thirteen were in Cyrillic, twelve were in Latin, and five were common characters. This alphabet consisted of the following letters:

a	b	c	d	e	f	g	x	i	j	k	l	m	n	o
п	p	s	t	u	v	z	љ	њ	ђ	ћ	ж	ч	ш	џ

The author concluded his short book by stating that it was necessary to establish a new tradition in order to mark the beginning of a common Yugoslav history: "We want to build a new tradition by respecting the traditions that should be honored and by replacing those that need to be removed. We know that by establishing a single alphabet for all a great stone will be laid in the foundation of our new building" (ibid.; my translation). Such was the optimistic hope of a convinced advocate of the spiritual, political and cultural unity of the peoples that composed Yugoslavia.

5.6 Reactions to the "mixed alphabet" proposals

In a later issue of the journal *Život i Rad*, D. Aranđelović[53], a physician by profession, published a commentary on the subject of the "Yugoslav alphabet" in an article entitled "Two Opinions on the Yugoslav Alphabet" ("Dva mišljenja o jugoslovenskoj azbuci"). The text revealed itself to be particularly critical and sharp, so much so that the editors of the magazine themselves stated in a note that they had decided to publish it even though they did not agree with the thoughts expressed in it. It began with the following statements:

> The Yugoslav alphabet! Of course, if the "Yugoslav fundamentalists" give up the Serbian, Croatian and Slovenian names, if they do not want to know anything about the Serbo-Croatian or Slovene language, but only about the

---

53 It was not possible to determine the full first name of this author.

"Yugoslav" one, if the history of Yugoslavia is already being written and not the secular history of the Serbs, Croats and Slovenes [...], then why not renounce Cyrillic and Latin and create a 'Yugoslav alphabet'? (Aranđelović 1934: 861; my translation)

The author claimed that, if this new mixed alphabet were adopted, all the joys and sufferings experienced by the three peoples over the centuries, along with the precious traditions of the past, would be in fact undone, all in vain. To the eyes of "Yugoslav fundamentalists" such considerations were clearly meaningless, since they "wanted to build everything from scratch, even the alphabet!" (ibid.; my translation). With his proposal, Aranđelović argued, Stojanović made a major mistake by failing to take into account the sensitivities of the Serbs, Croats and Slovenes, who would continue to exist as peoples despite attempts to impose an exclusively Yugoslav ideology and identity:

Seriously, what is Mr. Stojanović trying to attain with this mixture of Cyrillic and Latin letters? To convince Serbs, Croats and Slovenes of "Yugoslav fundamentalism"? I don't think it will be achieved this way [...] For centuries the Serbian, Croatian and Slovenian names and languages, together with the Cyrillic and Latin alphabets, have been preserved, defended, [...] persecuted and celebrated, and therefore it will take centuries to let all this be forgotten through the adoption of some "'Yugoslav fundamentalism," accompanied by a Yugoslav language and alphabet. (Aranđelović 1934: 861; my translation)

At the end of his article, Aranđelović provocatively allowed himself to give Stojanović advice on how to improve his "Yugoslav alphabet." If the aim was to make it innovative, then both Cyrillic and Latin needed to be completely abandoned: in order to break with the past, one must create an entirely new writing system, with brand new letters. Surely, the author added, there were inspired and willing Yugoslavs who could help to develop a suitable alphabet for such purposes. "Why use an ugly mixture of Cyrillic and Latin letters, like a mixture of two good wines that makes a third bad one?" And above all, Aranđelović wondered, with regard to Vuk Karadžić's Serbian alphabet, "[w]hy ruin the ingenious creation of our Cyrillic alphabet, the simplest, most beautiful and easiest alphabet?", when the invention of a new writing system would result in a revolutionary work that could be aesthetically pleasing, or at least not "as ridiculous as this unlikely mixture of Latin and Cyrillic characters" in the form of a "Yugoslav alphabet" (ibid., 862; my translation)?

Aranđelović's text was followed one year later by a commentary by the eminent linguist and philologist Aleksandar Belić, entitled "New Alphabet" ("Nova azbuka"), published in the first issue of the journal *Our Language* (*Naš jezik*). Belić introduced the delicate topic of the new alphabet controversy by recalling how the 19th century had been marked by the struggle to achieve important agreements on a common literary language and on the alphabet: it was the "alphabet war" or the "ABC struggle," which had involved "the two sides of the common nation" (Belić 1935: 1; my translation).

Belić recalled some details of these "alphabet wars," reminding his audience of Vuk Karadžić's endeavors to defend his spelling reform. These had lasted 50 years, from 1818, when Karadžić first introduced it in his work, until 1868, after his death, when the last restrictions on its use were lifted. Similarly, Belić recalled, Ljudevit Gaj had formulated his orthographic reform of the Latin alphabet in 1830, but this reform was not accepted until 1892. The Slovenian alphabet was not adapted to the principles of Gaj's alphabet until 1848, but even then the struggle was far from over. By referring to these events, Belić attested to the importance of questions of writing and spelling for the Yugoslav people: although they "may seem trivial matters, matters of convention, common usage, and agreement, in reality the slightest interference with their foundations provokes the resistance of society" (Belić 1935: 1; my translation). It was not surprising, therefore, to witness complaints and oppositions to certain writing practices in Yugoslavia. At that time, although a not insignificant number of people were familiar with both alphabets, the majority of the population were certainly not, a fact that Belić regretted: "[t]hat is a great pity: because it not only slows down our cultural harmonization, but also tears apart our cultural strength and hides from the sight of part of the population what is happening in the other" (Belić 1935: 2; my translation).

Nevertheless, what Belić was advocating was not the establishment of a new or single writing system, but the transformation of the situation of official "biscriptality" into one of "biliteracy": his ideal was that the equal use of both alphabets should become normal among the entire population, through a state policy that would encourage to the maximum extent possible the interchangeable use of Cyrillic and Latin. In this way, both writing systems would be perceived by all parts of the country as their own, automatically diminishing ethnic nationalist feelings.

Unlike Aranđelović, however, Belić seemed to admit the merits of the bizarre solution of a mixed alphabet: the "third way" could indeed help appease rivalries between different ethnic groups, leading to a victory "without winners or losers" (ibid.; my translation). In itself, Belić argued, such a proposal was not unfeasible, partly because the Latin and Cyrillic alphabets had the same origin, having both descended from the Greek alphabet. Hence, there were undoubtedly positive aspects in the proposals made by Kujundžić, Stojanović and Radivojević. Furthermore, Belić argued, the very principle of combining characters from two or more writing systems to create a new one had often been applied to old and new, foreign, as well as regional alphabets (Belić 1935: 2). Belić thus recalled that Vuk Karadžić himself had adopted the letter <j> directly from the Latin alphabet, a fact that had been widely criticized by many (cf. Stančić 2005). While acknowledging the merits of a "compromise" position, he nevertheless confirmed that the solution of a "Yugoslav alphabet" would not be the most appropriate solution for the issue of digraphia in the country:

> Is it really necessary, even in the twentieth century, to wage an "alphabet war," which would inevitably ensue if we were to attempt to replace our Cyrillic, praised by the whole world as one of the most perfect alphabets, and our Latin, which fully corresponds to it, with a third alphabet, albeit composed of elements of both? (Belić 1935: 3; my translation)

There was no doubt for Belić that the introduction of a third alphabet would have entailed many difficulties, as well as the considerable distancing of the people from all works which had hitherto been written in the Latin or Cyrillic alphabets. Indeed, the masses could not be expected to acquaint themselves with the other writing systems, in addition to learning the Yugoslav alphabet. Nevertheless, as we have seen, the defenders of the new Yugoslav alphabet insisted on this very point, highlighting the fact that the effort required to learn the few remaining characters of both writing systems was minimal.

Belić concluded his article by stating that the emergence of various proposals to create a new alphabet embodied "a commendable effort" and a supporting factor on the path to the cultural unification of the Yugoslav people. According to him, attempts like that of creating the new Yugoslav alphabet would not stop until the Cyrillic and Latin alphabets attained full official equality, both being "felt" by the whole nation as their own (ibid.). Belić's statement represented thus a full substantiation of the need to achieve a situation of "biscriptality" and "biliteracy" at both the official and private levels, embarking on the difficult path of the "ideological coexistence" of these two writing systems.

5.7 Živaljević's rejection of the Yugoslav alphabet and Trivunac's defense of Cyrillic

In the context of the script debates, Danilo A. Živaljević, a writer and literary historian, published in Belgrade a pamphlet in 1935 entitled *Cyrillic and Latin* (*Ćirilica i Latinica*), which dealt in particular with the proposals for a "Yugoslav alphabet" made by Stojanović, Kujundžić and Radivojević: "[t]hree proposals – three alphabets. Each tried to claim his proposal was the best," wrote Živaljević, who then ironically wondered: "which of these three new alphabets should we adopt?" (Živaljević 1935: 28; my translation). Živaljević was the only one who provided very concrete examples of the application of these three writing systems. For example, he reported the name of the Yugoslav capital, written in Latin as *Beograd*, and in Cyrillic as *Београд*:

a) According to Kujundžić's alphabet, this would appear written as "Beogpad."
b) According to Stojanović's alphabet as "Београд."

c) According to Radivojević's alphabet as "Beogpad."

The famous verses of the poet Njegoš, "God is angry at the Serbs, because of their mortal sins," written in Cyrillic as "Бог се драги на Србе разљути/За њихова смртна сагрјешења" and in Latin as "Bog se dragi na Srbe razljuti/Za njihova smrtna sagrješenja" appeared as the following:

a) According to Kujundžić: "Bog se dpagi на Spbe pazљuti/ Za њixova smptna sagpjeшења."
b) According to Stojanović: "Бog se dpagi na Spбe pazљuti / Za њixова smptna sagpješења."
c) According to Radivojević: "Bog se dpagi na Spbe pazљuti/ Za њixova smptna sagpjeшења."

Živaljević downplayed, both theoretically and practically, the potential benefits of a mixed writing system for the problems his country faced; instead, he debunked the illusion that such an alphabet would be able to stop the "tribal antagonism" that plagued many parts of the country and that it would also contribute to reducing the writing and reading issues of the elderly population. The unexpected benefit of the proposals for a new script, according to Živaljević, consisted in the fact that they united Serbs, Croats, and Slovenes in a common cause: one against the imposition of the Yugoslav alphabet. After all, "Yugoslav society has great tasks ahead of it, and it certainly does not have the time to deal with issues that had already been decided in the previous century." Moreover, in line with Belić's statement, Živaljević declared that the two alphabets could safely coexist, as there was no urgent need to resolve the country's characteristic digraphic situation:

> The two alphabets do not interfere with each other. […]. Cyrillic does not exclude Latin, just as Latin does not exclude Cyrillic. Let us thus respect both. Let us not place one above the other. Time, which creates and destroys, will also resolve the question of the two alphabets for our people. Regardless of what the new alphabet is called, whether Yugoslav *latinica*, the Yugoslav Alphabet or Cyrillic in *latinica*. (Živaljević 1935: 34; my translation)

In addition, for a good part of his publication, Živaljević defended the Cyrillic alphabet against the Latinizing movements that tried to downgrade its status as one of the two official alphabets. The author specified the importance of Cyrillic, attributing to it the capacity to preserve the Serbs as a nation through the centuries under the foreign yoke, to set them eventually free from the enemy, and to help other peoples in the Slavic South to join the struggle. He also pointed out that the Cyrillic alphabet was much more widespread than the Latin one and was increasingly used by the Muslims in Bosnia (since it was also "their alphabet," in the form of "Bosnian Cyrillic," i.e. *bosančica*), and even by the Jewish segment of the population. In particular, he recalled how the Turkish government in Bosnia and Herzegovina had shown great respect for the Cyrillic script: in 1866, the Ottoman authorities in Sarajevo began to print the newspaper *Bosna*, half of which appeared in Turkish (with Arabic characters) and half in Serbian with Cyrillic letters. This publication continued to be issued during the period of Habsburg occupation until the Austrian authorities, who "had always feared Cyrillic," banned the Cyrillic alphabet at the time of the First World War (ibid., 7).

According to statistics reported by the author, 70% of the population in Yugoslavia employed Cyrillic and 30% Latin (ibid., 36-37), figures that do not seem to correspond to the situation of the period. Živaljević also noted that the degree of Cyrillic diffusion should be taken into account in relation to the Slavic world, since "three quarters of all Slavs used this writing system." Finally, the author based his defense of the Serbian alphabet on the fact that, according to his information, many Croatian scholars printed their works directly in Cyrillic, often legal scholars and literary specialists, since this alphabet was "much more readable than Latin and more widespread."

Živaljević also observed that no one had proposed replacing the Greek alphabet in Greece, although it was not such a widespread writing system (ibid., 18-19). Curiously, this same statement would echo again many decades later during the new phase of the "script controversies" in Bulgaria at the turn of the century. With regard to the example of the Turkish alphabet reform, Živaljević, in contrast other authors active in the Cyrillic/Latin debate, did not praise it at all, and instead argued that it was unsuitable and imperfect, and described (in fact, in an almost completely inaccurate way) the letters of the new writing system:

> The letter <y> appears in it, as do apostrophes. In addition to the common <a>, there is <â> with a circumflex accent. With this accent, the letters <î> and <û> appear. In addition, there is the <ü> with two dots and the normal <u>; the <ö> with two dots also appears, the <g> appears both normal and with a pipe, and in addition to the common <n> there is also the one with the accent <ń>. In addition to all this, there are the double <ll>, <kk>, <dd>, <nn>, <rr>, <yy>, <tt>, <ss> – this is how Latin was patched up for the Turks, and how the Turkish language could easily be written with Cyrillic! (Živaljević 1935: 20-21; my translation).

Živaljević objected to the existence of a movement to adopt the Latin alphabet in Russia, which, in his opinion, was not adapted to the spirit and peculiarities of that language. The author was probably not aware of the debate that had taken place in Bulgaria a few years earlier, since he claimed that the Bulgarians did not consider replacing their Cyrillic alphabet with the Latin alphabet. Apart from that, Živaljević rejected the idea that the adoption of the Latin alphabet would imply a genuine rapprochement with Western Europe:

> Ivanišević is mistaken, like many others before him, when he thinks that, by adopting the Latin alphabet, we would become closer to the other peoples of Europe. Nor would we be drawing closer to the Czechs or the Poles. Croatian *latinica* is not the same as Czech or Polish *latinica*, just as the latter two are different from each other. [...] For foreigners, learning the Cyrillic script has not been a problem so far. It is much easier for foreigners to learn Cyrillic than Latin, because they find a separate letter for each sound.

In short, Živaljević's opinion was that one must learn to respect both alphabets and strive to achieve the unity of pure and correct speech as soon as possible, since there were still considerable discrepancies. The strength of the various peoples within Yugoslavia depended "neither on Latin nor on Cyrillic, but on the sincere love, loyalty and willingness of all its children to make every sacrifice for the progress and defense of the fatherland." Both alphabets had become national writing systems, and it was appropriate to let everyone decide freely which one to use: Latin or Cyrillic.

A similar position was defended by, among others, Miloš Trivunac, a professor at the University of Belgrade, who, although not expressing himself explicitly on the Yugoslav alphabet proposals, participated in the debate on alphabet reform and expressed his views in a 1931 pamphlet entitled *Cyrillic or Latin? (Ćirilica ili Latinica?)*. Like Belić and Živaljević, Trivunac asserted the need to retain both alphabets and criticized Skerlić's 1914 proposal. In fact, the acceptance of the Eastern variant by one side was in no way comparable to the acceptance of the Latin alphabet by the other. Trivunac noted that, after the war, during which the Serbs had suffered deep injustice and wounds, significant changes had taken place: if, on the one hand, an even more intense affection for the Cyrillic alphabet had developed, on the other there was now a decidedly different feeling towards the Latin alphabet, imposed during the war by the enemy powers (see also Radojčić 1930: 2): "[t]he enemies had devised new ways of striking at the feelings of the Serbs in the most sensitive places, and every time they looked for these they targeted the Cyrillic alphabet" (Trivunac 1931: 10; my translation). After the attacks against Cyrillic during the war, it was understandable that the Orthodox part of the population manifested its disapproval at the introduction of the Latin alphabet (ibid., 10).

Moreover, affirmed Trivunac, since the Romanians had replaced it with the Latin alphabet, Cyrillic had become an "exclusively Slavic" alphabet. Present among Bosnians and Croats for many centuries, it was now also a "Yugoslav" alphabet (ibid.). In any case, Cyrillic was not to be imposed as the sole writing system: the habits and practices of the population that used Latin were also to be taken into account. Trivunac hence seemed to approach a position backing official biscriptality and biliteracy:

> The harm lies not in the fact that we have two alphabets, but that one is perceived as a Western alphabet and the other as the alphabet of the Eastern part of the nation. In the interest of unity, this feeling must cease. And it will cease only when, over a long number of years, both alphabets will be equally respected in all parts of the nation, especially if in schools both alphabets will be represented in the reading material of the national language [...] Only in this way can we eventually build a generation that feels both alphabets as their own. This path may seem slow, but it is the safe path. (Trivunac 1931: 13; my translation)

The learning of both alphabets would mean enormous benefits at both the moral and political levels, as well as at the material one, since citizens would have access to everything written and printed in both alphabets: it was obviously fairer to expect everyone to make the "minimal effort" to learn to read an additional alphabet to which they were not accustomed than to demand that half the nation abandon its writing system. In short, it was reasonable, in the interests of national unity, to retain both alphabets and to ensure that they were "ingrained" in the population as a whole: thus, biliteracy, though an unusual path with no parallel elsewhere in Europe, was the only realistic one to pursue.

5.8 Conclusions: the developments of the alphabet question in Yugoslavia

During the times of the Kingdom of Serbs, Croats and Slovenes, and then the Kingdom of Yugoslavia, the most salient "schismatic" elements within the Serbo-Croatian language corresponded to the *ekavian/ijekavian* variants as well as to the Cyrillic alphabet as opposed to the Latin one. Both these aspects played a significant role in the discourse and debates between what could be described as two opposing factions: the more nationalist one, which used these elements to emphasize the diversity and incompatibility of the ethnic groups in question, especially the Serbs and Croats, and the "unitarian" one (linguistically, politically and culturally), which often clashed with these elements of the language, viewing them as obstacles to the realization of its unifying ideals. To some degree, these divisions and antagonisms persisted through the century.

While in the interwar period ethnic divisions were downplayed as much as possible, albeit often artificially, as part of the official policy of the Yugoslav unitary state, towards the end of this period these divisions were instead deliberately exaggerated and pursued programmatically, especially in Croatia, where, with the establishment of the so-called Croatian independent state (1941-1945), the Croatian language was altered and manipulated to make it as different as possible from Serbian. The interventions in the language emphasized the primacy of the etymological principle over the "Vukovian" phonemic one, revived forgotten Croatian archaisms, and invented "native" words to replace international ones. In parallel, a campaign was launched to belittle the historical and literary relevance of Cyrillic. This topic will be discussed in detail in the following chapter.

6. CYRILLIC AT WAR: SCRIPT IDEOLOGIES IN THE INDEPENDENT STATE OF CROATIA, 1941-1945

6.1 From unitarian ideologies to assertions of difference in the language field

As mentioned in the previous chapter, the official language policy of the Kingdom of Serbs, Croats and Slovenes and then of the Kingdom of Yugoslavia was to promote the unification of the Serbian and Croatian languages and to support the parallel existence of the Cyrillic and Latin alphabets. Advocates of this unitarian vision were scholars such as the linguist Aleksandar Belić, who in his *Orthography of the Literary Serbo-Croatian Language* (*Pravopis srpskohrvatskog književnog jezika*) (1923) supported the adoption of the phonemic principle to achieve orthographic consistency, and the Croatian lexicographer Tomislav Maretić, who in his *Croatian or Serbian Language Informer* (*Hrvatski ili srpski jezični savjetnik*) (1924) strove to eliminate the lexical differences between the two languages (cf. Langston & Peti-Stantić 2014: 102). A number of philologists of Serbian and Croatian origin referred in their writings to the unification of the Serbo-Croatian language as a *fait accompli* and minimized the differences between the two languages.[54]

Nevertheless, during the interwar period, a part of the Croatian intellectual world started to manifest political discontent at the unitarian attempts and the Yugoslav cause, especially because of the high degree of political centralism implemented by the institutions in Belgrade (cf. Tanner 2001: 128).[55] Croatian newspapers like *Review* (*Obzor*) and *Croat* (*Hrvat*) often informed the population about the so-called "Cyrillization"[56] process that was gaining momentum in the Croatian territories, i.e. the penetration of Serbian

---

54 As for example Franjo Fancev, cit. in Samardžija 2008: 16.
55 In particular in, 1921 the *Sabor*, that is, the main Croatian governmental institution, was eliminated.
56 Defined in Croatian as "ćirilizacija," "ćiriliziranje" or sometimes also "ćirilizovanje."

Cyrillic into areas where it had remained completely unknown, sometimes accompanied by its imposition on the Croatian Latin alphabet (Samardžija 2008: 16). For example, an article entitled "The Equality of Writing Systems" ("Ravnopravnost pisma"), which appeared in the daily *Review* in September 1923, stated:

> When a Serb refers to the equality of Latin and Cyrillic, he means that Serbs do not have to write in Latin script and that Croats must write in Cyrillic. Not only is the equality of these two scripts neglected in Serbia, but the goal is that of Cyrillic propaganda [...] But woe to the Croat who dares to neglect Cyrillic if this is required by "equality. (cit. in Samardžija 2008: 16; my translation)

On the political level, the assassination of Stjepan Radić, the leader of the influential agrarian party Croatian People's Peasant Party (Hrvatska pučka seljačka stranka) in 1928 in the Belgrade Parliament was a shock to the Croats; the subsequent establishment of King Aleksandar's dictatorship led to increased repression of Croatian political opposition (Banac 1984: 241). The desire for linguistic standardization on the part of the official authorities persisted unaltered even during this period, as evidenced by the publication in 1929 of the new orthography *Orthographic Instructions* (*Pravopisno uputstvo*), based on Belić's recommendations, in all schools of the Kingdom. At the official level, the promotion of a kind of state biscriptality was maintained, according to which both alphabets, Cyrillic and Latin, enjoyed equal recognition:

> In the Serbo-Croatian language, both Cyrillic and Latin alphabets are equivalent. The Latin alphabet will be used in the way it has been used so far in schools by the people of the Western regions, and the Cyrillic in the way defined by Vuk. (*Pravopisno uputstvo* 1929: 4; my translation)

In the course of the following years, resistance to linguistic and orthographic standardization in Croatia intensified radically, and in 1937 the Croatian Language Society (*Hrvatski Jezik*) was founded with its journal, followed by the Movement for the Croatian Literary Language (*Pokret za hrvatski književni jezik*) in 1938, a movement aimed at removing Serbian influences on the Croatian language imposed during the years of a common linguistic policy (cf. Langston & Peti-Stantić 2014: 104). Moreover, demonstrations of intolerance towards Cyrillic by the more nationalist factions of Croatian society started to emerge; one example was the case of a Serbian professor, Srećko Zagliu, who was confronted with animated protests by members of right-wing student movements when presenting his law textbook, printed in Cyrillic, in Zagreb in 1936 (cit. in Yeomans 2013: 33).

Stjepan Radić's successor, Vladko Maček, was firmly committed to the principles of a Croatian national identity and state autonomy. In 1939, in an attempt to grant greater autonomy to the Croats within the Kingdom of Yugoslavia, the autonomous Banovina of Croatia was established, encompassing most of the territory considered "historical," including Dubrovnik. The common 1929 orthography, which had met with strong opposition in the region, was immediately replaced with the Broz-Boranić version, which had previously been in force since 1892.

The following year, the linguists Petar Guberina and Kruno Krstić published the book *Differences between the Croatian and Serbian Literary Languages* (*Razlike između hrvatskoga i srpskoga književnog jezika*), edited by the *Matica Hrvatska*, in which they listed and described Serbian and Croatian variants at every linguistic level, along with a dictionary of the various lexical forms. With this work, Guberina and Krstić concluded that Croats and Serbs represented two different nations with two distinct literary languages (Guberina and Krstić 1940).

After Germany declared war on Yugoslavia in April 1941, a Nazi puppet regime was established in the Croatian territories, known as the Independent State of Croatia (Nezavisna Država Hrvatska [NDH]), led by the chief of the Ustasha movement, Ante Pavelić. In their program, announced in the official Ustasha newspaper *Croatian People* (*Hrvatski narod*) in June 1941 (but initially published as early as 1933), the idea was defended that the Croatian people constituted a separate, autonomous national (ethnic) community, one not associable with any other people in the national sense. In the very early phase of the NDH, in pursuit of the greatest possible differentiation from the Serbian language, an extreme purist linguistic policy was implemented, leading to a veritable campaign of "linguistic propaganda" (Samardžija 1993: 16-17), which aimed to de-legitimize any idea of unity with the Serbian element.

6.2 The development of the language situation before the NDH

In the context of nation-building, at the level of collective psychology, the tracing of boundaries, both material and symbolic, plays a prominent role: in this respect, acts of institutionalized differentiation regarding language (including the writing domain) serve to nourish specific collective constructions of identity based on an "exclusionary" principle (in Croatian *isključivost*; see Lešaja 2012: 415-441). In linguistics, there is no doubt that Serbian and Croatian are variants of the same language (cf. Kordić 2010), yet it is not linguistic criteria that determine the existence of different languages, but political considerations, often accompanied by the attitudes of speakers. As regards these delicate "extralinguistic" factors, we find evidence of this process of the "ideologization" of language matters in the above-mentioned book by Guberina and Krstić, *Differences between the Croatian and Serbian Literary Languages* (1940), which, although a decidedly "technical" work, appears to be dictated by the political and ideological will to demarcate the Croatian nation from the Serbian one and to legitimize an independent identity and political projects.

The statements of scholars and philologists like Guberina and Krstić referred to the Croatian language as a distinct Slavic language, separate from Serbian from a linguistic, historical and cultural point of view. The long independent history of the Croatian language was emphasized in contrast to Serbian, which was portrayed as a recently codified language whose beginning dated with the orthographic reform of Vuk Karadžić.[57] In opposition to such "anti-unitarian" language ideologies, Aleksandar Belić, co-author

---

57 Interestingly, such claims are still being made by major cultural institutions in Croatia such as HAZU (the Croatian Academy of Sciences and Arts). See Langston & Peti-Stantić 2015: 149-153.

with Andra Žeželj of the *Grammar of the Serbo-Croatian Language for the First Grade of High School* (*Gramatika srpskohrvatskog jezika za I razred srednjih škola*), wrote in 1940:

> Do all Yugoslavs write only in Cyrillic? Do our Croatian and Slovenian brothers also write in Cyrillic? — No, they use a different alphabet — the Latin alphabet. As you can see, we Yugoslavs have two writing systems: we Serbs use the old Slavic alphabet, Cyrillic, created after the death of the Holy Brothers Cyril and Methodius and adapted to our language by Vuk Karadžić, while our Croatian and Slovenian brothers have adopted the Latin alphabet, *latinica*, which was reformed by Vuk's contemporary, Ljudevit Gaj. (Belić & Žeželj 1940: 10; my translation)

Before the establishment of the Independent State of Croatia, Croatian linguists and philologists were divided into two main schools of thought regarding matters of spelling. One side upheld the principles of orthography on phonological grounds, while the other, under the influence of an "anti-unitarian" political will, attempted to establish an etymological orthography, named *korienski*, which went hand in hand with the ideal of the "linguistic purity" of the Croatian language: "[t]he former operated according to the arguments of science, the latter according to the arguments of power" (Samardžija 2008: 34; my translation). Predictably, with the establishment of the NDH, it was the latter that prevailed, using language as the medium and object of propaganda itself. In the introductory pages of the book *Differences between the Croatian and Serbian Literary Languages*, Guberina and Krstić acknowledged the emotional value of language: "[a]s the eternal companion of life, language goes hand in hand with the people: affection and hatred are reflected in it, and national unity gives it an indelible sign" (Guberina & Krstić 1940: 9; my translation).

The newspaper *Croatian People*, founded in 1939, presents an extremely valuable source for the reconstruction of instances of this linguistic propaganda. For example, on 19 January 1940, we find an article entitled "School Questions: High School Students and Cyrillic" ("Školska pitanja. Srednjoskolci i ćirilica"),[58] which includes

---

58 Appeared on *Hrvatski narod*, no. 50, 19 January 1940, p. 5.

two texts written by young citizens on the question of Cyrillic use in school. The first begins with the following words:

> Dear Editor. You are aware of the previous government's school instruction, still in effect today, according to which every other Croatian-language assignment must be written in Cyrillic script. This year, however, there is a movement among students advocating for the elimination of the Cyrillic script [...] from schoolwork altogether. I have heard that in a few cases students have written in Latin script even though they had to write in Cyrillic script, but some are afraid to do so again, fearing the school administration. Our class [...] had a Croatian assignment and we all wrote in Latin script except for two people. The teacher was very strict about that and told us that we would be punished for it. Our headmaster even gave us a lecture on the subject [...]. I think the issue of Cyrillic deserves to be brought to the public, that is why I am also sending you the article "High School Students and Cyrillic." Please, Mr. Editor, comment on it. (The letter is signed "S. P., high school student") (in: Hrvatski narod 1940: 5; my translation).

The second text, written by another young reader, stated that Belgrade's educational policy of the last twenty years was characterized by intellectual imperialism of the worst kind, whose aim was to eradicate genuine "Croatian national thinking" from Croatian youth, from elementary school pupils to high school students. The means of this "Yugoslavization" ("Jugoslaviranje") were known to all, but the Cyrillic alphabet occupied a privileged place in this process. It was therefore recalled that this alphabet had been defined by Ante Starčević as a "patchwork of Croatian and Greek letters"; the student thus affirmed:

> We leave to others the question of how far this "patchwork" is of cultural significance to us [...] and how far it is a Croatian alphabet. We are more willing to reflect on the extent to which this "patchwork" is an obstacle to educational progress. (in: Hrvatski narod 1940: 5; my translation)

According to the student, during the twenty-year regime, Croatian students endured the "Cyrillization" of educational policy and suffered insults and discrimination for their cultural identity, even in the textbooks in use. In light of recent political changes, rebellious students increasingly wrote in Latin letters exclusively. The article concluded: "[c]ould it not be stipulated that the Croatian population write only in Latin script, and the Orthodox in Cyrillic? And if the Orthodox also want to write in the Latin alphabet—let them do so, since it is a much more useful and necessary alphabet" (ibid.; my translation).

From this brief example, it appears clear that, on the eve of the proclamation of the NDH, the alphabet issue was particularly thorny and sensitive, embodying a fundamental topic to which Croatian linguists and philologists would return several times in the course of the following years, as we read for example in Kruno Krstić's article "The Question of Serbisms" ("Pitanje srbizama"), published in 1942:

> After the founding of Yugoslavia, the Ministry of Education in Belgrade explicitly sought to equalize the literary language of Croats and Serbs in schools and textbooks, and all other Yugoslav state institutions thoughtlessly spread Serbian terminology and other Serbian language doctrines, along with the *ekavian* form — and Cyrillic — throughout the country. [...]. (Krstić 1942a: 296; my translation)

6.3 "Cyrillicide" in the Independent State of Croatia

The Independent State of Croatia was established on 10 April 1941 after the Axis invasion of the Yugoslav territories. Its "birth certificate" defined the state according to "historical and ethnographic criteria"[59] and compared its founding to the Christian resurrection, as it fell on Easter that year. Only 14 days after the proclamation of the NDH, on 24 April 1941, Ante Pavelić, the fascist leader in charge of the state (called *poglavnik*), issued as one of the very first laws a specific decree against the use of the Cyrillic alphabet, in what appeared as a form of revenge against the Serb population, perceived as an alien and unwelcome element (Tomasevich 2002: 531). This fact led to the official prohibition of the Serbian Cyrillic alphabet and its replacement by the Croatian Latin alphabet.

This "cyrillicide" — in Serbo-Croatian "ćirilicocid" (see Zbiljić & Ivanović 2014) — took place only in the Croatian territories that were part of the NDH; in the Serbian ones under Nazi-German occupation Cyrillic was not forbidden. A precedent of Cyrillic script removal from the public sphere had taken place during the First World War, when the occupying Austro-Hungarian army

---

59 *Hrvatski Narod* special edition, 10 April 1941.

prohibited its use and enforced the exclusive use of the Latin alphabet for all publications in the occupied territories of the region (ibid., 111-120). In this context, on 13 October 1914, the Croatian *Sabor* was the first to apply the law (which was to come into force in 1915) banning this script in the Croatian territories (ibid.).[60]

Other attempts to eliminate Cyrillic from the public sphere had occurred further in the past, especially towards the end of Maria Theresa's rule (1779), when a decree was issued preventing the Serbian population in Vojvodina, with the exception of the Orthodox ecclesiastical authorities, from using this alphabet. This move was motivated by the idea of linking the culture of this region more closely with that of Slavonia and Croatia (Belić 1949: 20). There were hence many precedents for the law, named the "Legal Provision on the Prohibition of Cyrillic" (*Zakonska odredba o zabrani ćirilice*), which consisted of only two articles:

> Article 1: On the territory of the Independent Croatian State the use of the Cyrillic script is prohibited.
>
> Article 2: This legal regulation shall enter into force on the day of its publication in the "Official Gazette" and its implementation shall be entrusted to the Ministry of Internal Affairs. (Ustaški zakon 2000 [1941]: 15; my translation)

This legislative decree did not provide any explanation of the reasons for the prohibition of this writing system, nor was this specified in the regulations for its application, which listed the financial and penal sanctions for those who transgressed this order. An additional ordinance was issued on the matter, drafted by Andrija Artuković, Minister of Interior Affairs:

> Article 1: The use of the Cyrillic alphabet is prohibited throughout the territory of the Independent State of Croatia. This applies in particular to the

---

60 Significantly, at the same time, the Austro-Hungarian authorities banned the Cyrillic alphabet from education and printing for the Ruthenian language in the Carpathians: a special order of the Ministry of Education restricted its presence even in churches. In 1915, a campaign to eliminate the Cyrillic alphabet was carried out in the columns of Hungarian newspapers, requiring the Budapest newspaper *Nedelja*, published in Carpatho-Rusyn, to be transcribed into a Hungarian-style Latin alphabet (cf. Duličenko 2001: 178).

> activities of all governmental and administrative bodies, public order offices, shops [...], as well as to all correspondence and public signs.
>
> Therefore, I hereby order that throughout the entire area of the Independent State of Croatia, all use of the Cyrillic alphabet in public and private life shall cease. All printing of books in the Cyrillic alphabet is prohibited. All public signs in Cyrillic shall be [...] removed within three days at the latest.
>
> Article 2: Violations of this regulation are punishable by a fine according to the administrative divisions of 10,000 dinars and imprisonment for up to one month. (Ustaški zakoni 2000 [1941]: 16; my translation)

As can be deduced from the above-described ideological context, the Cyrillic alphabet in Croatia was closely associated with the Serbian Orthodox Church and with the idea of Serbian expansionism in the fields of education, literature and public media, and had therefore been unwanted by many Croats, especially those with a nationalist political orientation, long before the war. It is not surprising that Pavelić decided to target the entire Serbian ethnic community in a highly symbolic way, by damaging one of the most salient and constitutive elements of its collective identity.

The Ministry of the Interior was charged with ensuring that the elimination of the Cyrillic script from all domains, public and private, was effective. After the Ustasha regional authorities took over Serbian businesses and shops in the spring of 1941, one of the first measures was to replace shop signs written in Cyrillic script with the Latin alphabet (Yeomans 2013: 264). In May 1941, a little over a month after the establishment of the NDH and the enactment of the law against the use of the Cyrillic script, a group of Ustasha students from the University of Zagreb arrived in the Herzegovinian town of Trebinje, where, with the help of the local Ustasha youth organization, they removed all Cyrillic signs and then attacked Serbian and Yugoslav monuments (ibid., 51). All this was followed by the beginnings of the physical extermination of members of the Serbian population.

No trace of the visible presence of Serbian culture and identity was to remain: even books written in the Serbian Cyrillic script were banned and destroyed by the authorities (ibid., 250). The great majority of periodical publications were issued in Croatian, a small number in German and Italian, while only one was printed in Hungarian. All of them were in Latin characters and not a single one in Cyrillic letters, although Serbs made up a very high percentage of the population in the NDH.[61] From the list of publications we also see that the adjective "Serbian" does not appear in any of them, a fact that is certainly not surprising (in: Njegovan 2008). Most of the periodical press also appears in Croatian according to a *korienski* spelling, that is, based not on a phonemic principle, but rather on an "etymological" one.

In fact, other campaigns to "purify" the Croatian linguistic space were already taking over, especially in the writing sphere, and were to develop into a kind of control mania aimed at distancing the Croatian language as much as possible from Serbian. As is well known, such attempts at "linguistic purification" were by no means exclusive attributes of the Croatian fascist regime; quite the contrary. In Italy, special attention was paid by Mussolini to the preservation of the "Italianness" of the language, and, much more influential for this context, in Germany this "purification obsession" at the linguistic level materialized in some peculiar cases of "Germanic alphabet affirmation" (Kemplerer 2011 [1947]).[62] As regards the latter, indeed, in parallel to the emergence of National Socialism, a revival of the Gothic alphabet known as German blackletter (an angular form of Latin letters that had spread during the Middle Ages and later to many countries) occurred in the 1930s. Otto Jespersen mentions this writing system in his introduction to the 1934 volume *L'adoption universelle des caractères latins*, lamenting the predominance of exclusionary motives at the writing level over the ideals of simplifying international communication, a fact that isolated some countries (not only Germany, but also Ireland) from the "civilized world" (Jespersen 1934: 15).

---

61   1.8 million of the approximately 7 million total, according to *Hrvatski Narod*.
62   As illustrated by Kemplerer's famous work, *Lingua Tertii Imperi*, some important innovations had also been introduced in Germany during the Nazi era at an "alphabetic" level, first and foremost the revitalization of certain characters of Guido von List's ancient Germanic runic alphabet at both the "symbolic" and "practical" level.

Although this same writing system was later, at the beginning of the 1940s, unwelcome to Hitler (see Bunčić 2017: 34), this fact is in any case indicative of the degree of penetration of nationalist ideology into writing practices and demonstrates that, even in Western Europe, the symbolic value of writing systems was affirmed on several occasions in connection with major historical and political changes. In this case, one should not underestimate the link at the level of ideologies and writing practices between Hitler's Germany and Pavelić's Croatia where, predictably, in parallel to the elimination of any trace of the Serbian language and script, special recognition and importance was conferred to the language of the Nazi allies.

6.4 Writing ideologies between purism and denialism

It has been argued that "purist" attitudes at the level of language can be interpreted as a manifestation of a nationalist conception, i.e. as the linguistic equivalent of xenophobia (Coulmas 1996: 83 cited in Kordić 2010: 11). The reason for this is that such behaviors coincide with the affirmation of a desire for demarcation and distinction from the "Other," often from a "neighboring antagonist" perceived as "disturbingly" close and similar, sometimes also with a will to suppress any form of "identity ambiguity" in the writing domain (cf. Mac Giolla Chriost 2003: 167). As we have seen, in the formulation of the "new internal enemy," special importance was attached by the NDH authorities to the most visible and manifest sign of "Otherness" and diversity, namely the Cyrillic alphabet, in what could be defined also as a form of "graphic purism." This involved not only the anti-Cyrillic restrictions, but also the definition of new orthographic rules for the Croatian language in order to secure its prestige and legitimacy (cf. Samardžija 2008: 35). Not surprisingly, these interventions in the written domain of the language were consistently accompanied by a program to spread literacy as widely as possible among the Croatian population.

In the linguistic propaganda of the NDH, the notion of the existence of a single correct way of writing and speaking the Croatian language was, in a sense, taken to extremes. In fact, writing fulfilled its symbolic function as a unifying sign and as a barrier against members of the group perceived as different, i.e. the Serbian population, a fact that confirms that, in the context of nationalism, language often becomes both the means and the message of this ideology (cf. Fishman 1972: 224ff). While the legal decree banning the Cyrillic script and its complementary Implementing Order of 25 April 1941 represented the emblem of what the Ustasha regime rejected and denied in terms of identity in the field of writing, the enactment of the legal decrees creating the Croatian State Bureau for Language (Hrvatski Državni ured za Jezik [HDUJ]), a few days later (28 April 1941) embodied the essence of language policy in terms of identity assertion (cf. Samardžija 2008: 37-39).

The main tasks of the HDUJ were to devise a new Croatian orthography and then urgently develop it into a manual; in addition, the HDUJ researched and propagated linguistic correctness at all levels. On 30 April 1941, two days after the founding of this state bureau, Kruno Krstić, co-author of *Differences between the Croatian and Serbian Literary Languages*, published an article in *Croatian People*[63] entitled "Croatian Language Legislation" ("Hrvatsko jezično zakonodavstvo"), expressing his views on the national language, which, according to him, needed tighter control through strong legislative intervention. This article also contained historical reflections on the peculiarity of Croatian, especially in its written form, with reference to the work of Cyril and Methodius and its impact on the further development of the language.

Krstić argued that the tradition of writing in the Croatian vernacular through the centuries was a reflection of the resistance of the "spirit of freedom of the Croatian popular soul": a rebellious attitude, a desire for autonomy. Krstić projected the beginning of the Croatian people's contact with the written word into the distant past, that of Cyril and Methodius, which, though it did not involve the use of the Croatian vernacular, nevertheless legitimized the assertion of the existence of a "prestigious" tradition of writing (cf. Cardona 2009a: 90-93). Thus, on its way to self-affirmation,

---

63 Cit. in Samardžija 2008: 164ff.

affirmed the scholar, the spirit of the Croatian people had to determine and trace its linguistic boundaries more accurately:

> The independent Croatian state must pay special attention to the rapid creation of Croatian language legislation. By studying our literature from the Illyrian movement to the present, we must achieve a codification of the Croatian language, as well as a new vocabulary and orthography [...]. The inapplicable and meaningless saying "write like you speak" must be replaced by the real and progressive saying "one language for one people." (Krstić 1941: 11; my translation)

The final insistence on the necessity of defining "one language for one people" expressed the crucial principle of restoring the original identity borders of the Croatian nation and of clearly distinguishing it from the internal and external enemy, namely the Serbian element, by imposing a series of symbolic markers that had practical effect. Applying Fredrik Barth's principle of organizing cultural difference (Barth 1969), we see that the ethnic barrier, in this case embodied and fomented above all by "script diversity," represented a privileged element for maintaining the boundary with the Serbian group. This also made language the homogeneous field in which the particular vision of the nation was reflected.

In a similar way, the linguist Blaž Jurišić, in his article "In the Name of the Croatian Language" ("O imenu hrvatskoga jezika") published on 8 May 1941, argued that the name "Croatian" needed to be fully restored after a century of "concealment" through the misleading designations of "Serbo-Croatian" or even "Serbian," for which a part of the Slavic Studies world was responsible, Vuk Karadžić and his Slovenian friend Jernej Kopitar above all (Jurišić cit. in Samardžija 2008: 173). In his article, Jurišić targeted the Serbian writing tradition and belittled its value in light of Croatian literary history: in contrast to the authoritative 750-year tradition of Croatian autochthonous writing, Serbs had achieved official recognition of their written language only in 1868, that is, just 72 years earlier (ibid., 174).

The motif of the profound gap between a Croatian writing tradition in the popular language and a newly emerged Serbian is a recurring one in many other articles by various scholars of the time.

The concept is that no real literature in Serbian existed before Vuk, a vision that represents the affirmation par excellence of the prejudice about the "absence of writing" in the "Other" (cf. De Certeau 2005), aimed at asserting a national superiority in this very prestigious and legitimizing domain. This negative conception confers a triumphant victory on the Croatian language, elevated to the key symbol of a nation possessing the genuine tradition of writing, over those who, until recently, lacked a consistent writing system. Furthermore, this view constitutes precisely the paradigmatic justification that colonialist rulers resorted to in order to legitimize their conquests and subjugate populations depicted as "illiterate" (cf. Cardona 1986: 17, Fabietti 2014). Through this representational strategy, Serbs emerged as a more effectively "controllable" subject, thus being denigrated as a people possessing only an "irrelevant history of writing."

6.5 The "Orientality" of the Serbs and the role of the Glagolitic alphabet

As briefly mentioned earlier, one of the concerns of the writing control ideology of the Pavelić regime was the attainment of literacy among as many Croatian citizens as possible. Indeed, in parallel with the language ordinances, a law was passed aimed at increasing the literacy level among the population. In the areas that became part of the NDH, there were about 7 million inhabitants, including about 4.8 million "Croats," Catholics and Muslims, about 1.85 million Serbs, 145,000 Germans, 70,000 Hungarians (cf. Samardžija 2008: 36). Of the total population 42% appeared to be illiterate.[64]

On 11 September 1941, a legislative decree entitled *Legal Provision on Spreading Literacy among the People and Organization of Classes for the Illiterate* ("Zakonska odredba o širenju pismenosti u narodu i održavanju tečajeva za nepismene") was issued. It stated (art. 1) that all illiterate Croatians who had not attended public school but were mentally and physically capable of doing so and

---

[64] Information appeared in *Hrvatski Narod* III (96), on 19 May 1941.

had not yet reached the age of fifty were obliged to learn to read and write within the next six years (cit. in: Samardzija 2008: 142). This duty was considered both a "private" and a "national" interest. Hence, courses were set up for illiterate people, in which everyone could participate, including Muslims, but predictably not Serbs (or Jews): *"biti pismen"* ("to be literate") was the motto to be followed, although in the Ustasha way.

The ideologically oriented publications of those years pointed out that, during the last century of "coercion" by the Serbian phonological orthographic model, the so-called *korienski pravopis*, that is, the etymological orthography, remained alive in the usage of many influential writers and intellectuals, as well as politically important exponents such as Stjepan Radić and Ante Starčević. The latter, to whom not only all the intellectuals involved in the work of "linguistic purification," but also Pavelić himself referred, had played a crucial political role in Croatia in the second half of the 19th century, paving the way for the later development of Croatian nationalism by founding the right-wing Croatian Party of Rights (*Hrvatska Stranka Prava*), which still exists in Croatia. Pavelić himself had been a member and secretary of this party before it was dissolved by King Aleksandar in 1929.

Ante Starčević had been heavily involved in language issues and was firmly opposed to the Vienna Agreement of 1850 and to the language conceptions of Vuk Karadžić and Ljudevit Gaj. In a series of articles published in 1852, he expressed a position of absolute denial of Serbian identity, disparaging the value of its language and writing tradition:

> Where are the writers, where are the letters of this Serbian people? Where is this language? To be honest, with a few minor exceptions, until yesterday only the Slavic ecclesiastical language was written in Cyrillic, while Croatian had both its own church and its own language before we even knew about the Serbs. (Starčević 1852; my translation)

Starčević's negation of Serbian identity coincided with the ascription of "Western" values to Croatian cultural history, as opposed to the "Balkan" and "Asiatic" worlds the Serbs were associated with.

Similarly, in the writings of Croatian intellectuals of the NDH era, it is not uncommon to find terms such as "barbaric," "primitive," and "Balkan" pejoratively employed as synonyms for "Serbian." On the contrary, affiliation to the Catholic religion, the uninterrupted tradition of writing, the Glagolitic alphabet were all elements used to elevate the "civilizational" status of Croatia and contributed to its representation as a wholly "Western" country, and at the same time entirely distinct from all others.

The motif of the "Westernness" of the Croats in contrast to the "Eastern" and "Balkan" Serbs was actually a recurrent one in the ideological history of the country. For example, in addition to the aforementioned Starčević, Stjepan Radić, head of the Croatian Party of Rights at the time of the Kingdom of Serbs, Croats and Slovenes, had similarly stated that the geographical position of the country necessitated an orientation towards Hungary, a fact that would enable the Croats not to become dependent on the Balkans, which constituted an "extension of Asia" (in: Cohen 1995: 15). The task of the Croats was therefore "to Europeanise the Balkans, and not to Balkanise the Croats and Slovenes" (ibid.).

This process of identity ascription coincides precisely with the one described Milica Bakić-Hayden in her famous text, which she defines as "nesting orientalism": the ethnic groups in the Balkan region define their significant "Other" as "their own Orient" and try to disassociate themselves from it to all possible extents through a series of ideological formulations. And so, paradoxically, the "designation of 'other' has been appropriated and manipulated by those who have themselves been designated as such in orientalist discourse" (Bakić-Hayden, 1995: 922). In defining the relationship with the Serb minority in the country, the NDH regime also made use of the ideas of scholars such as the archeologist Ciro Truhelka, who argued for the "Vlach" origin of the Serbian population. In this, once again, Ante Starčević's ideas proved to be very supportive, as Truhelka advocated very similar positions aimed at denying the existence of a specific Slavic historical and cultural identity of the Serbs (cf. Bartulin 2006: 70).

In this context, the constant affirmation of the Croatian "primacy of writing" through the evidence of the Glagolitic alphabet's use validated support for ideologies of cultural superiority. It should be noted that this script, created in the second half of the 9th century by the missionary brothers Cyril and Methodius as the first writing system for translating the Holy Scriptures for the Slavs, survived and remained in use for a longer time in some parts of Croatia, where it was employed in the church liturgy in some coastal areas until the 19th century. This phenomenon is related to the privilege granted in 1248 to the Croats of southern Dalmatia by Pope Innocent IV to use their own language and script for the liturgy in the Roman rite. Such writing freedom was later extended to the entire Croatian territories of that period.

In an article published in the newspaper *Croatian People* some days after the establishment of the NDH in late April 1941, entitled "The Sense of the Croatian Spiritual Revolution" ("Smisao hrvatske duhovne revolucije"), the writer and journalist Ivo Lendić claimed that the "enemies of the Croatian nation" had made systematic attempts to destroy its spirit by plundering the country's cultural wealth and attempting to take it over (Lendić cit. in Bartulin 2006: 302). In particular, Lendić dwelt on the heritage of writing, stating that the Croats possessed their own Old Croatian language, their own Old Croatian alphabet, their own Old Croatian Glagolitic literature, something that no other "so-called Slavic people" could boast of. However, according to Lendić, the Croats were not allowed to express this sense of pride, since Czech, Serbian, Russian and Yugoslav scholars "proclaimed that language as the Old Slavic one, the Glagolitic literature as Old Slavic literature, the Glagolitic alphabet as the Old Slavic alphabet" (ibid.)

It was the other Slavic peoples, including the Serbs, who undermined the "Croatianness" of this basic element of Croatian historical identity at the writing level, namely the Glagolitic alphabet. It was clear that the Glagolitic alphabet had to be defended and promoted in the new historical era. Traces of this ideological thinking can be found in the writings of the above-mentioned intellectuals, such as Kruno Krstić, in which special attention was paid to the Glagolitic alphabet, treated as a distinctive sign of "Croatianness" even at the moment when it was first used (see Krstić 1942b: 412-420).

In relation to the Glagolitic alphabet, a noteworthy fact in the NDH years was the creation of a huge commemorative inscription in this script in Zagreb Cathedral, on the right rear wall, celebrating 1,300 years since the Christianization of the Croatian people. This example of public writing, engraved with the letters of the typical Croatian angular Glagolitic alphabet, although dated 1941, was officially presented to the public on 17 September 1944. This work is apparently (or at least so far) the largest Glagolitic inscription in the world, as well as the largest monumental inscription in Croatia.

The inscription in the Zagreb Cathedral represented the affirmation of the symbolic value of Glagolitic (cf. Tandarić 1985: 1973), at a time when it was no longer part of the living tradition of writing, but presented itself as an "extinct" alphabet (ibid.). This monumental inscription was erected as a sign of the Croatian people's "love for the Christian faith and for the Catholic Church," which had exceptionally allowed their ancestors to use the vernacular language and script in the liturgy (Getliher 1994: 5). At the same time, this monument was also presented as a testimony to Croats and foreigners of "the living faith of the Croatian people, its spiritual commitment and its national indissolubility" (ibid.).

SECTION III

FROM THE GLAGOLITIC REVIVAL TO THE NEW DISCRIMINATIONS AGAINST CYRILLIC IN CROATIA

7. THE REDISCOVERY OF GLAGOLITIC: FROM REGIONAL TO NATIONAL PHENOMENON

7.1 The new signification context of the Glagolitic alphabet

When dealing with the issues of alphabet ideologization and politicization in the post-socialist and post-Yugoslav era, special attention should be paid to the analysis of the phenomenon of the Glagolitic alphabet's rediscovery in Croatia. In spite of being an extinct alphabet (although with exceptions), many factors point to the importance this script plays in the construction and affirmation of a specific Croatian identity. In assessing the contemporary Croatian writing context, it is also necessary to specify how the marginalization of Serbian Cyrillic coincided with the revaluation and revival of the Glagolitic at the national level, as a new element in a discourse until then almost exclusively anchored to the dualism of the Cyrillic/Latin opposition. The tendency of cultural and political elites to rediscover part of their national past had, as we have seen, already been active to some extent in the period between the two world wars, also in relation to this writing system (see the end of the previous chapter). It then intensified from the 1970s onwards, and received a strong boost in the 1990s, in a process that has not yet concluded.

In Croatia, the Glagolitic alphabet is considered a unique cultural phenomenon due to its linguistic, ethnological and semiotic attributes. This fact was evidenced, for instance, by the 2014 decision by the Ministry of Culture to formally include it in the intangible cultural heritage of the country. This alphabet, present in Croatian history for more than a millennium, is considered the fundamental element in the cultural representation of the nation, having permeated its liturgical life, legislation, science and literature. The symbolic value of the Glagolitic alphabet should therefore be explored in more detail to understand how it comes to attract increasing popular attention, how it is used as a recurring motif in a wide variety of cultural settings, how it is transformed by modern commercial dynamics, and how it is related to new educational needs. Although the formally extinct alphabet is not officially used as a writing system for the transcription of the Croatian language, there are some major exceptions, such as contemporary Glagolitic printing, school courses and some evidence of public writing, which contribute to make this writing system's use an interesting topic also for sociolinguistic research.

In addition, it is worth mentioning that there are various levels of reappropriation of the discourse on the Glagolitic alphabet: these are initiated not only by representatives of the intellectual world, but also by politicians, tourism workers, and ordinary citizens. The combination of these different levels has produced both ideological manipulations (claims of exclusivity regarding the "national character" of the alphabet) and popular dissemination, such as the monumental works of the Glagolitic Alley (*Aleja glagoljaša*) in Istria and the Baška Glagolitic Alphabet Trail (*Baščanska staza glagoljice*) on the island of Krk.

7.2 The alphabet issue during the period of socialist Yugoslavia

In post-war socialist Yugoslavia, attempts aimed at achieving orthographic standardization, inspired by the work of the linguist Aleksandar Belić, were again encouraged from the 1950s onwards, and found legitimization in the 1954 Novi Sad Agreement (Banac 1984: 247). This declared the equivalence of the "two varieties" of the language as well as of its two existing writing systems, Cyrillic and Latin, and affirmed the necessity to expose schoolchildren to both equally:

> Both scripts, Latin and Cyrillic, are of equal value; and that is why efforts must be made to ensure that both Croats and Serbs learn both alphabets in the same manner, a goal to be achieved primarily by means of school instruction. (Novosadski dogovor 1954: 65; my translation)

In 1960, a new orthographic manual was simultaneously issued in Novi Sad (Cyrillic edition) and in Zagreb (Latin alphabet edition). However, the publication of the first two volumes of the joint dictionary (*Rječnik hrvatskosrpskoga/ srpskohrvatskog književnog jezika*) in 1967 triggered strong reactions in Croatia (Langston & Peti-Stantić 2014: 108). Moreover, the main Croatian cultural institutions issued the Declaration on the Name and Status of the Croatian Literary Language (*Deklaracija o nazivu i položaju hrvatskog književnog jezika*), calling for the official recognition of Croatian as a separate language in its own right and not as a variant of "Croatian-Serbian" (Banac 1984: 248). Although the Serbian Cyrillic version of the dictionary was published in the planned six volumes without incident, the production of the first two volumes of the Latin alphabet version in Zagreb was heavily criticized by Croatian linguists for what was perceived as its pro-Serbian bias (Bugarski 2004b: 50-51), a fact which provoked the interruption of the printing of the remaining ones.

Shortly thereafter, the so-called "Croatian Spring Movement" (*Maspok*) began, one of whose main goals was to achieve greater autonomy for the Croatian republic within the Yugoslav federation (Wachtel 1998: 85). This was actively supported by cultural representatives, student groups and the Catholic Church, all contributing to revive the link between Catholicism, the Latin alphabet and Croatian nationality (Denich 1993: 51, Guzina 2000: 31n). In this context, not coincidentally, some demonstrations against the Cyrillic alphabet used by the Serbs in Croatia took place (Crampton 2002: 133).

In the meantime, Croatian intellectuals and academics began to mobilize increasingly for the autonomous designation of the Croatian language. In 1971, the main Croatian cultural institution, the *Matica Hrvatska*, officially renounced the Novi Sad Agreement and encouraged the production of a new spelling manual, simply called "Croatian Orthography" (*Hrvatski Pravopis*). However, the central authorities blocked the distribution of this text and went so far as to destroy almost all of its copies; one secretly made its way to London, where it was published in a photographic reproduction and went down in history as the "londonac" (Greenberg 2004: 118).

In those same years, another event of symbolic value took place, concomitantly with the 1970 celebrations of the 300th anniversary of the founding of the University of Zagreb. On that occasion, a bronze copy of the sculpture created in 1932 by Ivan Meštrović (1883-1962) was placed at the main entrance of the Faculty of Law, where the rector's office was also located. Meštrović, a world-famous Croatian artist, had created the sculpture to visually interpret and symbolize the history of the Croatian people (cf. Črnja 1962: 332): it depicted a mother holding in her lap the stone tablet representing the book "History of the Croats," whose title, engraved on the spine, appeared written in the ancient Glagolitic script.

After 1974, following the introduction of the new Yugoslav Constitution, citizens were subjected to new pressures to identify themselves with a specific nationality and it became more difficult to select the category of "Yugoslav." The new constitution of the Croatian Socialist Republic declared the official language as "the Croatian literary language, the standardized form of the popular language that is called Croatian or Serbian" (Ustav SRH 1974: 138; my translation). Although this did not imply freedom to express a separate linguistic identity, the "Croatian literary language" had nevertheless obtained administrative recognition, and regulatory measures were therefore taken to try to ensure its separate standardization (Bugarski 2004a: 28).

It was in this complicated and animated context that the rediscovery of the Glagolitic heritage in Istria took place, a phenomenon that in many ways seemed to be independent of the broader national dynamics that characterized Croatian autonomy movements.

7.3 The creation of the *Aleja Glagoljaša* in Istria and the role of Zvane Črnja

On the multiethnic and multicultural territory of Istria, the Glagolitic alphabet began its "renaissance path" in the 1970s, through the collaborative work of local artists and intellectuals. The most significant outcome of these joint efforts consisted in the so-called "Glagolitic Alley," the *Aleja Glagoljaša*, a memorial path stretching for 7 km along the road connecting the villages of Roč and Hum in the northern part of the peninsula. This includes eleven sculptures and memorial plaques honoring the Croatian origins of the Glagolitic alphabet.

The *Aleja Glagoljaša* was symbolically erected in 1976, on the 500th anniversary of the first mention of a Croatian printed book (cf. Bratulić 2009), and was intended to testify to the roots of Slavic writing and the continuity of this alphabet from Constantine-Cyril to the present day (Bratulić 1983: 23). The sculptures, created by the artist Želimir Janeš, paid tribute to historical religious figures who had contributed to the invention or maintenance of this writing system over the centuries, such as Cyril and Methodius, the Glagolite (*Glagoljaši*) priests (who were active in Croatia and kept Glagolitic in use in the church liturgy), Clement of Ohrid, and others.

One of the main protagonists of this process of revaluation of the local Istrian cultural heritage, especially in relation to the Glagolitic element, was the writer Zvane Črnja, born in the town of Žminj in 1920. He was, among other things, the founder of the so-called *čakavski sabor* (Biletić 2001: 9), i.e. the Chakavian Parliament, named after one of the dialects of Serbo-Croatian, spoken in Istria, in the Kvarner Bay and on most of the Dalmatian islands. This institution was established in 1969 as a local project aimed at promoting autochthonous cultural priorities and affirming the value of Istrian history. During the repressions by the Yugoslav authorities that followed the Croatian Spring movement, the activities of the *čakavski sabor* were also targeted, in particular in relation to the involvement of representatives of the ecclesiastical world (Bratulić 2009).

For Črnja, the institution of the Chakavian Parliament epitomized the valorization of cultural and local diversity, according to a conception that saw national essence not as an abstract and uniform category, but as a concrete, living fact that consisted of heterogeneous phenomena and nonequivalent experiences (Črnja 1971: 308). Unsurprising in this context is the extent to which the values and ideals associated with the Glagolitic alphabet's heritage permeate Črnja's entire oeuvre, in which the 1966 collection of poems *The*

Book of Žminj (*Žminjski Libar*) stands out, its verses inspired by the inscriptions in angular Glagolitic engraved on ancient monumental stones scattered throughout the Istrian land (cf. Biletić 2010: 20-21).

In Črnja's vision, the Glagolitic alphabet represented a means of defending traditional and cultural specificities in areas where Western European urban structures directly threatened the spiritual and material elements of Croatian folk life (Črnja 1977: 265). From the sixteenth century onwards, he believed, the use of Glagolitic became connected with the manifestation of a will to safeguard local tradition against various potentially assimilatory elements, mainly consisting of papal Latinity and the Italian influence (ibid., 268).

7.4 The rebellious and democratic character of Glagolitic

In many of his texts, Črnja emphasized the idea of a close relationship between the monuments of the Istrian and Croatian Glagolitic past and a specific form of cultural identity: the tradition of writing in this alphabet embodied a "rebellious" attitude towards European culture, aimed at the affirmation of original and unique cultural elements in the context of the Old continent (Črnja 1971: 263-279). Črnja developed this concept more concretely in his essay "The Democratic Message of Glagolism" ("Demokratska poruka glagoljaštva") included in his 1978 work *Cultural History of Croatia* (*Kulturna Povijest Hrvatske*). According to Črnja, at the time of the invention of the Glagolitic alphabet, the Slavs, characterized by an untamable nature, a predisposition for freedom, and an ambition to resist any foreign domination, were undoubtedly the only actor capable of setting European culture on a new path. Cyril had taken on the task of inventing a new writing system, different from the Greek script and even more from the Latin in the hope that the Slavs would accept his alphabet as their own, as a precious cultural tool unencumbered by foreign influences (Črnja 1978a: 122-124).

Nevertheless, Črnja acknowledged that, with regard to Glagolitic, the Croatian situation later acquired a completely different cultural, political and ideological content. If the ideas of the two

Slavic Apostles were aimed at strengthening the independent Slavic states and their effective political rise, the Croatian Glagolitic movement in the second half of the eleventh century took on an opposite, anti-state connotation, becoming identified with the oppressed masses (Črnja 1978a: 148). Therefore, in this view, Glagolitic was no longer a weapon for asserting Slavic civilization within the European cultural space, but rather a spontaneous instrument of resistance that contributed to the preservation of this particular society and its folk spirit at the regional level (Črnja 1971: 265). According to Črnja, the Croatian language and alphabet testified to the Slavic presence on the coastal territories, along with their culture, which was not Latin but "Slavic, Croatian, Glagolitic" (Črnja Bertoša 1968: 130).

Črnja's statements about the ideological implications of the sociopolitical dynamics that enabled the maintenance of the Glagolitic alphabet appear particularly consequential, and it would be possible to draw interesting parallels to the current processes of Europeanization faced by Croatia today and the role of Glagolitic in preserving and legitimizing a specific image of the country. One could also ask to what extent Črnja projected some of the dynamics active in the Yugoslav context into a distant past of Glagolitic resistance.

Certainly, the Glagolitic used along the Croatian coast eventually differed from the original alphabet, by virtue of the privilege conceded by the Pope allowing its continued use: over the course of time, a new variant emerged, the so-called angular form. It is thus possible to see in the persistence of the Glagolitic and Old Slavonic liturgy in these territories a confirmation of the particularism of the eastern Adriatic coast. It was linguistically Slavic, but tried to distinguish itself both from a common Slavic world and from a Roman-Latin one (Zakhos-Papazahariou 1972: 160). According to Črnja, one the reasons why the Glagolitic script tradition was so firmly rooted in the foundations of Croatian culture lay in the anti-Roman, anti-Latin and even "heretical" essence that characterized it since its appearance in this part of Europe.

Under such conditions, Glagolitic writing became closely linked to the conservatism of Croatian "anti-urban" folk culture and grew into a kind of political program, enforced at all costs in a minority context. The tradition of Glagolitic, which extended over the entire sphere of public life, conferred on it a Slavic character and separated it from the influence of "Latinism" precisely in those areas which, because of their proximity to Italy and its culture, could more easily succumb to assimilation (Črnja Bertoša 1968: 138-9). The Glagolitic alphabet thus stood as a form of spontaneous, popular resistance to the process of Europeanization that threatened Croatia (Črnja 1971: 265).

The Glagolitic heritage was praised by Črnja in terms of its capacity to give rise to elaborate patterns of "non-homogenization," which made it one of the most original and beautiful phenomena in Croatian and Yugoslav cultural history. Despite its resistance to the processes of Europeanization, from a long-term historical perspective, "thanks to the Glagolitic alphabet (...) the Slavs were called to the banquet of European high civilization, of which the alphabet is a fundamental sign, in relation to written culture" (Ekl & Fučić 1968: 35; my translation).

Črnja regretted the fact that, in the course of Croatian historical development, given the advance of the Latin alphabet in the urban context of Dubrovnik literature, Glagolitic eventually proved less practical and convenient:

> It reminded them too much of the poor archaic world outside the cities, as well as of old fights, priests' rooms and monks' cells, at a time when they were turning instead to new cultural perspectives. [...] Hence, Glagolitic did not become an urban alphabet, nor a national alphabet in the modern sense of the word. The Renaissance did not adopt it and instead let it languish around village churches, where life remained almost unchanged, as though Dante, Petrarch and Marulić had never been born. (Črnja 1978a: 158; my translation)

The author observed that, until the 20th century, the Glagolite Priests resisted capitalist civilization by addressing their people in the ancient language: Latinity represented the element of Western European culture, which they stubbornly opposed, until the end, drawing ever closer to the people (Črnja 1978a: 137). In the course of the 19th century, a political struggle did indeed develop between the defenders of the Glagolitic script in the Catholic liturgy and its opponents. Not surprisingly, the latter position was defended by the Italians, whose imagological processes began to give rise to ideals and prejudices of cultural superiority to other peoples and nations, associating their "prestigious" culture with that of urban centers and civilization, and denigrating Slavic cultures as rural, uncivilized and illiterate (Ashbrook 2011: 876).

The survival of this Glagolitic culture until the recent challenges, i.e. the Italian fascist occupation in the interwar period, is also a topic for Črnja, who recalled the damage inflicted by the Italianization campaign in Istria also in the field of writing (Črnja 1971: 37-40). The territory endured intense fascist persecution, which attempted to deny the Slavic presence in the area and emphasize an exclusively Italian identity (Črnja Bertoša 1968: 52). The occupation, which began in 1922, forbade the official use of Slavic languages from 1926; in 1928, all schools with Croatian or Slovene language instruction were closed (cf. Bratulić 2009).

In this period, all the Slavic names of towns or settlements were Italianized, and even inscriptions on gravestones in Slovene or Croatian prohibited, in the very land where the Glagolitic script had left so much evidence of its antiquity (Bratulić 1983: 20-21). In this context, it is also worth mentioning that many traces of the Glagolitic past were severely damaged at the hands of the Italians. During the period of fascist occupation, some Glagolitic monuments in Hum were barbarically devastated. Hence, what remains in Istria of the cultural heritage of the Glagolitic script today is only a small part of its past glory, as we read in a text by the writer Josip Bratulić, also an active member of the Chakavian Parliament:

> With the arrival of the fascists in the Buzet area and especially in Hum, the stone monuments were also targeted. They were struck violently, in the most brutal way, with a mason's hammer, in order to remove the last traces of a culture that had flourished here during the Middle Ages and which—like every culture—had enriched human life by promoting beauty and goodness. (Bratulić 1983: 20; my translation)

7.5 The universal value of regional Istrian culture

By examining Črnja's engagement with the valorization of the local specificities of his Istrian land, it is possible to reconstruct his overall vision of the development that Yugoslavia should undertake: it was precisely diversity, rather than uniformity or "monovalency," that enabled the conditions under which socialism, as a "liberating spiritual force," could finally emancipate itself from monolithic statism and nationalism (Črnja 1971: 308). With this as a reference, we can state that, throughout his cultural and political engagement, Črnja always favored the regional Istrian, chakavian heritage first, and only then the Croatian and Yugoslav context. In his vision, however, one did not exclude the other, and the various levels, in his imagination, were eventually integrated into the broader European and global structure according to their value in terms of cultural and intellectual creativity (Biletić 2010: 7).

This is evidenced, for instance, in a speech delivered at the *čakavski sabor* entitled "The Conditionality of Croatianness" ("Uvjetovanost Hrvatstva") in 1970, in which Črnja supported the idea of the equality of the chakavian dialect with the kajkavian and shtokavian ones (the latter also spoken in the area), maintaining that "national synthesis arises at a supra-regional level, it is the result of all our cultural and human strengths" (in: Črnja 1971: 318ff; my translation). In a sense, the multicultural and multiethnic Istrian identity, which included Croats, Slovenes, Italians, Istro-Romanians and other groups, challenged at its root the very Croatian national identity, and this would become even more pronounced in the 1990s, after the dissolution of Yugoslavia (Bellamy 2003: 122).

The concept of *chakavian* and Istrian identity that Črnja so meaningfully linked to the "rebellious" and "democratic" tradition of the Glagolitic alphabet did not embody a form of "centrifugal regionalism" (Črnja 1971: 319) or an adherence to a fossilized or fictional regional identity: it was rather inscribed in a process of historical development in terms of cultural differentiation and variation. Črnja was not opposed to processes of modernization and change, and in his view, the Yugoslav context did not necessarily mean restrictions on the valorization of local heritage, obviously as long as the latter did not take on political connotations. It is worth noting that in the context of the valorization of the local Glagolitic heritage, references to "Yugoslav brotherhood" often appeared, demonstrating that this alphabet could prove to be a valuable tool in the process of cultural memory referring to a common writing space. For example, we read in the description of the monument honoring St. Clement of Ohrid in the *Aleja Glagoljaša*:

> The installation of the monumental work dedicated to St. Clement of Ohrid was supported by the generous financial contribution of the Macedonian Academy of Sciences and Arts [...] It participated in the project in the best possible way, affirming the work of Cyril and Methodius, Clement of Ohrid and the Istrian Glagolites, and confirming the brotherhood of the South Slavic peoples—those of Macedonia—with those of the westernmost Slavic world, Istria. (Bratulić 1983: 40; my translation)

Certainly, Črnja affirmed the idea of a multicultural and multiethnic Istria, in which different peoples found themselves with common elements, including the Glagolitic script:

> The Croatian Chakavs and the Slovenes in Istria have long been close. The Croats have adopted some peculiarities of the Slovene language and the Slovenes some peculiarities of the Chakavian dialect, mainly due to the fact that during the Middle Ages, but also later, the Glagolitic alphabet of the Croatian Chakavian variant was in use also for the literary language of the Slovenes. (Črnja Bertoša 1968: 70; my translation)

The monuments in the Istrian hinterland testified to the establishment of the Glagolitic tradition at a time when the area was not yet politically part of a Croatian state. Moreover, Črnja showed how this heritage had also reached the Italian territories inhabited by significant Slavic communities: another path of the Glagolitic script extended to Trieste, and from there had arrived to Gorizia and the surrounding areas. Thus, thanks to the Glagolitic script, the Slovenes were under the strong influence of the Croatian version of the old Slavic ecclesiastical language of the region (Črnja Bertoša 1968: 133).

In its specificity, Istria also represented the symbiosis of Croatian, Slovenian and Italian elements and an important model of coexistence to be valued (Črnja 1971: 320-321): this "non-exclusionary" vision of identity also had an impact on the vision of Glagolitic culture. It too represented a culturally productive synthesis, a unique phenomenon at the European level, as has been affirmed: "though Catholic (and therefore separated from Orthodox Slavdom), Croatia continually resisted the Latin universalisms of the Roman Church, and was therefore hardly a typical representative of the trends in Catholic Slavic countries. The Cyrllo-Methodian tradition of Glagolism was part of the tendency towards maintaining some links with the Slavic East" (Banac 1984: 215-216). This was also the position maintained by Picchio (cf. 1984: 3), according to whom the area of Glagolitic influence in Croatia had always constituted an area of mixed and overlapping influences between the two cultural worlds he defined as *Slavia Orthodoxa* and the *Slavia Romana*, whose boundary lines were never clearly or definitively fixed.

7.6 The Glagolitic as a marker of continuity and prestige after the end of Yugoslavia

With the collapse of Yugoslavia in the early 1990s, new political realities emerged, constituted according to principles corresponding to those of the nation-state. Following this, the process of European integration began, which, at least in theory, was supposed to reduce the influence of the nation-state. In the Croatian media, Croatia was described (as in the past) as an integral part of Europe, and Europe in turn as a long-standing community determined by its own historical destiny—and founded on Christian values (cf. Busch & Holmes 2004: 3).

As regards the Croatian Istrian region, during the disintegration of Yugoslavia, many of its inhabitants, while supporting the country's independence, mainly for economic reasons, did not adhere to the nationalist ideals of the new state and defended instead their specific regional identity. An example of this is the limited success encountered by Franjo Tudjman's Croatian Democratic Union (Hrvatska Demokratska Zajednica [HDV]) party in the region in the 1990s, as well as the rejection of the centralization policies imposed by the Zagreb authorities, expressed in the desire to maintain some form of autonomy together with the official practice and recognition of multilingualism (Ashbrook 2011: 879, Bellamy 2003: 121-122).

Undoubtedly, the concept of identity in the countries that emerged from the Yugoslav Federation became associated with new notions of borders that grew increasingly restrictive. Certain cultural elements, such as language and the alphabet, played an active role in the process of representing the different nations, becoming "ideologized" and turned into markers aimed at emphasizing ethnonational differences. These cultural symbols also supported the tracing of new identity boundaries (especially linguistic ones) in the territory, through which the legitimacy of the new state was socially and ideologically affirmed.

This quest for "distinctiveness" had paramount repercussions in the linguistic sphere, with the emergence of an increasingly "Croatianized" language, stripped of all elements that could be associated with the Serbian counterpart. Moreover, in a way, the Glagolitic alphabet too was included in this process, as this writing system, perceived as genuinely "autochthonous," embodied an indispensable element in the determination of the value and continuity of the national culture. Thus, it comes as no surprise that, starting in the post-Yugoslav period, literature, art and other cultural phenomena in Croatia began to politically construct a specific identity discourse based on the use of the old writing system (cf. Selvelli 2015c: 97).

In the promotion of Glagolitic on the national level, the activities of some cultural organizations, poets, artists and writers were decisive. A major step was the foundation of the Society of Friends of Glagolitic (*Društvo Prijatelja Glagoljice*) in Zagreb in 1993, supported by Croatian intellectuals and academics, whose main ambition was (and remains) encouraging the knowledge of this alphabet and its use in modern contexts. To this end, the Society organizes exhibitions, urges the use of the Glagolitic Missal, offers courses on learning to read and write in this alphabet, and is active in organizing cultural events related to its writing heritage.

In recent years, a new commemorative path inspired by the letters of the Glagolitic alphabet, the Baška Glagolitic Alphabet Trail (*Bašćanska staza glagoljice*), was erected on the island of Krk, consisting of 34 sculptures representing the letters of this alphabet. This island was chosen as a suitable location for this project, as the famous Baška Tablet (*Bašćanska Ploča*) from the early 12th century was discovered there, the importance of which stems from the fact that it is one of the oldest monuments bearing an inscription in Glagolitic script and the first to mention the ethnonym "Croatian." This cultural element has also become one of the most popular cultural symbols in recent years, appearing reproduced on a series of gadgets sold in the country and on innumerable surfaces.

In its process of nation-building, Croatia has developed a specific rhetoric about this alphabet, presenting it as an essentially Croatian element, a feature of historical continuity and distinction that, linked to Catholicism, has enabled the maintenance of national identity over the centuries. Furthermore, it now allows the country to distinguish itself from its neighbors, with whom it shared a common state until thirty years ago. Thus, its meaning is directly proportionate to the so-called "ethnohistory" it contains (Barth 1969: 12, Smith 2009), making it a precise marker of identification and a symbolic boundary of "Croatianness." This writing system serves equally to consolidate a sense of collective identity among internal members and to represent the nation to external observers.

The Glagolitic alphabet has also been institutionally elevated to the status of national symbol, appearing on banknotes, postage stamps, national soccer team jerseys, etc. A special day is now celebrated to mark the significance of this alphabet and the people who have contributed to preserve it throughout the centuries: the Day of Croatian Glagolitic and Glagolism, established by the Croatian parliament on the initiative of the Institute for Croatian Language and Linguistics in 2019 and marked on the 22nd of February, the date on which the first Croatian book was printed in 1483, the *Missale Romanum Glagolitice* ("*Misal po zakonu rimskoga dvora*") (Lazić 2019). On a popular level, this alphabet appears as a recurrent motif in a variety of contexts, such as tattoos on the arms of national athletes, creative street signs, gadgets, fashion items turned into an element of the "inscription" of national consciousness.

In light of this, we can determine that Zvane Črnja's ideas regarding the promotion of Istrian cultural heritage in the form of the Glagolitic script have been realized to some extent since the collapse of Yugoslavia: the popularization of the alphabet in the national and even European context appears today an evident reality. Nevertheless, the parallel glorification of Glagolitic and deprecation of the writing identities other than Croatian is in sharp contradiction with the principles and values expressed by the Chakavian Parliament and by Črnja. While their Istrian "regionalist" conception promoted an idea of multilingualism and multiculturalism as constitutive factors in the history of the peninsula, the Croatian nationalist vision instead envisages a focus on the struggle for the autochthonous nation, in a mono-ethnic sense, downplaying the contribution offered by other cultures and promoting, above all, the idea of a single culture and language (Ashbrook 2011: 880).

Moreover, it is important to note that the institution of the *čakavski sabor* was gradually marginalized after 1990, a condition that seems not to have changed in recent years (Bratulić 2009). Ironically, its isolation coincides with a kind of national appropriation of one of the elements it had contributed most to reviving and promoting, namely the Glagolitic alphabet.

7.7 The institutionalization of the Glagolitic alphabet by the Croatian state

The relationship between Glagolitic and politics, as mentioned in the previous chapter, had already become evident at the time of the independent Croatian state, especially through a valorization of this alphabet also on a visual level, which took the form of the huge inscription in Zagreb Cathedral in 1944. In more recent times, in 2003, during his visit to Croatia, John Paul II received a copy of the old Glagolitic 14th-century book *Glagolitic Breviary of Vitus of Omisalj* (*Glagoljški brevijar Vida Omišljanina*), specifically created by the academic Branko Fučić, a gift which testified to the indissoluble ties between Croatia and the Holy See. In the post-socialist period, various parties, including HDZ itself, the party founded by Tudjman in 1989, have used this script as an element in their rhetoric or even as a symbol. On the website of the HDZ, for example, one can read some statements about the Glagolitic alphabet, described as an element through which the Croatian people kept alive "not only their language, but also the old folk spirituality," an expression which in some measure echoes the ideas of Črnja. Two parties have used Glagolitic in their logos: the Croatian Democratic Party (HD), based in Zagreb, founded in 2002 and active until 2009 (the letter D of this script) and the Party of the Liberal Democrats (LIBRA—Stranka liberalnih demokrata), founded in 2002 in Zagreb and active until 2005 (the letter L of the Glagolitic alphabet) (in: Heimer 2011: 482).

In addition to these examples associated with political parties, as a symbol and as a means of communication, Glagolitic is now being popularized on the official level with unprecedented intensity, and countless institutions are including the letters of this alphabet in their logos.[65] Glagolitic thus lends itself to new writing and reading contexts: the Croatian dictionary of Church Slavonic, published by the Old Church Slavonic Institute (*Staroslavenski Institut*), contains a section in Glagolitic, and its journal *Heritage* (*Baščina*) also offers texts in this alphabet among its articles. There are numerous initiatives and games for teaching how to write and read its characters, aimed mainly at the very young, but not only them; the website of the Society of Friends of Glagolitic contains the texts of many contemporary poets who compose their verses in the Glagolitic alphabet; many restaurants, especially in Istria, have menus with transliteration in the Glagolitic script, and these characters are employed

---

65 Such as the Faculty of Philosophy at the University of Zagreb, the National Library, the Zagreb University Library, the Croatian Philological Society, the Agency for Education and Training, and of course the Society of Friends of Glagolitic. Glagolitic letters also appear on the logos of other institutions that are not directly connected with the philological and cultural heritage of the country, such as the Apolonija Dental Clinic (Stomatološka Poliklinika Apolonija), some shops, etc.

even in a number of Croatian culinary products (see Tyran 2019: 288ff).

According to Marica Čunčić, director of the Old Church Slavonic Institute, the pre-eminent scientific institution dealing with the Glagolitic heritage, one can speak of a continuity of the Croatian Glagolitic alphabet from the 9th to the 21st centuries, since it is still used today, although for secondary and not directly communicative purposes (Čunčić 2003: 3). A significant fact of recent years is also the declaration of the art of "reading, writing and printing the Glagolitic" as an element of the intangible cultural heritage of the country by the Directorate for the Protection of Cultural Heritage of the Croatian Ministry of Culture (Rješenje 2014). The aim is to promote the function and importance of these traditions in society and to incorporate their protection into specific programs, as well as to ensure their availability to the public (ibid.), a fact that shows the recognition of the double value of this alphabet, symbolically and also communicatively. Particularly relevant for this goal, then, is the cooperation of communities and social groups that, through their popularization and valorization work with electronic media, literacy courses and other initiatives, ensure that this intangible heritage is passed on, cared for, defended and preserved (ibid.).

The Small Glagolitic Academy Juri Žakan (*Mala glagoljska akademija Juri Žakan*), founded in 1993 in the village of Roč in Istria – where, thanks to the Glagolitic Alley, traces of the Glagolitic written heritage are a living reality – organizes an annual summer course attended by about forty young students from all over the country. But this is not the only place where this alphabet is taught: in various Croatian schools, foundations and associations it is possible to get acquainted with literacy practices in Glagolitic through specific courses. The ministerial document lists indeed fifty-five institutions concerned with the cultural transmission of the alphabet: besides the Small Glagolitic Academy Juri Žakan, we find, for example, the *čakavski sabor* and the Society of Friends of Glagolitic, as well as the Old Church Slavonic Institute. The last institution is the most important actor working for the preservation of the Glagolitic heritage, and even offers a modern online program for teaching the different varieties of Glagolitic.[66] As already noted, from a sociolinguistic perspective, it is very interesting to observe that, despite being an extinct alphabet, the revival of Glagolitic has been successful from a practical and communicative point of view in terms of "script revitalization" (see Brooks 2010), and we can expect that more and more Glagolitic courses will take place in the future, for both "internal" and "external" audiences.

7.8 Glagolitic as a national symbol in an "exclusivist" sense

It has been argued that, in the practice of "banal nationalism" active in newly established state entities, there is a strong need to affirm the nation through symbols of collective belonging that are continuously recalled to people in everyday life (cf. Billig 1995: 8). In this respect, it is striking the extent to which Glagolitic has expanded its dominion since the establishment of an independent Croatia; we could perhaps interpret this phenomenon as a further validation of what has been described as the value and power of writing on collective consciousness (cf. Martin 1998). Within any society, there is a certain competition in terms of what counts as "cultural": in relation to writing, it is evident that different communities and societies, past and present, designate and hence limit the forms of writing recognized as legitimate (cf. Barton Papen 2010: 18). In the specific case of the Glagolitic script, its revival was initiated by the enthusiasm of a small cultural circle in a region, Istria, but thanks to its efforts, important effects were achieved on a national level too. As a consequence, the Glagolitic script has by no means disappeared; on the contrary, it seems to be increasingly asserting itself as a literary, aesthetic, artistic and, above all, identity-forming motif

---

66 Available at the following link: http://glagoljica.stin.hr/index.php?menu=10 (last access: 3/11/21). For those who prefer to learn Glagolitic from a textbook, one of the most recent is *Glagoljica za osnovce* by Martina Valec Rebić, published in 2013.

through its "reactivated" use, so that it sounds a bit inappropriate to define it as "extinct."[67]

A series of websites[68] provide numerous instances of the public and personal use of the Glagolitic alphabet by Croats, through images illustrating the presence of this writing system on various surfaces and in multiple contexts. Examples of public use include some public signage in some cities, as well as some institutional plaques appearing at the entrances of state buildings. As mentioned, it is often scholars and academics who contribute to the popularization of this alphabet: an example is the philologist Anica Nazor, with her numerous collaborations in projects and exhibitions related to Glagolitic, her participation in radio broadcasts and other initiatives such as the selection of Glagolitic motifs for some fashion creations. In her book *The Book of Croatian Glagolitic: By Knowing the Word I Speak* (*Knjiga o hrvatskoj glagoljici. 'Ja slovo znajući govorim...'*), published in 2008, the author presents the history of the Glagolitic alphabet, including a detailed section on its contemporary use. In the introduction, she states:

> Before you is a living book that should remind us in our everyday lives of the numerous meanings and values of the thousand-year-old Croatian Glagolite culture, of its continuous connections with the world, right up to the present day, when we rightly consider it one of the symbols of our people and our country. (Nazor 2008: 10)

According to Nazor, Glagolitic represents a "distinctive feature of Croatian culture and hence of its national identity" (Nazor 2008: 5), as it laid the foundation for Croatian literature and the Croatian literary language. Moreover, this writing system is no longer a "dead alphabet," but has become a source of inspiration in artistic, musical and cultural spheres.

Another important representative of the cultural world involved in the promotion of Glagolitic is Jasna Horvat, author of the

---

67   See also the entry on Glagolitic in the Atlas of Endangered Alphabets: www.endangeredalphabets.net/alphabets/glagolitic (last access: 3/11/21).
68   Among which is the website of the Society of Friends of Glagolitic: http://www.croatianhistory.net/glagoljica/dpg.html (last access: 3/11/21).

novel *Az*[69] (2009), whose events revolve around the moments of the invention of the Glagolitic alphabet by Cyril and Methodius, and in which the letters are connected with symbolic and numerological levels of interpretation. In addition to her literary activity, Horvat has also participated in the creation of several murals dedicated to this writing system at the Faculty of Economics at the University of Osijek. This institution states on its website that "[i]n establishing the Atrium of the Glagolitic Alphabet as a monument to the Glagolitic alphabet, the Faculty of Economics in Osijek joins the protectors of the Glagolitic alphabet in the safeguarding of intangible cultural heritage."[70]

The interior of the faculty has effectively become the largest institutional space housing the characters of this alphabet, after the Zagreb Cathedral, which was discussed at the end of the previous chapter. This initiative aims to attract public attention to the "philosophy and symbolism of the traditional Croatian writing system." Furthermore, the murals on the walls of the faculty are an example of how "lost parts of Croatian identity can now give rise to new cultural and creative products." The visuality of the Glagolitic alphabet is thus confirmed and legitimized, and Croatian space proves to be increasingly imbued with Glagolitic elements that stimulate the concept of a specific and unique identity on a semiotic level.

As has been affirmed (cf. McLuhan 1976: 6), the emergence of writing in antiquity essentially took place through the shift from the auditory to the visual realm as a transition from oral discourse. Later, letterpress printing linked the written word even more intimately to the visual component (Ong 2009: 69), a principle that holds unchanged in our own time, where the dominance and power of the visual sense manifests itself in all its intensity. (Peyró 2016: 196-197, Arnheim 1974). By representing ideas and words that precede writing itself, the alphabet in a sense duplicates them, establishing a new version that acquires a certain autonomy in

---

69 The name of the first letter of the Glagolitic Alphabet.
70 Available at: http://www.efos.unios.hr/aule/en/the-atrium-of-the-glagolitic-alphabet/ (last access: 3/11/21).

relation to the original message (Jensen 1969: 15-23). Keeping this in mind, we can better grasp the various implications of the use of Glagolitic script on several levels: countless surfaces can be turned into a space for hosting its alphabetic signs, confirming the fact that human beings can write "anywhere" if motivated by powerful symbolic and communicative objectives. Cardona remarks in this regard:

> Wherever a surface has been offered to it, writing has covered the most diverse materials. [...] besides covering specifically designed surfaces, writing can cover any object of use, and this often shows us that writing has other purposes besides the immediate one. (Cardona 1982: 76; my translation)

And similarly, Armando Petrucci:

> Everything, or almost everything, can become a writing surface. [...] These are all experiences and products that show that, if we ignore conventions and rules, we can write anywhere and arrange our text in the way that is most convenient for it and for us. (Petrucci 2007: 16; my translation)

The personal use of the alphabet as symbol (tattoos, t-shirts, jewelry) is an important phenomenon to take into account, since through its analysis we can better understand the nature of the encounter between the national rhetoric in relation to writing and the world of the reader or receptor (cf. Chartier 1992: 50). If we conceive the space of a nation-state in a semiotic sense as a context densely filled with meanings that are passed on to the population, then it is crucial to consider how these are in turn received and re-appropriated by the public of "readers." It is hence possible to measure the attraction and real influence of certain ideological drives promoted by ruling elites on different segments of the population.

While examples of the use of Glagolitic characters in amulets and talismans appeared in the past, serving to safeguard against disease and evil influences, the symbolic element of the alphabet is today linked to its materialization as a consumer object, as an accessory. We are faced with the interesting practices of self-representation in the visual field, a fact further exemplified in the use of this alphabet even in the personal space of the human body, which testifies to its significance as a symbol, despite the scarce, even minimal knowledge of the phonetic value of its characters on the simply communicative level.

The power of the Glagolitic alphabet in the collective imagination of the Croats can partly be explained by the peculiar aesthetic nature of its letters, which can also become the object of speculative thinking. An interesting work in this respect, aimed at highlighting the aesthetic, mystical and philosophical value of the Glagolitic alphabet is represented by the book *The Solemnity of the Glagolitic* (*Svečanost Glagoljice*), published as a collaboration between the philologist Josip Bratulić, the painter Branko Čačić, the sculptor Želimir Janeš, the graphic designer and academic Frane Paro and the poet Slavko Jendričko in 1987. In this work, which combines art and philosophical speculation, Glagolitic reveals itself both as an object and as a means of transmitting symbolic elements; the title is written in Glagolitic, and a number of poems by Slavko Jendričko dedicated to this alphabet appear in the book, some with a Glagolitic version. There is also an illustrative table at the end of the book showing how to write Glagolitic characters correctly.

Josip Bratulić, in turn, has noted that Glagolitic can be considered a magnificent alphabet possessing a sort of "ideographic" dimension, imbued with the "theological" idea of its inventor Constantine-Cyril:

> He fought for the icons in the churches and against the iconoclasts, and he incorporated all his intellectual faculties into this writing system [...]. When we speak of Glagolitic, we often do not have in mind the fact that Glagolitic is an alphabet that at the same time shaped the language — the language shapes the alphabet, and the alphabet shapes the language. (Bratulić 2009; my translation)

In a sense, the value that emerges from the use of this alphabet in contemporary Croatia is explained by its conveying meanings associated with precise notions of "Croatianness," which continue to be preserved thanks to its re-actualization, in line with a vision that affirms the historical continuity of the Croatian nation. The Glagolitic alphabet is now regarded in the country as an inalienable symbol of national identity: as we have seen, the Croatian rhetoric referring to this alphabet emphasizes its historical continuity, its Catholic aspect and its belonging to the Western European cultural space. Quite neglected is its association with the Eastern Christian aspect, despite its past use in other Slavic countries and its parallel symbolic revival in another Balkan country, Bulgaria[71] (see also chapter 10). These factors prove to be particularly relevant to the analysis of the contemporary Croatian ethnopsychological context, as they constitute some of the strongest motifs of the national identity discourse, constructed largely in opposition to specific cultural traits attributed to the Serbian neighbor, which will be discussed in more detail in the next chapter.

---

71   But also in Central European countries such as Slovakia and the Czech Republic.

8. THE MODIFIED STATUS OF CYRILLIC IN POST-SOCIALIST CROATIA AND SERBIA

8.1 Introduction: Issues of biscriptality

The outward appearance of a language, although conceivable as a purely technical and functional element (corresponding to both the orthography and the writing system), is in reality the bearer of an extremely powerful ideological and symbolic dimension, linked to the cultural orientation and/or tradition of a nation (Fishman 1977: xv, Durand 2014: 205). In hypothetical terms, each language could be represented by any writing system (Wellish 1978: 19); yet the adoption of a script is largely due to "extralinguistic" factors (cf. Fishman 1977: xii) and is a significant indicator of religious and political aspects.

During the times of socialist Yugoslavia, the parallel existence at an official level of the Latin and Cyrillic scripts constituted one of the most peculiar elements of the linguistic landscape. Being exposed in varying degrees to such a "bialphabetical" context (Richer 2004: 78) most citizens, consequently, became able to read and write in both alphabets, thus being "biliterate," although with peculiarities among the various republics (cf. Greenberg 2004: 43). In all elementary schools of Yugoslavia, pupils learned to write and read the two scripts (cf. Feldman & Barac-Cikoja 1996: 769, Mitrović 1999: 127); as a rule, however, educational manuals in the Cyrillic alphabet were not employed in Croatia, as the script that dominated in Croatian schools was Latin (cf. Owen-Jackson 2015: 85). Moreover, in many other contexts, as in legal transactions, Cyrillic was never used in the country.

In addition to this, it is important to remember that the Latin alphabet was the official one used by the Yugoslav's People Army (*Jugoslovenska narodna armija* [JNA]) for the entire course of its existence. Hence, in Croatia the knowledge of Cyrillic was mostly limited to those wanting access to the written production coming from the neighboring Republic of Serbia. This was not the case among the Serbian communities in Croatia, to whom the right to use the Cyrillic alphabet as the main writing system in education had been guaranteed from the end of the Second World War in the areas where this community composed the majority (Memorandum SANU 1986).

8.2 The first changes in the status of the Cyrillic alphabet

In considering the last 150 years of Serbian and Croatian history, we can easily point out how the differences between the Serbian and the Croatian languages have been diminished or highlighted as identity rhetoric varied and according to the dominant ideologies operative at different political moments (Richter 2004: 80). Certainly, in phases characterized by animosity between the two political entities, the idea of a common language was one of the first victims to be sacrificed, and it is not surprising that, since the dissolution of Yugoslavia, we have observed the development of a strong repudiation of the previous "digraphic" conditions present in various areas of the country. The use of one script rather than another has indeed started to be associated with a strictly symbolic practice of ethnic identification (Hammel 2000: 26).

In Serbia, from the 1980s onwards, concern was expressed that the Latin alphabet was gaining dominance over the Cyrillic alphabet in an increasing number of popular and scholarly publications (Greenberg 2004: 61-62, Denich 1993: 52). A few years before the outbreak of the war, in 1986, the Serbian Academy of Sciences and Arts, chaired by the writer Dobrica Ćosić, issued a now famous memorandum arguing that the right to use the Cyrillic alphabet in Croatia was under serious threat, due to what was denounced as a clear attempt to assimilate Serb minorities (Memorandum SANU 1986). In light of the language policy pursued, the memorandum stated, the Cyrillic alphabet had to be taught more extensively in the Croatian Republic: "[t]he fanatical zeal to create a separate Croatian language, as opposed to any idea of a common language of Croats and Serbs, leaves little hope in the long run that the Serbian people in Croatia will be able to preserve their national identity" (SANU Memorandum 1986). This document maintained that the Cyrillic alphabet found itself in a perilous situation, presenting the alphabet issue as one of fundamental political importance and legitimizing Cyrillic as a marker of Serbian identity within Yugoslavia (Greenberg 2004: 61).

As is well known, relations between Serbs and Croats began to deteriorate rapidly from the end of the 1980s: as an example, when the HDZ came to power in Croatia in 1990, one of the first moves made by the national authorities was to declare the Latin alphabet as the only official one, removing all signs bearing inscriptions in Cyrillic.[72] This script was then removed from school curricula in the educational institutions of the country (Bugajski 2000: 85). The new Croatian Constitution in late 1990 abolished the status of Serbs as a constitutive nation (see Hayden 1992), as it referred only to the "Croatian language in the Latin alphabet," although providing for some exceptions (Ustav RH 1990, art. 12). At an institutional level, this change entailed the modified status of the non-majority populations, which became identified as national minorities, with important consequences in ideological and identitarian terms. Furthermore, not only was Cyrillic eradicated from the public space of the country, but also many words of Serbian origin were stigmatized as "verba non grata" and substituted with Croatian archaisms or brand new, artificially created words (Langston & Peti—Stantić 2014: 175-180, Greenberg 2004: 48-49).

A sort of symbolic program of "Croatization" was inaugurated, which "represented the primacy of a separate (from the Serbian) Croatian identity based on (re-)expressions of Croatia's

---

72 Apparently, in 1990, the founder of the Serbian Democratic Party in Croatia (SDS), Jovan Rašković, asked Tudjman to grant the Serbs in Croatia, as Orthodox Christians, the right to continue using the Cyrillic alphabet. When Tudjman refused this request, Rašković responded by saying, "Serbs are a crazy people" (Bjelić 2011: 16). With this claim, Rašković emphasized that, if they were prevented from using the Cyrillic alphabet, which is crucial for maintaining their identity, "the Serbs would go mad, and seized by madness, would start a war with the Croatian government." Rašković insisted on "small linguistic differences between Croats and Serbs [...] as a precondition for peace" (ibid.).

historical past, together with other pragmatic measures such as ensuring the predominance within the Republic of a distinct Croatian language in the Latin script" (Roe 2005: 101). A symmetrical phenomenon took place when, as a consequence of the self-proclaimed Republika Srpska of Bosnia in 1992, the use of Latin characters was forbidden by governmental decree. With the abandonment of the Latin alphabet and the *ijekavian* variant of the language, Bosnian Serbs began to move further and further away from an essential part of their cultural heritage (Richter 2004: 78, Sen 2009: 416-417).[73]

The post-Yugoslav context shows that new collective constructions of identity defended and maintained their own space through the use of language and the alphabet, embodying elements capable of enforcing a vision of separation by making social and ethnic differences explicit (cf. Bourdieu 1990: 138). In this respect, the phenomenon of "de-Cyrillization"/"cyrillophobia" (see Scarcia 1999: 182 on the Russian case) and linguistic "purification" active from the early 1990s in Croatia was in many respects similar to what had occured fifty years earlier during the time of the NDH, especially in relation to the ideology of recovering an authentic Croatian tradition by radically transforming the language (Garde 2004: 221).

After the end of the Yugoslav wars, the delicate question concerning the linguistic educational rights of the Serb minority in Croatia remained open: starting in 1995, Serbian representatives in Eastern Slavonia tried to institute separate primary schools with instruction in the Serbian language and using the Cyrillic alphabet, but with little success. However, it is important to note that, according to many reports, before the collapse of Yugoslavia, the majority of the Serbian communities living in the Krajina region of Croatia availed themselves of the Latin alphabet and not the Cyrillic (Roe 2005: 118, Greenberg 2004: 43).

---

[73] Since the Republika Srpska was not separated from the rest of Bosnia and Herzegovina by borders or checkpoints, the importance of symbols as identity markers became crucial in representing difference. Cyrillic thus embodied a symbol of the difference and "perfection" of Serbian as opposed to Bosnian and Croatian, which are not immediately distinguishable from each other since they both use the Latin alphabet.

The possibility of having their own school institutions was formally guaranteed to all national minorities. There were, for example, Hungarian-language schools in Eastern Slavonia and Italian-language schools in Istria; nevertheless, an application in September 2002 for the official registration of schools with Serbian-language teaching provoked a displeased reaction from the then Deputy Prime Minister, Goran Granić (MRG Report 2003: 25). In fact, the politician spoke out against the establishment of schools for this minority, justifying his position by the fear of possible segregation of ethnic Serb pupils from the surrounding social context (ibid.). In this way, the Croatian government could therefore impose school instruction in the Croatian language and in the Latin script exclusively, banning Cyrillic from every sector of the public life of the country (Magner 2001: 21).

The open question about the status of the Cyrillic alphabet in Croatia can be interpreted both as a sign of the persistent hardening of identity in the country (at the level of rejection of any symbols and elements of common history with the Serbian neighbor) and as the "symmetrical" reaction to the glorification of the Cyrillic alphabet in Serbia by political exponents and intellectuals associated with more or less pronounced nationalist thinking.

It has been noted that "(...) in order to become emancipated Europeans, the Balkans had first to pathologize their own geography, cut organic ties with other ethnic groups, accept mono-ethnic nation states, and legalize ethnic differentiation" (Bjelić 2011: 2), in a process defined by Bob Hayden (1992) as "constitutional nationalism." In Croatia, past political experiences with Belgrade as the dominant center (in Yugoslavia and in the former Kingdom), and the "Germanization" and "Magyarization" attempts endured during the time of Habsburg rule in the 19th century, made the dominant national rhetoric very sensitive to issues of cultural and linguistic identity and prone to protect specific interests as a nation understood in a homogeneous sense (Batovic 2009: 16).

8.3 The Serbian case: will bialphabetism survive?

As regards the relationship with the (alphabetic) "Other" in the post-Yugoslav context, the situation in the Republic of Serbia appears to be even more complex than the Croatian case due to the persisting co-presence of both alphabets. Notwithstanding the changes at an ideological level with respect to the status of the Latin alphabet inaugurated in the 1990s, the country is still characterized by a peculiar situation of "bialphabetism" (cf. Đurđević Milin Feldman 2013), or "biscriptality" (Bunčić 2016) (in Serbian, "dvoazbučnost" [Bugarski 1997: 38, 91]), in which both scripts are used interchangeably, making most people perfectly "biliterate."

The Latin alphabet played a key role during the Yugoslav period, being used in numerous official publications, and also, as mentioned, constituting the official writing system of the Yugoslav People's Army. Nevertheless, in 1990, the Constitution of the Republic of Serbia decided to officially downgrade the status of the Latin alphabet and introduce a sort of "alphabetic hierarchy." This was soon manifested in the printing of banknotes in Cyrillic script exclusively, a policy that reflected "the Milošević's regime underlying agenda of advancing the cause of a Greater Serbia" (Greenberg 2004: 62). As we read in the 1990 Constitution of the Republic of Serbia, Article 8:

> In the Republic of Serbia, the Serbo-Croatian language and the Cyrillic alphabet are in official use, and the Latin alphabet is in official use in the manner established by law.

> In the areas of the Republic of Serbia where [other] nationalities live, their languages and alphabets are also in official use in the manner established by law. (Ustav RS 1990; my translation)

With the outbreak of war in 1991, Serbian nationalists increasingly pursued a campaign aimed at restricting the use of the Latin script. Shortly after Croatia and Slovenia declared independence, rumors circulated in Belgrade that "letters mailed domestically would only be delivered if they were addressed in Cyrillic script" (Greenberg 2004: 60n), predictably creating some difficulties for the population. In this period, many journals and magazines that had previously used the Latin alphabet began to appear in Cyrillic script (Garde 2004: 224). In a sense, it seemed that Belgrade was compensating for the loss of its status as the Yugoslav center by expressing more intensely a specifically Serbian nationality. In parallel to this, in the changed socio-political and cultural context, the idea of a "correct" Serbian language became intertwined with the exclusive use of the Cyrillic alphabet; the idea of Cyrillic as the "most perfect alphabet in the world" was increasingly asserted (Bugarski 1997: 39).

In the following years, however, in contrast to neighboring Croatia, both writing systems continued to be present in the school curricula in Serbia and Montenegro and were mastered by the vast majority of the population as a legacy of Yugoslav education (Richter 2004: 79, Feldman & Barac-Cikoja 1998: 769). Extreme measures, such as "Cyrillization," were not proposed by linguists, but rather by individual nationalists; and, at this time, in response to the strong promotion of Cyrillic, the use of the Latin alphabet represented for some a way of demonstrating their "anti-nationalism" (Garde 2004: 224).

Following the dissolution of Serbia and Montenegro, the new Serbian Constitution of 2006, at Article 10 (Ustav RS 2006), declared Cyrillic as the only official alphabet in the country, a fact that, basically, minimized the status of the Latin script, even if the latter was recognized as legitimate in areas inhabited by minorities that used it and in the context of inscriptions in public spaces, along with Cyrillic (cf. Selvelli 2015d: 167). The Latin alphabet is still included in the educational curricula starting from the second year of primary school, and continues to be taught to children for writing both Serbian and foreign languages such as English.

In more recent years, the rhetoric of defending Cyrillic has gained new momentum, as Serbian nationalists organized a series of actions to fight against "Latinization" threats perceived as imminent (see Jovanović 2018), in particular through the activities of the *Ćirilica* associations, in the cities of Belgrade and Novi Sad. Members of these associations even advocated the elimination of the character <j> introduced in the 19th century by Vuk Karadžić into the Cyrillic alphabet, considering it some sort of Latin intrusion (see Brehmen

2015: 59). According to authors and scholars closer to nationalist positions (see, for example, Zbiljić 2002), the Latin script is indissolubly linked to Croatian identity and thus constitutes a threat to "Serbianness." In this view, part of the responsibility for the parallel existence of both scripts in the country is ascribable to those linguists who mistakenly consider *latinica* as a "Serbian Latin alphabet" (Đorđević 2012). The persistence of a situation in which Serbs are "the only bialphabetic nation in the world" would, according to these views, foster a critical state of "cultural and social schizophrenia" (Đorđević 2014: 354ff).

Claims like these are contradicted by intellectuals and linguists who disagree with associating the Latin alphabet used in Serbia to Croatian culture. An example is the popular linguist Ivan Klajn, who, together with other colleagues, defends the historical existence of a genuine tradition of Serbian *latinica*, which includes the literary tradition of Dubrovnik, from the 17th century to the present. In a 2006 interview with the Serbian daily newspaper *Politika*, published concurrently with the new normative laws on matters of language and the alphabet, Klajn expressed his view on the situation of biscriptality in the country, pointing out that Serbia was the only country in Europe to possess the peculiar feature of a "double alphabet" (Klajn 2006).

Klajn warned that a "monoalphabetic" solution would not only affect the writing rights of citizens, but also have no realistic chance of being practically applied in daily life. On the other hand, the legislative recognition of the parallel existence of Cyrillic and Latin was nothing new, as the same principle had been in force for decades in the time of Yugoslavia. A provision to impose Cyrillic exclusively, Klajn noted, would lead to a regression of the Cyrillic alphabet vis-à-vis the Latin, since these two alphabets were by no means symmetrical. The Latin one was necessary for English, for most foreign languages taught in the country, for mathematics, physics, chemistry, as well as for correspondence with foreign countries, for emails, the Internet, text messages and so on. Cyrillic, on the contrary, could not be used for any of these functions: with it one could ("and had to") write only the Serbian language. Cyrillic had to be preserved, albeit not for utilitarian but for "cultural and historical" reasons. In considering the status of the Latin alphabet in the examples of public writing in Serbia, Klajn also added:

> The same alarming statistics that the *Ćirilica* Association denounces — almost 80% of public signs in Belgrade in the Latin script, advertisements exclusively in the Latin script, etc. — are proof that the Serbs also consider the Latin alphabet their own: surely, they did not borrow it out of love of the Croats. (Klajn 2006; my translation)

Klajn thus declared the possibility of a non-exclusive choice in the field of writing, and asserted that biscriptality was the only possible path to follow: it was the "destiny of the country," and the law must find the proper way to "save Cyrillic from extinction" (Klajn 2006).

It can be argued that, in the Republic of Serbia, one of the main features of Serbo-Croatian lives on to some extent, as the language in its written form still includes the two alphabetic variants. A clear distinction between the Cyrillic and Latin writing domains is not reflected in public documents nor in public or private use. The Radio Television of Serbia public broadcaster uses the Cyrillic alphabet almost exclusively, while private TV channels employ mainly Latin. Although a defense of the Serbian Cyrillic alphabet is carried out at the official level, it is rather the Latin one that dominates the streets of the main urban centers of the country today. Undoubtedly, many more books are printed exclusively in Cyrillic script nowadays than in the times before the disintegration of Yugoslavia, especially works dealing with Serbian history and culture. Some people actively strive to write and read in this alphabet, especially in the context of modern technologies, so as not to lose their immediate familiarity with it, managing to maintain a perfect balance of "biliteracy."[74] In addition, school facilities may receive visits from Department of Education officials explaining the rules about which alphabet to use in different domains. Class registers, for example, must be written in Serbian Cyrillic, with the exception of those for foreign language courses.[75]

---

74 Personal communication from an academic at the University of Novi Sad.
75 Personal communication from an academic and teacher working in Belgrade.

Nevertheless, the largest publishing house in the country, Laguna, now publishes almost exclusively in the Latin script, not for ideological reasons, but for entirely practical ones, that is, the greater availability of typefaces and the possibility of wider distribution in other countries of the former Yugoslavia: Bosnia and Herzegovina, Croatia, Montenegro. The publisher sometimes receives letters of protest from citizens complaining about its "Latinophile" policy, and there are cases of authors who refuse to publish with it, not wanting to see their works printed in this alphabet.[76]

8.4 The destruction of allographic traditions

In his analysis of the relationship between language and nationalism, Bugarski confirms that the ideology of the nation-state has succeeded in imposing the condition of homogeneity as an ideal on the members of post-Yugoslav communities: it is desirable that all use the same language or variety, as well as the same alphabet, which is necessarily different from those of neighboring communities, which are generally very similar (Bugarski 1997: 106). In this way, language, even in its graphic form, connects with the nationalist dimension, sharing two crucial functions: a communicative one, i.e. including a certain number of people in a given community, and a symbolic one, demarcating the relation with other communities considered external. In the context of the former Yugoslavia, the symbolic aspect of language, among whose elements the alphabet occupies a privileged role, is exaggerated to the detriment of the communicative one, becoming one of the cornerstones of national identity.

All the states that emerged from the former Yugoslavia, and more generally in the Balkans, have undertaken a process to legitimize their identity through the "mythographic" use of a certain part of their history: in this process, as we have seen, language and the alphabet contribute to the goal of institutionalizing an idea of unity or, in some cases, of destroying a whole section of the history

---

76   Personal communication from an employee working at Laguna.

created and experienced by previous generations. As a consequence, whole cultural traditions can be swept away (Richter 2004: 82), works disappear from the shelves of bookshops and from school desks (cf. Lešaja 2012), monuments are destroyed, and street names are changed (cf. Ugrešić 2004).

During the collapse of Yugoslavia, a specific phenomenon of social conflict manifested itself in the destruction of cultural and monumental elements associated with an unwanted "Other," as sadly occurred in the form of the "urbicide" (cf. Bogdanović 1995) perpetrated by Yugoslav Serb forces on cities such as Dubrovnik, Sarajevo and Vukovar. Furthermore, this phenomenon manifested itself also in the annihilation of the written presence of the "Other," that is, of "allographic" traditions: several were indeed destructive acts targeting the written tradition in the alphabets of the various peoples, perpetrated not only by Yugoslav Serb forces, but also by Croats. A relatively unknown case is one described in the book *Bibliocide* (*Knjigocid*) (2012) by Ante Lešaja, dealing with the forced removal from Croatian public and school libraries, in the first years after the war, of almost three million books considered "dangerous" for ethnic and ideological reasons.

These were the books written in Cyrillic script, in the *ekavian* variant or by Serbian authors (approx. 13.8% of the total stock), whose disappearance provoked a sort of "de-Cyrillization" and "de-Serbization" of the country's bibliographic heritage (see also Kordić 2010: 17), which could be associated with the "exclusionist" tendency in Croatian society in the 1990s. Lešaja defines this "bibliocide," i.e. the destruction of the written memory of Croatian (and Bosnian-Croatian) cities, a phenomenon of manifestly symbolic character, comparable to a "blow to memory," symptomatic of the desire to erase any trace of a common past with the Serbian people (Lešaja 2012: 12).

Further acts of destruction of Cyrillic books occurred in other parts of the former Yugoslavia, such as in the National Library in the Croatian part of the city of Mostar, where a large number of volumes were removed on the grounds of eliminating the "pests" that had infested them. The local media commented ironically on the events at the time, noting that the insects only attacked books by Serbian authors or those in Cyrillic script (ibid., 200n).

Of course, it should be noted that acts of "bibliocide" were not limited to the Croatian side. Indeed, the greatest damage inflicted on the Yugoslav bibliographic heritage was by the Yugoslav Army's onslaughts during the wars, especially in Dubrovnik and Sarajevo (Riedlmayer 2007). In this last city, the Vijećnica national library had 90% of its holdings destroyed in August 1993, an immense loss of the historical evidence of the Bosnian multicultural heritage. A few months earlier, in May, the library of the Oriental Institute had been targeted: 5,263 manuscripts in Arabic, Persian, Ottoman Turkish and *arebica* (Bosnian in Arabic characters) were devastated, along with 200,000 documents from the Ottoman provincial archives and several Bosnian newspapers (van der Hoeven 1996: 18). During the Bosnian war, numerous elements of the Islamic cultural heritage were struck by the destroyers of the cities, who symbolically wanted to target the sites of the Ottoman past, including examples of public writing in Arabic script. Apart from the libraries, the most important places that fell victim to such destructive acts were Muslim cemeteries.

Serb attackers had perhaps forgotten the price Serbian culture had to pay fifty years earlier in the form of bibliographic losses when, in April 1941, as a result of the German occupation, the National Library in Belgrade was almost completely razed by bombs. At that time, some 1,300 Cyrillic manuscripts from the 12th to the 18th centuries had been reduced to ash, along with important books by Serbian authors and scholars, incunabula and old printed works, as well as Serbian books from the period between 1832 and 1941 (Van der Hoeven 1996: 14).

8.5 Croatian reactions to the bialphabetic plaques in Vukovar

Some twenty-five years after the end of the war in Croatia, the recent case of the destruction of the Cyrillic panels in Vukovar is indicative of a troubled relationship with the Serbian alphabet, viewed by many as the paramount symbol of the war and siege of the 1990s. The protests against the public legitimization of the Cyrillic alphabet in Croatia, which took place between 2013 and 2015, represented the most critical stage of Serbian/Croatian relations since 1997.

Ethnic Serbs, most of whom are Orthodox Christians, constitute by far the largest minority in Croatia:[77] according to the 2011 census, the Serb presence numbers 186,633 people or 4.4 percent of the total population. Since the 1991 census, when it represented 12.2 percent of the population, the Serb community has declined drastically, mainly as a direct result of the war and the exodus following Operation *Oluja* in 1995, during which the Croats regained power over the territories of the self-proclaimed Serb Republic of Krajina (1991-1995).

In 2011, the results of the census showed that Serbs constituted more than 33% of the population of Vukovar, a fact entailing the introduction of bilingual and especially "bialphabetic" signs. In 2002, the Constitutional Act on the Rights of National Minorities (*Ustavni zakon o pravima nacionalnih manjina*) replaced the previous laws regulating the linguistic rights of national minorities as a fundamental step in Croatia's rapprochement with international European principles in view of joining the Union. This document affirmed the right of national minorities to use their own language and alphabet, both privately and publicly, including in the field of education (Ustavni Zakon 2002). According to Article 12 of the Croatian Constitution, the official language in Croatia is Croatian, written in the Latin alphabet (Ustav RH 1990, art. 12). The Serbian language, together with its Cyrillic alphabet, may be used as a minority language if the conditions set out in both the Constitutional Act

---

[77] The Serbs originally moved to the territories of present-day Croatia as border guards during the period of Habsburg rule, being settled in the so-called "military border" (*Vojna Krajina*) to defend it against the Ottoman Empire from the 16th century onwards. Following the abolition of the border at the end of the 19th century (1881), the Serbs were placed under the authority of the Principality of Croatia-Slavonia, which remained part of the Habsburg Empire until 1918.

and the Law on the Use of National Minority Languages of the Republic of Croatia are met.

However, in trying to meet the requirement to adopt the appropriate measures to guarantee the rights of the Serb minority, the introduction of bilingual and bialphabetic signs was rejected by large segments of the population, both in the city of Vukovar and in the rest of the country, triggering a series of intense protests that erupted in autumn 2013. The explanation for the rejection of bilingual signs was rather ironic, as it was stated that such a law could not apply if a minority language was identical to that of the majority (see Langston & Peti—Stantić 2014: 131). Indeed, if Serbian and Croatian were considered a single language, there would be no need to enforce a law on bilingualism, but simply to transliterate from Latin to Cyrillic (see Šarić & Radanović Felberg 2017: 54n). Nevertheless, the prime minister at the time, Zoran Milanović (of the social-democratic party SDP) insisted on implementing the Constitutional Act on the rights of ethnic minorities.

Widespread demonstrations began in Vukovar on the night of 2 September 2013, when a series of bilingual signs, written in the Croatian with Latin characters and in Serbian with Cyrillic script, were put on a series of institutional buildings. The Committee for the Defense of Croatian Vukovar (Stožer za obranu hrvatskog Vukovara), consisting of war veterans, together with members of the nationalist right (a total of about a thousand people), immediately expressed their outrage by pummeling a plaque installed on the Public Treasury building. The protesters also destroyed a sign located at the entrance to the police station and removed a third one from the wall of the state administration building. The remaining signs were protected by police units specially brought in from Osijek.

Following this event, the Committee for the Defense of Croatian Vukovar managed to collect the required number of signatures to launch a referendum on the issue (more than 650,000). The request submitted to Parliament called for the linguistic rights of minorities regarding public signage to be respected only in local government units where at least half of the population belonged to an ethnic minority. However, Prime Minister Milanović confirmed that the government would not abandon the placement of the Cyrillic plaques, while the leader of the opposition HDZ, Tomislav Karamarko, called on the government to remove them. According to Karamarko, Article 8 of the Constitutional Act on the Rights of National Minorities stipulated that a law could only be adopted on the basis of understanding, cooperation and dialogue between the majority and minority communities: conditions that, in his opinion, were not present in Vukovar.

Numerous statements condemning the erection of bilingual signs came from various right-wing politicians, such as Ruža Tomašić, then leader of the nationalist party Croatian Party of Rights Dr. Ante Starčević (*Hrvatska stranka prava Dr. Ante Starčević*) and vice president of the Parliamentary Committee for Human Rights and National Minorities. In a statement released in February 2013, Tomašić stated that "Cyrillic in Vukovar means cannons, tanks, destruction, murder and rape. The wounds of war have not yet healed and the time is not yet ripe for Cyrillic."

The Croatian Movement for Life and the Family (*Hrvatski pokret za život i porodicu*), an association known for extremist statements, declared their preparedness to do anything to prevent bilingualism in the public signage, releasing a highly controversial message targeting the Serbs in Croatia, which completely belittled their cultural and historical identity:

> It is a well-known historical fact that the present-day Serbs did not come to Croatia from Serbia as Serbs, nor even speaking the Serbian language from Serbia, but settled here as Vlachs, speaking the Vlach language [...]. By what logic is the forcible introduction of a foreign language and a foreign alphabet from the Republic of Serbia now being demanded for the entire Serb minority?[78]

In this context of renewed interethnic tensions and extremist discourse, the alignment of a part of the Croatian Catholic Church, especially Cardinal Josip Bozanić, Archbishop of Zagreb, with the most nationalistic and intolerant elements in society, appeared

---

78 https://www.novosti.rs/vesti/planeta.300.html:416512-HDZ-Cirilica-u-Vukovaru--sramotan-zahtev (last access: 3/11/21).

highly controversial. Instead of calling for peace, tolerance and respect for the law, church leaders denounced the Milanović government for its intention to defend the law on bilingualism. The Church leadership not only refused to counter the countless manifestations of ethnic hatred, but also avoided any reference to the fact that, in its Croatian variant called *hrvatska ćirilica*,[79] Cyrillic, together with Glagolitic, had been a writing system used in the country's Catholic Church records for many centuries. Furthermore, the Croatian bishops came to fully support the referendum against the Cyrillic alphabet called by the Committee for the Defense of Croatian Vukovar.[80]

As a result of the institutions' failure to condemn the various expressions of hatred towards the Serbs, ethnic intolerance also spread to the level of informal public writing in cities across the country. Nazi graffiti, fascist symbols and Ustasha messages, explicitly calling for physical violence against the Serbs have unfortunately become common in public areas of many urban centers:[81] "Vukovar nikad neće biti Вуковар" ("Vukovar will never be Вуковар" — the latter representing the Cyrillic version of the city's name, which, however, contains characters that can be read in the Latin alphabet but with a different phonological value), "Stop ćirilici u Vukovaru" ("Stop Cyrillic in Vukovar), etc. (Opačić 2014: 6). Moreover, from September 2013 to February 2014, in Vukovar alone thirty-five Cyrillic panels were destroyed in twenty-six different assaults (Reinkowski 2019: 210).

---

79 The one that Bosnians call *bosančica*.
80 https://www.blic.rs/vesti/svet/zoran-pusic-zastrasujuca-je-podrska-katolicke-crkve-referendumu-protiv-cililice/wl52f29 (last access: 3/11/21).
81 In 2014, in Vukovar, a Cyrillic panel placed in the building housing the offices of the Independent Democratic Serb Party (SDSS) was damaged. The premises of the *Prosvjeta* Serbian cultural association in Split were also targeted, leaving the glass of its front door shattered. On 5 December 2014, offensive graffiti with Ustasha symbols and messages of hatred appeared on the façade of the parish house of the Serbian Orthodox Church in Vinkovci. During the same year, there was also the destruction of a sign with Cyrillic inscription on the building of the Serbian Minority Council in Pula on Orthodox Christmas Eve.

Even though the campaign supporters managed to collect the necessary number of signatures, the Croatian Constitutional Court declared the referendum question unconstitutional in April 2014. Nevertheless, even after this decision, resistance to the use of the Cyrillic alphabet as well as forced removal and destruction of bilingual signs on the buildings of Serbian state bodies and institutions continued throughout the year, mainly in Vukovar, but also elsewhere in the country (Opačić 2014: 34).

8.6 The Serb minority in Croatia as the "Other"

According to the Vukovar City Statute of 2009, the Cyrillic script legally constituted one of the two official alphabets in the city since 16 July 2009, recognized in particular in Article 61, paragraph 3 of this document (Statut grada Vukovar 2009). However, in August 2015, the City Council, under the leadership of the new HDZ mayor Ivan Penava, decided to amend the Statute by deleting the reference to the obligation to display bilingual signs in Latin and Cyrillic scripts on public buildings, in the squares and streets. The modification of the Statute provoked a reaction from the Council of Europe, which expressed its regret at this decision.

During the period of the most intense anti-Cyrillic demonstrations, the Serbs of Vukovar refrained from a public reaction, so as to avoid a further escalation of violence by the most extreme factions.[82] In this context, the Serb minority weekly *News* (*Novosti*) published a copy of the Croatian Ustasha regime's April 1941 announcement of the ban on the use of the Cyrillic alphabet on the territory of the Independent State of Croatia, stating that the fight against the alphabet of a minority was not an "original idea of Tomislav Josić and his Committee for the Defense of Croatian Vukovar," but could count on sad precedents in the recent history of the country.[83]

---

[82] However, the Serb People's Party of Vukovar, in condemning the vandalism of the Cyrillic signs, stated that this was an attack on the Serbian people of the city.

[83] http://www.portalnovosti.com/reakcija-na-rehabilitaciju-ustastva (last access: 3/11/21). My translation.

It appears evident that, in Croatia, both Vukovar and Cyrillic embody two symbols that are in opposition to each other in the prevailing national vision. The alphabet in question is indeed linked to the culture and identity of those who subjected Vukovar to a devastating siege that left a deep trauma in the collective memory (Malešević 2002: 227). According to this view, Cyrillic stands in opposition to all those values on which the Croats have constituted themselves as a nation and asserted themselves in history, and embodies the symbol of a foreign and hostile culture. In this regard, a significant statement was made by Zdravko Komšić, spokesman for the Committee for the Defense of Croatian Vukovar:

> The Cyrillic alphabet bothers us because all those barbarians who came from the East [...] wrote their accusations in Cyrillic. Think of our houses when we were expelled from Vukovar. On them was written, in Cyrillic: occupied, Serbian. Therefore, we believe that accepting anything written in Cyrillic script in Vukovar is a defeat in peacetime.[84]

As the writer Miljenko Jergović notes in his article on this topic, the "doggedness" regarding the Cyrillic alphabet is part of a process of constructing an "Other" which is exclusively connected with the Serbian element. We can indeed remark that the rights to bilingual signs appear to be respected in the areas inhabited by the Italian minority in Istria, or in the those populated by Hungarian communities, but not always in the areas inhabited by Serbs. However, the association of this alphabet with the war does not exactly correspond to reality, since the tanks of the Yugoslav Army actually bore writings in Latin letters:

> The question of the Other and of diversity in Croatia concerns only and exclusively the relationship with the Serbs. All other minorities are marginal, any other tolerance is a total fantasy. The relationship with Cyrillic is the relationship with the Serbs, not with the sufferings of 1991. Besides, Vukovar was shelled by Latin-charactered tanks and cannons. In case we have forgotten it, the official alphabet of the Yugoslav National Army was Latin. (Jergović 2013; my translation)[85]

---

84 http://www.slobodnaevropa.org/a/pravo-na-dvojezicnost-od-primjene-don egiranja/24936733.html (last access: 3/11/21). My translation.
85 http://www.jergovic.com/sumnjivo-lice/ako-je-kad-i-bila-cirilica-odavno-nij e-hrvatsko-pismo/ (last access: 3/11/21)..

The need to find a solution to the issues affecting the public visibility of the Cyrillic script has also been noted by international bodies: in April 2014, both the Council of Europe and the United Nations Human Rights Committee called on Croatia to guarantee the right of minorities to use their own language and alphabet. Concern was also expressed regarding the referendum question, considering it a possible act of violation of national minority rights standards, both at the national and European level, according to the European Charter for Regional and Minority Languages.[86]

In April 2015, the Committee of Ministers of the Council of Europe urged Croatian authorities to persevere in their efforts to promote tolerance towards minority languages: in particular, this could be achieved by including "signs and traditional local names with inscriptions in Cyrillic script, based on the conclusions of the Committee of Experts (...), and the cultures they represent as an integral part of the cultural heritage of Croatia, both in the general curriculum at all educational stages and in the media" (Recommendation 2015). In another press release of 21 August 2015, the Council of Europe, alerted by the decision of the Vukovar City Council to amend its statute in an "anti-Cyrillic" direction, strongly deplored the removal of signboards in minority languages through acts of vandalism and by formal decisions aimed at limiting their presence in the public space. It therefore solicited all relevant public authorities in the country to fully enforce the provisions of the European Charter for Regional or Minority Languages.

Such recommendations continue to be nonetheless ignored. As of this writing, there are still no examples of public writing in Cyrillic alphabet in Vukovar, and the institutional buildings still bear the traces of the panels violently removed during the protests. Vukovar appears to be a deeply divided city where reconciliation and recovery from the wounds of the 1990s are still far away. Ethnic communities are polarized due to mistrust, disillusion and the separation of their institutions, as in the case of separate instruction for

---

86   http://minorityrights.org/2014/04/24/croatia-should-test-merits-of-proposed-anti-minority-referendum-mrg-says/ (last access: 3/11/21).

Croatian and Serbian children, similar to what is happening in many parts of Bosnia and Herzegovina.

8.7 The relevance of the public writing context

Each society expresses a specific vision of what is considered "cultural": in relation to the writing domain, different communities and nations design and limit forms of writing that are recognized as legitimate (cf. Barton & Papen 2010: 18). The official use of a minority language in the public sphere implies a series of rights, including having inscriptions and other information of a public nature in the minority language, as well as local toponymy, street names and other topographical information. In this sense, the Council of Europe's recommendations on the use of minority languages on official signs are indicative of the extent to which the presence of public inscriptions can exert a positive impact on the perception of the prestige and legitimacy of a minority language, and thus on the self-esteem of the same minority community. The presence of signs in Cyrillic script in areas inhabited by Serb communities is not just a formality: we can rather consider it a necessary factor in the construction of a society capable of hosting its "Other" in a symbolic way. Certainly, the erection of bialphabetic public signs would help the nation deal with its contradictions and history, by undermining the basis of a homogeneous identity construction still impacted by painful taboos and unhealed wounds.

Landry and Bourhis (1997) have employed the term "linguistic landscape" when referring to the relationship between language salience and ethnic vitality in the context of public inscription. In their view, the ability of users to avail themselves of a given language (and script) by enforcing it in their environment would be directly proportional to the status accorded to it at the official level. The inclusion of a language in the public sphere can thus have a positive effect on its degree of vitality, which involves its ability to perform the more mundane communicative functions. Moreover, the elevation of the minority language status at the official level also entails a symbolic dimension that contributes to the signification of a particular social geography: through its visibility in the public space, the community of users is recognized and legitimized by the rest of the linguistic context. Languages and alphabets that differ from those of the majority can therefore play a role in affirming a certain type of territory that is also "marked" in an ethno-linguistic sense, in relation to both internal and external observers.

In a post-conflict environment where strong power dynamics are at work, public inscriptions represent one of the tools that provide greater representation to the social: this is not only the case in the Balkans, but also elsewhere in Eastern Europe (see, for example, Eglitis 2002: 141-144) and of course beyond. The analysis of public inscriptions is therefore particularly useful for identifying power relations and salient markers of identity in a shared public context, as well as national ideologies about languages and minorities. It is undeniable that minority groups often feel the need to symbolically demarcate their social space through writing and monuments in which a distinct language or alphabet appears. Examples of public scripts reveal a lot about a country (cf. Kramer, Ivković & Friedman 2014: 14), above all in relation to their linguistic and, in a sense, identity issues: the degree of multilingualism is also and especially expressed in the form of public inscriptions. An example of this is the city of Novi Sad in Vojvodina, a rare case of a multilingual public setting, representative of an autonomous, historically and "intentionally" multicultural region.[87] However, this attitude is rather an exception in Serbia, a fact that can be deduced by considering the official public inscriptions in the Serbian capital, most of which appear written exclusively in the Serbian Cyrillic alphabet, although other public signs reveal the presence of foreign languages such as Chinese, Russian and English for tourism purposes (see Canakis 2018: 236).

In relation to the context of public writing and multigraphism in Vukovar, an interesting proposal was the one made by the

---

[87] Nevertheless, even in this case we can highlight a significant absence: that of the Romani language from the four, five or even six languages that appear on public inscriptions, in spite of the fact that the Roma community is numerically and institutionally very significant in Vojvodina.

members of the association The City is Also Us (*Grad, to smo mi*), which, in September 2014, after the regrettable events related to the destruction of bilingual plaques in their city, suggested that the dispute could be resolved by adopting a more creative solution. The proposal was to place a Latin-alphabet plaque on the right side of the entrance to the institutional buildings and another one on the left side with inscriptions not only in the Cyrillic alphabet and the Serbian language, but also in the languages of all other national minorities living in this city characterized by a long multicultural tradition, namely Hungarians, Germans, Russians and Ukrainians, in alphabetical order. According to the president of this association, the initiative represented the only possible solution to the tense situation that had arisen in the city, according both with its present reality as well as with its past history of multiethnic coexistence.[88] Unfortunately, the inclusive and reconciliatory solution proposed by this association did not receive proper consideration by local and national authorities.

8.8 The multigraphic character of the Croatian writing tradition

In Croatia, the ideologization of the Cyrillic alphabet impacted not only the practical life of members of the Serb minority, and citizens in general, but also the field of knowledge. In particular, it exerted great influence on disciplines such as the philological sciences, which do not seem to be able to overcome a "monolithic" or "one-dimensional" view of historical events (cf. Žagar 2012). Even before the outbreak of the Vukovar protests, in an interview appeared on the journal *The Wreath* (*Vijenac*) published by *Matica Hrvatska*, the scholar Mateo Žagar[89] affirmed that "anti-Cyrillic rigidity" could be explained by a sort of Freudian interpretation, as a symptom of Croatia's fear of "seeing itself in the Other." One of the consequences of such an unresolved condition was the lack of appreciation or

---

[88] http://www.vecernji.hr/slavonija/inicijativa-gradana-vukovara-o-dvojezicn osti-upucena-i-celnicima-drzave-963224 (last access: 3/11/21).

[89] Chair of Old Church Slavonic and Croatian Glagolism (Staroslavenski jezik i hrvatsko glagoljaštvo) at the University of Zagreb and member of HAZU.

knowledge of the local tradition written in a variant of the Cyrillic alphabet commonly known as *hrvatska ćirilica, zapadna ćirilica* or *bosančica*.[90] According to Žagar, many people were willing to suppress a part of their cultural past, just to avoid the risk of identifying themselves with the Cyrillic tradition, because for decades the Croats had associated that alphabet almost exclusively with the Serbian writing sphere:

> Cyrillic is perceived primarily as an alphabet of the Serbs and Orthodox Slavs [...] However, it is also considered entirely justified not to teach it at school or in any other domain [...] In narrow-minded school programs as well as in traditional philology, it is obviously difficult to find any support in this direction. (Žagar 2012; my translation)

Žagar maintains that both Serbs and Croats adopted problematic patterns of mutual communication, constantly finding reasons for arguing and accusing each other of some "cultural usurpation." In the context of this debate on the Cyrillic alphabet, the philologist Josip Bratulić points out that, unlike other European peoples and their writing culture, which was in essence "monoalphabetic," the Croatian one was "trigraphic" since its inception. The Croatian language was indeed written in Latin, Glagolitic and Cyrillic scripts, often simultaneously, sometimes even for similar purposes (Bratulić 2014: 17).

In a similar vein, the writer Marijan Vogrinec, a member of the *Matica Hrvatska*, in an article wittily entitled "The Petty Politician's Squaring of the Cyrillic Circle" ("Politikantska kvadratura ćiriličnog kruga") declared the necessity of affirming the "polycentrism" of Croatian culture, unmasking the irrationality of the persecution of an alphabet, whose outcome was the condemnation of the entire Serbian population. The alphabet was not responsible for any of the fatalities during the Yugoslav wars, neither in Vukovar

---

90   And others such as *hrvatkica, arvatica*. The denomination of this variant of the Cyillic alphabet is also the cause of many controversies, especially among Croatian and Bosnian philologists. In Bosnia and Herzegovina, this is commonly known as *bosančica*, while in Croatia it is mostly called *hrvatska ćirilica* or *zapadna ćirilica*, and each has accused the other of wanting to "appropriate" this tradition. See, on this topic, Lomagistro 2004: 132-133.

nor in any other part of the world, "since no writing system is responsible for such a crime."

Surely, the cultural element of the alphabet in itself is never the real focus of attention in the narratives of one side or the other (the Croatian-Serbian one in this case): its significance lies rather in the fact that it embodies a powerful symbol which is efficaciously included at the level of the national imagination. However, in light of recent events, Vogrinec thinks it appropriate to bring Cyrillic back into the realm where it belonged: not politics, but the field of culture and philological studies. He also refers to the words of Bojan Glavašević, son of the famous writer and radio correspondent Siniša Glavašević (author of the famous book *Stories of Vukovar*, 1992), who died during the war: "If my father was alive today, he would certainly not be against Cyrillic in Vukovar."

In relation to the reception of the Cyrillic script in Croatia, its modified status depended not only on historical and cultural changes in the country, but above all on the new ideological context, capable of exerting new influences on various areas of social life. As a consequence, what once considered Croatian could suddenly cease to be so. As Miljenko Jergović says: "Cyrillic was once Croatian, but today it is no longer so" (Jergović 2013; my translation). Attempts at integrating bialphabetic practices into Croatian daily social life are undertaken in the weekly *News* published in Zagreb by the Serbian National Council (*Srpsko Narodno Vijeće*), an organization founded in 1997 that promotes human rights in the country, mainly concerned with issues of the participation of the Serb community in Croatian society. Since its first publication in 1999, the weekly newspaper *News* has adopted a policy of linguistic and alphabetic pluralism by issuing articles both in Croatian and Serbian and by offering mixed sections printed in Latin and Cyrillic. The title and logo of the magazine appear in both alphabets as a symbolic communion of these writing systems, and this example represents a happy synthesis of the possibilities of communication and dialogue between the two cultures, a model of what could happen on a broader level in other social and written spaces of Croatian society.

In winter 2016, some positive signs emerged in Croatia, indicating a possible step towards the acceptance of the Cyrillic alphabet in the public sphere. Damir Boras, rector of the University of Zagreb, publicly affirmed that Cyrillic constituted an integral part of Croatian history and recommended that it be reintroduced into the country's primary schools (see Reinkowski 2019: 195). The rector's wish was to make use of the Cyrillic script a generic fact, removing from it any political implication.[91] This proposal was judged by Milorad Pupovac, President of the Serb National Council (*Srpsko Narodno Vijeće*) as "noble and praiseworthy."[92] Pupovac also added that it was necessary to "recognize Cyrillic as an alphabet in Croatia and put an end to the campaign against it" by learning to regard it not only as the writing system of the Serb minority in the country, but also as a Croatian historical script, and a Slavic one.

The HDZ reacted ambiguously to the rector's proposal: the party leader and then deputy prime minister Tomislav Karamarko spoke out in favor of teaching the Cyrillic script, but only as an elective subject. *Sabor* chairman Željko Reiner (HDZ) welcomed the opening of a public debate on the issue and assessed the appropriateness of reintroducing the Cyrillic script as a way of alleviating social tensions. Significantly, after the opening of the debate, the rector of the University of Zagreb also declared his intention to propose Glagolitic as an elective alphabet in school classrooms. To date, however, the proposal on reintroducing Cyrillic has not resulted in practical application in Croatian schools.

8.9 Conclusions: patterns of symmetrical differentiation

In the years following the dissolution of Yugoslavia, a process of "symmetrical differentiation" took hold in both the Croatian and Serbian ideological contexts. If in Croatia it found expression in the (quite successful) attempts to modify the grammar of the language,

---

91 http://www.novosti.rs/vesti/naslovna/drustvo/aktuelno.290.html:587197-Prof-Boras-Cirilicu-odvojiti-od-politike (last access: 3/11/21).
92 http://www.kurir.rs/vesti/drustvo/milorad-pupovac-za-kurir-sto-pre-prekinuti-kampanju-protiv-cirilice-u-hrvatskoj-clanak-2101817 (last access: 3/11/21).

in Serbia its realization proved somewhat easier thanks to the visual advantage (cf. Drücker, 1995: 11) of a different alphabet such as Cyrillic, which immediately catches the eye of the observer. Consequently, the Cyrillic alphabet's importance in the post-conflict context, as a privileged element of the new nation-building processes based on a contrast to significant neighbors, both in Croatia (as a means to "suppress") and in Serbia (as a means to "glorify"), comes as no surprise.

As mentioned above, in recent years a number of associations were created in the Republic of Serbia with the goal of safeguarding the use of the Cyrillic alphabet. These have published various materials (see, for example, Janjatović 2011) and are active in promoting a Serbian Cyrillic identity directed against the Latin alphabet, seen as a symbol of Croatian expansionism, especially by members of the *Udruženje* "*'Ćirilica*," in Novi Sad, and the *Srpsko Udruženje* "*Ćirilica*," based in Belgrade. The insistence on the exclusive use of the Cyrillic script at the institutional level has led to some significant repercussions, such as in the case of the April 2012 elections, when some voters in the south of Serbia had difficulty identifying their names in the lists because they appeared only in Cyrillic, a script they could not read[93] (Mermagen 2012: 7). The "glorification" of Cyrillic seems to have strengthened in recent years precisely in correspondence to the events of the destruction of Cyrillic panels in Vukovar in Croatia, as a symmetrical reaction aimed at the affirmation of Serbian national elements.[94]

---

93 By law, electoral cards have to be printed not only in Serbian and Cyrillic, but also in the native languages and scripts of the various minorities; however, this did not happen.
94 On 21 February 2015, on the occasion of International Mother Language Day, the Democratic Party of Serbia (DSS) announced the launch of an initiative to "save the Cyrillic alphabet and the Serbian language," proposing to exempt from VAT all books, magazines and newspapers printed in Cyrillic. In addition, companies and shops with names, plaques and advertisements written in Cyrillic would receive a 5% tax reduction. A similar initiative in 2013 by the same party had resulted in signs on city buses appearing exclusively in Cyrillic, and no longer in the Latin alphabet. The party's vice-president, Borko Ilić, stated that the Cyrillic issue was connected to the general appearance of the city of Novi Sad, noting that "keeping Cyrillic would preserve the old soul of the *Matica Srpska*, the Serbian national theater and the spirit of the Serbian Athens."

According to the relational approach characteristic of social science scholars like Fredrik Barth (1969) and Pierre Bourdieu (1989), the interpretation of the actions of groups must include consideration of their social reality, which consists of symbolic and material ties. Social actors construct their reality through the use of a "symbologenic" capacity, applied in particular to language, religion, myths. Through this mental prism, boundaries between groups are drawn, and individuals come to conceive of themselves as a kind of collectivity: national, ethnic, social, and so on.

In the Serbian-Croatian case, as already noted by Denich (1993), the theory of conflictuality between groups formulated by Gregory Bateson (1977 [1972]) and defined by the term "schismogenesis" is particularly useful for understanding a situation of hostility towards a neighbor perceived as uncanny, according to the psychological definition of *das Unheimliche* elaborated by Freud (1919). Bateson describes a pattern of communication characterized by increasing juxtaposition in the way each party responds to the other and to the other's reactions, in a mechanism that leads to an increasingly extreme diversification (including in symbolic terms) between the actors in play, in effect to a state of "schism."

Such a view is also very closely related to the idea of the "suggestibility of the hostile temper" in competing social groups, theorized by Georg Simmel within the framework of the sociology of conflict (Simmel 1904: 503). The response model seems to manifest itself in terms of "symmetrical differentiation" (Bateson 1977 [1972]: 102-103): each of the parties responds to the other by treating it as a threat, and in its reactions contributes to reinforcing the behavior perceived as threatening (Denich 1993). This applies very well to Croatia in relation to the Serbian neighbor, where during the 1990s various political and intellectual parties reinterpreted narratives about national history to legitimize their political programs (Bellamy 2003: 32ff), using (and abusing) language and the alphabet as privileged elements of identity affirmation.

See: http://www.b92.net/info/vesti/index.php?yyyy=2015&mm=02&dd=21&nav_id=960541 (last access: 3/11/21). My translation.

The script debates of the post-Yugoslav era manifest, on an ideological level, the degree of dissolution of the unity of the peoples that belonged to the former federation, a fact that is particularly evident in the new identity politics, starting with the official acts and communications of the main institutions. After decades of exposure to unitarian rhetoric, also in "affective" terms through the propaganda of a specific ideology, after the disintegration of Yugoslavia, individuals were massively involved in campaigns aimed at affirming the exclusivity of their own nation, using the most effective elements at the symbolic level for the construction of the new identitarian image. The concept of the common good of the Yugoslav people was thus replaced by the exclusive and exclusionary concept of the good of the nation.

In the Croatian nationalist vision, the Latin and Cyrillic alphabets are presented as privileged elements in their symbolic rendering. Cyrillic is "Byzantine," "communist," "Soviet" (cf. the following chapter on the Bulgarian case), while Latin is a "civilized," "Western," "European" writing system. This counterposition between the European and the "Asian" elements in the Croatian-Serbian relationship is in fact a constant in Croatian history, as already noted in Ante Starčević's statements and in those of the scholars at the time of the Independent State of Croatia (see chapter 6).

Of course, the thorny issue of the Cyrillic-Latin dispute in Serbia and Croatia does not end here, and much debate about language and script is also taking place in other countries of the former Yugoslavia, as in neighboring Montenegro, where some specific "local" phonemes (cf. Silić 2009: 7) have been introduced for both the Latin and Cyrillic alphabets. The new Montenegrin alphabet was adopted by the Ministry of Education on 9 June 2009, replacing the Serbian Cyrillic that had been officially used until then. Although the two new letters (<ś> and <ź> in Latin and <ć> e <з́> in Cyrillic) are supposed to replace the previous digraphs <sj> and <zj>, their adoption has mainly a symbolic value, as it establishes in the Montenegrin language a set of characters unique in the context of South Slavic languages (see Nikčević 2008, Greenberg 2004: 103).

It should also be noted that, although the new Cyrillic and Latin alphabets are formally equal under the law of the country, the government and the more nationalistic supporters of the Montenegrin language prefer to use the characters of the Latin alphabet to emphasize their distinctness from Serbian cultural identity:[95] a process which seems to be inversely proportional to that occurring in Serbia. In the post-Yugoslav territories, writing systems have been turned into tools for the expression of national feelings and for the objectification of difference: the disputes between the Cyrillic and Latin alphabets in Serbia, the anti-Cyrillic demonstrations in Croatia and the codification of the new Montenegrin alphabet are all paradigmatic expressions of these trends.

New alphabet debates are gaining ground in the territories of the former Yugoslavia, and as long as the region does not truly come to terms with its past, they are likely to continue, producing new cultural and identitarian phenomena that will certainly not be confined to mere alphabetic polemics. Any debate about the alphabet, and thus about language policy in the former Yugoslavia, must therefore take into account broader dynamics and "extralinguistic" factors related to borders, minorities and the creation of national identities. In particular, it is appropriate to question the role of language and the alphabet in creating new political borders and, symmetrically, the power of borders in legitimizing the codification of different languages and alphabets (see also Busch & Holmes 2004: 1).

---

95 http://www.balkaninsight.com/en/article/montenegrin-opposition-alleges-cyrillic-script-discrimination-06-13-2016 (last access: 3/11/21).

SECTION IV

THE NEW CHALLENGES OF CYRILLIC IN BULGARIA IN THE NEW MILLENNIUM

9. BULGARIAN CYRILLIC BETWEEN TRADITION AND MODERNITY: THE "KRONSTEINER AFFAIR"

9.1 Introduction: the post-socialist ideological context in Bulgaria

In Bulgaria, after the end of the Latinization debates of the early 1930s, the controversy over the complex issue of script reform resurfaced with force after the collapse of communism. As previously mentioned, in contrast to the policy and ideology of Latinization pursued in the 1920s, the change adopted by Stalin in the Soviet Union led to practices of forced Cyrillization (Wellish 1978: 105ff), with the exception of Georgian, Armenian and the Baltic languages. In this context, Bulgaria's ideological affiliation with the communist bloc and its alienation from the Western European countries after the Second World War also meant the extinction of any debate about the desirability of introducing the Latin alphabet in the country.

In considering the Cyrillic/Latin debate that began with the restoration of democratic politics in Bulgaria, it is natural to draw comparisons with the one that took place some seventy years earlier in the interwar period. Both moments indeed represent historical turning points bearing interesting similarities (cf. Barkey 1997: 104-109), and having significant implications for debates on identity issues, in which linguistic and alphabet issues are also involved. It is easy to see how both periods embodied for Bulgaria a historical moment of opening in which, after centuries (in the first case) or decades (in the second) of (more or less pronounced) isolation from the rest of the world, innovative and complex dynamics of identity affirmation were activated.

In both historical cases, the need to create and pursue a distinct national identity (Daskalov 2011: 75-76), to distinguish oneself from a certain part of one's past and to place oneself in a new setting in the eyes of the Western world, i.e. the so-called "significant

Others," occupied a prominent role. Moreover, a similar shift from an "Eastern" influence (in the first case Turkish-Ottoman, in the second Russian-Soviet) to a process of European integration occurred; in both moments, the two poles represented supposed values of "backwardness" (first the Turkish-Muslim world, then the Soviet-Communist one), as opposed to ideals of modernity and modernization associated with the West.

In the context of nation-building in the Balkans, both in the post-imperial and post-socialist situations, the most important elements of national identity were the ones associated with the traits of ethnic and cultural distinctness, especially language, customs, religion, folklore. According to this view, cultural identity represents a kind of memory of the past that must be honored and preserved, the traces of the nation's childhood that are part of the psyche and personality of the country; clearly, the element of writing belongs to this category (cf. Vezenkov 2013: 338).

In the years following the democratic changes in Bulgaria, many discussions took place involving the nature of the Cyrillic alphabet and its possible association, together with its related rituals, to the communist past (Spasov 2012b: 171). The identity factors at play in the delicate moment of post-socialist transition led to a kind of "hypersensitivity" to possible script changes in the country, and the debates on European integration thus became filled with metaphors relating to a very distant past, that of the Cyrillo-Methodian work of writing system invention. In a manner reminiscent of the debates held seventy years earlier, the new alphabet polemic was again shaped by the important concerns of modernization and European integration, and accompanied to a (somewhat) contradictory extent by conservative identity principles.

This dualism of arguments is particularly characteristic of Bulgarian society and, in a sense, it embodies a form of both temporal and spatial "bipolarity": between the past and the future, and to a considerable extent, also between Russia and Western Europe. The development of relations with the community of democratic European states was a primary goal of Bulgarian political forces: rapprochement with the West was a metaphor for political, social and economic development. However, relations with Russia by no means broke down; despite some friction over the years, related to the procedures of the country's accession to NATO (which began in 1997 and lasted until 2004), unlike the other countries of the communist bloc (with the exception of Serbia and, until recently, Montenegro), relations with Russia are still crucial on many levels: economic and political as well as religious and "ethno-psychological" (Giatzidis 2002: 145). The consciousness of belonging to a common Orthodox religious horizon, expressed more openly after the postsocialist political changes, constituted an important motif in the relations between the two states from the very beginning. In addition, there was also the "ethnic" factor, manifest in valorization of the common Slavic or "Pan-Slavic" element, in which the Cyrillic alphabet played a crucial role.

The main controversy over the Cyrillic/Latin dilemma in the country arose from the statements of a famous Austrian Bulgarianist, Otto Kronsteiner, who suggested that Bulgarians should adopt the Latin alphabet in parallel with the Cyrillic, after he himself had spent years defending the historical and cultural tradition of the latter at an academic level. Between 1999 and 2001, these statements caused quite a stir in Bulgaria, especially in relation to the fact that one of Kronsteiner's main arguments was that the Cyrillic alphabet was perceived by Western European countries as inseparable from the Soviet and communist world (see on this association also Durand 2014: 210-221). According to Kronsteiner, with the country's accession to the European Union, it was desirable that Bulgaria introduced practices of "bialphabetism" through the complementary presence of the Latin alphabet, (see also Aleksandrov 2000: 75) similarly to what the Serbs were already doing in their country. However, this proposal outraged part of the Bulgarian public, especially some academics and intellectuals, despite the fact that many Bulgarians already used the Latin alphabet for writing on the Internet (popularly called *Shljokavitsa* — *Шльокавица* in Cyrillic).

9.2 The first debates on writing issues in the late 1990s

In Bulgaria, the democratic changes of 1989 initiated a profound phase of rewriting the nation, in which numerous cultural elements of the past were openly valorized and revived, while others were more or less forgotten. In the field of writing, it is interesting to recall that on 24 May 1992, when Bulgaria celebrated the Holiday of Saints Cyril and Methodius, two parliamentarians from the Union of Democratic Forces drafted a bill to revive the old orthography of the Bulgarian language, i.e. the pre-1944 one (cf. Popova 1998, Stantchev 2015: 131n). The old orthography contained the archaic letters of the alphabet which had catalyzed much discussion in the 1920s after Omarchevski's brief reform (see the end of chapter 3). The proposal was submitted to the National Assembly, where the usual procedures for turning it into a law began the next day (see Guentcheva 1999: 369). In the draft law, it was envisaged that by 1993 the "sacred letters" *jat* and *jus* would be restored, together with the two *jer* appearing at the end of the word. According to its advocates, the old spelling represented "a bonding device for the whole Bulgarian nation, would enormously facilitate the Bulgarian diaspora's return to the culture of its homeland, and the restitution of the letter *jat* would 'fill in the empty gap which splits Bulgarian lands in two'" (Guentcheva, ibid.). Despite these premises, the bill was later abandoned.[96]

In 1998, about a year before the "Kronsteiner affair" began, the Bulgarian weekly *Culture* (*Kultura*) devoted a series of articles to current script issues in the country on the occasion of the May 24 holiday. One of them was a text entitled "Bulgarian Latin — no kidding" ("Латински български — bez maytap," containing words in both alphabets), written by Diana Popova, editor of the magazine and an expert on contemporary art, which provoked a first, small debate in this direction. Popova presented the idea of a possible

---

[96] Interestingly, in the same year, in Romania, following the political changes and the modified relationship with Russia, the letter <â> was reintroduced into the Romanian alphabet, after having been abolished in 1953.

switch to the Latin alphabet, at a time dominated by electronic modernization and promising international communication: "In recent times — with the penetration of computers and the Internet into our lives — the idea of introducing the Latin alphabet in Bulgaria appears to me more and more reasonable" (Popova 1998; my translation).

In fact, the availability of internet and email services in Bulgaria since the early 1990s had led to a number of difficulties in writing in Cyrillic characters, as no computer programs had been developed that could adequately encode the letters of the Cyrillic alphabet (cf. Spasov 2012a). As a consequence, people used Latin characters for communication on the internet and in SMS. Furthermore, for a long time, some versions of Microsoft Windows (XP) were not available in the Cyrillic alphabet, and it was not until October 2001 that this problem was resolved after lengthy discussions between Microsoft executives and Bulgarian officials.

In her article, Popova referred to a writer from her country (without specifying who) who had affirmed a few years earlier that, if it had not been for Cyril and Methodius, Bulgarians would have been able to write on the computer without feeling so "isolated from the world" (Popova 1998). Although anticipating the wave of outrage her remarks would cause among the conservative and patriotic segment of the public, Popova justified her position on the possible adoption of the Latin script by observing that the Serbian neighbors used both alphabets for internal political reasons, and by recalling that the adoption of this alphabet had greatly benefited the Turks in the process of modernization begun in the 1920s (ibid.).

Certainly, if the Serbian case could to some extent be accepted by the Bulgarians as an acceptable example, the Turkish one was bound to be perceived as problematic. In the author's opinion, if all historical, political and religious implications were removed from the equation, only practical advantages would result. Indeed, the introduction of the Latin alphabet in Bulgaria would facilitate the use of street, geographical and institutional signs for all, eliminating the persistent difficulties in transcribing foreign names as well as in the email system. Although a large proportion of Bulgarians knew some Western foreign languages written in Latin letters, the author acknowledged that Bulgarian in this alphabet still appeared foreign and disturbing: however, this was merely a matter of habit and therefore of education. Had Bulgarians been taught to write and read their own language in the Latin alphabet, this problem would not have arisen: at least in theory, nothing prevented Bulgarians from adapting their language to new, modern graphic requirements.

In addition to such technical considerations, in her article Popova also expressed some troubling comments about Bulgaria's national heritage, explicitly touching on the cardinal values of her country's identity. She indeed criticized the May 24 holiday, noting that the media's characterization of it as "the most Bulgarian holiday" constituted another "desperate search for strong support of Bulgarian identity" that brought the country's unresolved complexes to the surface. Moreover, she added, many Slavic peoples in Europe used the Latin characters, a fact that proved that "not all Slavs read the books we gave them" (ibid.).

Popova's article was followed by the critical reaction of Elka Mircheva, a representative of the Institute for the Bulgarian Language at the Bulgarian Academy of Sciences (BAN). Mircheva lamented the juxtaposition in the Bulgarian weekly *Culture* of an article in defense of the Latin script with the celebration of the Slavonic alphabet, as well as with the picture of Christ Pantocrator in the church in Bojana holding a book with the Cyrillic characters "that alienate us so much from the world" (Mircheva 1998). Mircheva's reaction suggested that both Diana Popova and the editors of the cultural weekly had simultaneously "desecrated" two of the sacred and inviolable pillars of Bulgarian national identity: the *civil* (or so it seemed) celebration of May 24 and the *religious* sanctity of the letters of the Cyrillic alphabet. It is clear that Mircheva's reasoning pointed to an emotional attachment to the symbols of Bulgarian identity and pride.

This attitude of defending the Cyrillic language by resorting to essentialist arguments represents the rhetoric on which the majority of institutional opinions regarding the Kronsteiner debate were based. Moreover, many foreign historians (cf. Crampton 1997: 5) also consider the invention of the Cyrillic (rather than the

Glagolitic) alphabet a fundamental fact of Bulgarian history, one which enabled the establishment of a form of national consciousness. According to this view, a sense of identity, though far removed from the modern concept of nationalism, had been strong enough to preserve an idea of Bulgaria as a distinct cultural and religious entity. Certainly, Popova's text represented an attempt on the part of the *Culture* magazine to actively stimulate discussion on various issues related to the Latin alphabet. However, with the exception of Mircheva's response, the debate quickly died out, even though this was only a "foretaste" of what was to come a couple of years later.

9.3 The origins of the "Kronsteiner affair"

Otto Kronsteiner, an Austrian professor of Bulgarian studies at the University of Salzburg, was a well-known and popular figure in the Balkan country, so much so that for his services in promoting the Bulgarian language in Western Europe, he was awarded the honorary title of Doctor Honoris Causa by the Saint Cyril and Methodius University in Veliko Tarnovo in 1990. This title was also conferred on him by Sofia University St. Kliment Ohridski in 1998. Finally, in August 2000, the Bulgarian President Petar Stoyanov awarded the professor the highest distinction in Bulgaria, the first degree "Stara Planina" Order.

In his thank you speech given on being conferred the title by the University of Veliko Tarnovo in 1990, in the context of the democratic changes in the country and the opening of Bulgaria to Western Europe, Kronsteiner drew meaningful analogies between the present and the past when Cyril and Methodius had worked to create a new alphabet in opposition to the Latin one. The work of the two brothers had indeed constituted an event of enormous importance for the linguistic and cultural future of the European area: it embodied the struggle against the domination of the three sacred languages: Biblical Hebrew, Greek and Latin (cf. Radev, Kenanov & Vasilev 2002: 19). Kronsteiner therefore argued that, since the linguistic situation in Europe at the end of the 20th century was dominated by English and Russian, it was appropriate to defend the equal rights of all European languages. According to his vision, European politics needed a pluralism of languages and writing systems, and, with its Cyrillic alphabet, Bulgarian could impose itself as a symbol against global homogenization, in defense of the principles of cultural diversity (cf. Radev, Kenanov & Vasilev 2002: 17-18). In short, the ideals of the 9th-century Cyrillo-Methodian mission were still current in the context of a reunited Europe at the end of the millennium.

Nevertheless, less than a decade after these statements, the same Kronsteiner began to formulate a series of ideas that were in contradiction to his earlier pronouncements. In reference to the issue of script change, Kronsteiner pointed out that for some time there had been an intense discussion in Bulgaria about the introduction of the Latin alphabet in parallel with the Cyrillic. According to him, the following positions existed on this issue:

- Something as sacred as the Cyrillic script should not be removed from the national self-esteem.

- It was Cyril who began to drive Bulgaria into isolation, making it a European outsider.

- Compromise: Bulgaria must become bialphabetic; those who want to can continue to use Cyrillic. (Kronsteiner 2000a:7; my translation)

At the turn of the new millennium, Kronsteiner's new statements made him an advocate for the third position, that of compromise, although he also kept oscillating towards the second. However, it should be recalled that, while Kronsteiner pointed to the alleged isolation of Bulgaria on account of the Cyrillic alphabet, and in some cases, as we shall see, his statements were decidedly questionable, they were never accompanied by a desire to "eliminate" the Cyrillic alphabet altogether.

Kronsteiner defended the parallel introduction of the Latin alphabet in Bulgaria by maintaining that this script appeared completely free of religious connotations: the association of the Latin alphabet with Catholicism was an anachronism, since "Catholics, Protestants, Muslims, Orthodox, Buddhists and Mormons" equally availed themselves of the Latin letters. Cyrillic, on the other hand, embodied, according to him, "a persistent symbol of Orthodoxy, with a growing (...) anti-European connotation" (Kronsteiner 2000a: 8; my translation).

The professor associated the Cyrillic alphabet with Orthodox Christianity only in the European context, since many non-Slavic peoples around the world used (and still use) the Cyrillic alphabet despite not being Orthodox believers, such as the Mongols, Chechens, Abkhaz, as well as the peoples of Central Asia, who not coincidentally began to consider a return to the Latin alphabet after the fall of the Soviet Union (having already adopted it, as already mentioned, in the 1920s). In the discussion of the Latin/Cyrillic question, Central Asia represents an interesting case, since in some of these countries the Latin alphabet was already reintroduced (in Turkmenistan in 1993, cf. Clement 2008) as the only official one, while in others, such as Kazakhstan, a form of "bialphabetism" started to be theorized (cf. Tanayeva 2007), receiving further confirmation in recent years (since 2017).

As for Bulgaria, Kronsteiner saw nothing strange in the possible introduction of Latin as a parallel writing system, and criticized Bulgaria for its "monoalphabetic" attitude, recalling the Latin alphabet's literary past and its existence in neighboring countries, such as Serbia, where two different writing systems were employed "without any fear":

> Bulgaria is the only exclusively Cyrillic country in Europe (...) Its Serbian neighbors are already bialphabetic. Bulgaria was the land of many alphabets. On such a small territory one could find the Greek, Latin, Proto-Bulgarian, Arabic, Glagolitic, Bulgarian Cyrillic and Russian Cyrillic alphabets. (Kronsteiner 2000a: 9; my translation)

The ideological incorporation of Bulgaria into what Kronsteiner called the "Cyrillic bloc" resulted in the disappearance of the tradition of multigraphism from the country's national consciousness. Bulgaria's changing political role over the centuries also led to transformation in writing practices: the varying positionings in relation to the dominant powers at different historical moments (the Byzantine Empire, Turkey, the Soviet Union) had important effects also in the field of script influences and ideologies (Kronsteiner 2000a: 7).

In problematizing the question of the existence of Cyrillic as an "ontological fact" of Bulgarian history, Kronsteiner also noted that the continuity of this alphabet was not an obvious reality, since for centuries the Greek alphabet had dominated in the Church and trade domains, while the Arabic alphabet ruled at the official state level. The fact that Cyrillic "in its Russian form" prevailed from the 19th century onwards did not constitute the only possible outcome of the writing issue, since the more "Westernophile" segments of society at that time might have preferred to adopt the Latin alphabet (Kronsteiner 2000a: 8).

In highlighting a secular link between language and the alphabet, Kronsteiner recalled the Turkish example, noting that Atatürk had opted for this writing system while building a new Western-oriented state, regardless of the religious and cultural context associated with the Arabic alphabet. Moreover, he maintained, Cyril had not invented the Cyrillic alphabet, which was essentially a Greek alphabet composed of many letters common to the Hellenic writing system. Finally, Kronsteiner claimed that Bulgarian could have been written with Latin or Greek letters without much difficulty (Kronsteiner 2000a: 11), a point that met with the displeasure of many Bulgarians and Bulgarianists. In their view, unlike the Ottoman Turkish or Greek alphabets, which were phonematically imperfect for transcribing their respective languages, the Bulgarian alphabet embodied an almost perfect example of sound-character correspondence and it was thus inappropriate to question its suitability and precision (cf. Radev, Kenanov & Vasilev 2002).

9.4 Bulgarian Cyrillic between "Europhilia" and "Russophilia"

By challenging the historical and ideological legitimacy of the Cyrillic alphabet, Kronsteiner touched on some of the most constitutive elements of Bulgarian cultural and national identity, and brought to the surface some of the crucial issues with which the Balkan country was cyclically confronted. His remarks thus acquired a variety of important connotations, especially of a political nature. In this context, Kronsteiner recalled that a specific ideology related to the revival of the glorious past of the Bulgarian Cyrillic alphabet, combined with the support of the Russians in the struggle for independence from the Ottoman Empire, played a crucial but negative role in the field of script choices.

Related to this are the close friendly, cultural and historical relations, not to be underestimated, that the Bulgarians developed with the Russians even before communism (cf. Peeva 2015). This influence remained strong in the years before the Second World War, although a more pro-Western current also developed during this period — as already seen in the debate on the possible introduction of the Latin alphabet in Bulgaria considered in chapter 3 — in a kind of "double conditioning" to which the country was simultaneously exposed.

With the end of the Second World War, Soviet Russia was glad to have Bulgaria as an inseparable part of a "common circulatory system" (see Giatzidis 2002: 133), and in return, after successive defeats in the two world wars, the Balkan country found in this ally a guarantee of security and protection on the international stage. At the beginning of the third millennium, sentimental attachment to Russia was still intense and strongly influenced the idea of retaining the Cyrillic alphabet, moving Kronsteiner to state: "[w]ithout the politically important Russia, Bulgarian Cyrillic would have died out long ago" (Kronsteiner 2000a: 10; my translation). According to Kronsteiner, the entry into the European Union could represent the third chance for graphic "Europeanization" offered by history to the country, after Tsar Boris I's decision in favor of the adoption of the Cyrillic alphabet at the end of the 9th century and the choice made following independence from the Ottoman Empire in 1878.

But what was the alphabetic situation in Russia and the former Soviet Empire at the beginning of the new millennium? Although Kronsteiner never referred to what was taking place there in his writings, he was probably very aware of it. The Cyrillic alphabet had already been dismantled along with Soviet rule in some countries of the former empire: first in Moldova and then in Azerbaijan (cf. King 1994). Tatarstan, a Turkic-speaking republic in the heart of Russia, was attempting a "rebellious" reform that would enable it to switch to the Latin alphabet: in that historical moment, the use of the Latin alphabet by the Turkic-speaking population was a decision that symbolized independence, Westernization, and pan-Turkish solidarity (cf. Wertheim 2012). Significantly, Sergey Aleksandrovich Arutyunov, the eminent ethnographer and member of the Russian Academy of Sciences, maintained in 1992 that the question of a general return of the non-Slavic languages of Russia to the Latin alphabet would be desirable and appropriate (in: Alpatov 2015: 9).[97] In 2001, Arutyunov confirmed this view, adding that a "universal" transition to the Latin alphabet of all languages, including Russian, was imminent. He based such judgments on arguments related to "civilization" and "globalization" issues, which appeared to be in opposition to the "harmful and reactionary" positions of the major powers in Russia (Arutyunov 2001).

Notwithstanding such premises, in November 2002, a law was passed in Russia banning the use of non-Cyrillic alphabets for state languages throughout the Federation, a fact closely related to the status of the Tatar language in the Republic of Tatarstan, whose struggles for the right to use the Latin script had provoked considerable tension. Vladimir Putin justified this decision by the need to prevent a script change that would have resulted in the Tatar population's alienation from the surrounding Russian context (Wertheim 2012: 75). The members of the State Committee of the Duma on National Affairs had previously rejected a bill that granted the different ethnic groups the right to choose for themselves the alphabet they wanted to use: hence, the country's ethnic

---

97 Despite Soviet insistence that Moldavian and Romanian were separate languages, the two are close dialects, though Moldavian was written in Cyrillic (Collin 2011: 55). The central government in Chișinău declared Moldavian in 1989 to be the national language and the Latin alphabet to be the official one (King 1994: 345), thus initiating a process of script reform. However, the self-declared independent republic of Transnistria promptly started a real "alphabet war" by adopting a law that made it illegal to transcribe the Moldavian/Romanian language in any alphabet other than Cyrillic and closing all schools using the Latin alphabet.

minorities found their "alphabetic rights" restricted, being forced to use Cyrillic exclusively (Sebba 2006: 110). This fact affected not only Tatar, but also other languages that had historically used the Latin script within Russia, such as German, Karelian, Estonian, Vepsian and many others. The ideology of state unity was again expressed, albeit in a different political context, in the desire to hold together a supposed integrity of the Russian people that would effectively incorporate minorities, precisely through the symbolic element of the Cyrillic alphabet.

Similarly, in Bulgaria, the more "Russophile" factions viewed Bulgarian national identity as inseparable from the Slavic, Orthodox, linguistic, and scriptural roots it shared with Russia. In light of this, Bulgaria undoubtedly possessed a number of specific features that distinguished it from other European states or EU candidates. Its cultural closeness to the largest Slavic country was evident in the common use of the Cyrillic alphabet, and the "Russophile" factor probably also played a role in the controversy surrounding the "Kronsteiner affair." In the years following the political changes in the country, these views were, as in the interwar period, opposed by the more "Europhilic" factions, the two sides gaining varying degrees of dominance, but basically maintaining a fairly stable balance (cf. Daskalov 2011: 72). In this regard, it is worth mentioning that this apparent contradiction is a matter of fact for most Bulgarians, as noted for example by the writer Angel Wagenstein:

> This bifurcation is centuries-old for Bulgaria—between the East and the West. We have never understood in which direction we should go—sometimes with the one, sometimes with the other. We celebrate the Birth of Christ with the Catholics, and the Resurrection of Christ with the Orthodox. (cit. in Selvelli 2017: 81; my translation)

9.5 The issue of alphabetic coexistence in the European context of pluralism

According to Kronsteiner, the parallel introduction of the Latin alphabet in Bulgaria would enable the country to join the community of "European Slavs" and to receive a warmer welcome than it had received in the course of recent history from Russia, for which

Bulgaria constituted no more than a small and uninteresting "marginal Cyrillic province" (Kronsteiner 2000a: 16; my translation). What Kronsteiner proposed, therefore, was the establishment of a condition of biscriptality that would facilitate international trade and communication: the parallel introduction of the Latin alphabet was considered sufficient to internationalize the country in a graphic sense.

Adopting the Latin alphabet on the "external" level would also simplify Bulgaria's exchanges with its Southeast European neighbors, such as the Turks, the Romanians, the Serbs and the Albanians. In this context, Kronsteiner proposed a Slavic-based model of transliteration into Latin characters, similar to the Czech, Slovak, Croatian and Slovenian orthographies (which he also applied in his 2000 "bialphabetic" text: Kronsteiner 2000b: 32ff).

In the new millennium, Kronsteiner argued, Bulgaria needed a new identity, as this could no longer be represented by the idea of a past "golden age." A great advocate of the European values of freedom and secularism, Kronsteiner saw the nation as a category destined to disintegrate within a short time, replaced by the idea of a supranational European identification. Bulgaria could find a proper collocation in Europe if it managed to take the step of integrating the Latin alphabet, viewed as the world's most important one (Kronsteiner 2000a: 4). Kronsteiner did not go so far as to call for the complete removal of Cyrillic, but stated that a parallel introduction of the Latin alphabet was necessary, while retaining the traditional Cyrillic alphabet for internal use. This position was repeated on several occasions. For example, we read in the article ("I am for Cyrillic, I am for Latin" ("Аз съм за кирилица, Az săm za Latinica," written in both scripts):

> Whether I am in favor of the Cyrillic or the Latin alphabet is not a scientific question at all, or at least it does not require scientific expertise [...] it is a personal decision. Moreover, this question does not arise as an "either/or," but as a "both/and" (both Latin and Cyrillic). (Kronsteiner 2000b: 34; my translation)

In short, the Cyrillic alphabet was not doomed to disappear. On the contrary, in a European and pluralist vision, Cyrillic was no longer to be considered a taboo, or a "heretical" alphabet, but rather to be integrated into a new common culture. The problem with the Cyrillic alphabet stemmed, according to Kronsteiner, from its association with Slavic Christian Orthodoxy: religion had always interfered in the fate of Europe, often in a dangerous way. The association of the alphabet with religion and with a particular political ideology had erected an enormous cultural barrier, preventing a genuine European unification process. In this sense, Kronsteiner interpreted the development of Cyrillic as compromised by extralinguistic elements of great historical importance.

As a foreign scholar, Kronsteiner attempted on several occasions to problematize the issue of "Bulgarian isolation" in alphabetic terms, but met with bitter resistance from the Bulgarian academic world, for whom the tradition of writing was still sacred and inviolable. In contrast to this attitude, the Austrian professor claimed that Bulgaria's future could not reside in an "eternal cult of Cyril" (Kronsteiner 2000a: 18; my translation). The exclusive link between Bulgarian national identity and the alphabet was by no means positive: the cult of Cyrillic needed to be overcome, and in this connection Kronsteiner cited the example of Turkey, which, by abandoning the Ottoman-Turkish alphabet, had also severed a certain kind of relationship with the Arab and Islamic world and thereby made itself truly "free."

Kronsteiner's statement about the need for Bulgarian society to be oriented more towards the future than towards the past constitutes perhaps the key to Bulgarian academia's negative reaction, since a national discourse so fixated on its "mythographic" narrative could not accept any endangerment of its system of values. The religious aspect of the alphabet does not appear to be similarly evident to Western peoples, since the Latin alphabet is used widely and massively in many different countries of the world, of all faiths and families of languages. No sacral or affective value is attributed to this script, since no one would be able to define its origins, contextualize its invention in a defined space or time or relate it to a precise creator. This aspect is probably one of the most important cultural factors in the definition of a difference between a Western and an Eastern world, already within Europe, but not exclusively (cf. Lörinczi 1982: 75). In the Slavic area, this observation is significantly linked to the question of *Slavia Latina* and *Slavia Orthodoxa* and to the use of the Latin and Cyrillic scripts corresponding to either Catholic or Orthodox religious affiliation, which emerged following the Cyrillo-Methodian mission and the progressive "marginalization" of the Glagolitic alphabet.

9.6 Cyrillic as a "communist" alphabet

In the "Kronsteiner affair," another critical point that contributed to triggering the reaction of the Bulgarian institutional world was the association of the Cyrillic alphabet and its cult with communism. Indeed, Kronsteiner argued that it was "the communists" who portrayed Cyril's mission as egalitarian and addressed to all Slavs, resulting in a "democratic alphabet" (Kronsteiner 2000a: 11). In truth, he argued, Glagolitic (the alphabet invented by Cyril) was "neither democratic nor addressed to the whole people, nor even to all Slavs" (ibid.; my translation). Kronsteiner argued that many in Europe considered Cyrillic to be a communist writing system and hence identified the Bulgarian people with the Russians. According to him, the appearance of Cyrillic "in the heart of Europe" after the Second World War was perceived as a threatening event in the Western world. In this context, he also referred to the moment the name of his home village of Losenstein appeared in Cyrillic on a road sign in 1945, a fact that left a deep impression on him as a child (Kronsteiner 2000a: 13).

The Cyrillic alphabet thus turned into a symbol of the Soviet Army, "the representative of communist power leading Eastern Europe" (ibid.; my translation), perceived as the emblem of the "Cyrillic proletariat" by other Central European countries such as Poland, Czechoslovakia, Germany, Hungary and Austria. In this way, the stigmatization of the script intensified, a fact which played a crucial role in Bulgaria's isolation within Europe, since Cyrillic marked a "graphic wall"[98] (Kronsteiner 2000a: 14).

Bulgaria was hence at a crossroads, facing the same issue of script choice that it did 1,200 years earlier: as in the 9th century, it had to decide between Latin and Cyrillic. According to Kronsteiner, while Bulgaria was no more than a "marginal Cyrillic province" to the Russians, it was on the contrary an important and interesting country in the eyes of Europe, and the most stable and tolerant in the Balkan region. In the European Union context, the exclusive use of the Cyrillic script, employed by eight million "economically not very powerful Southeast Europeans" would represent a problem when confronted with the parallel existence of the Latin script, used by 350 million Europeans. The adoption of the Latin alphabet as a parallel writing system, concluded Kronsteiner, implied a series of practical advantages, determining Bulgaria's final exit from the Russian sphere of influence and full participation in European political and cultural life (ibid.).

9.7 Bulgarian institutions against Kronsteiner

Kronsteiner's recommendations for the need to adopt a bialphabetic policy in Bulgaria and his provocative statements targeting elements of the country's cultural past initiated a series of reactions and discussions. While, in 1998, Diana Popova's text backing the use of the Latin script was criticized by the Bulgarian Academy of Sciences representative Mircheva mainly for the alleged lack of expertise of its author, Kronsteiner was confronted with sharper judgements and far greater consequences. This can be explained by his being a recognized and respected professor from a Western European country (cf. Spasov 2012a): the "wound" in this case was felt to be deeper, since it was inflicted by a representative of the "Significant Others."

---

98 Even at his Salzburg faculty, according to Kronsteiner, students of Slavistics were unable to read this alphabet and as a result only a few learned Bulgarian.

In rejecting Kronsteiner's proposal for script change, the professional community of Bulgarianists focused primarily on technical arguments, but avoided an in-depth discussion of the issue (BAN 2001). In June 2001, about two years after the appearance of Kronsteiner's first articles supporting the introduction of the Latin alphabet in Bulgaria, the Faculty Council of the University of Veliko Tarnovo came to the conclusion that removal of the honorary title conferred on the Austrian scholar was a necessary step to take. Consequently, a text advocating for this decision was drafted and approved during a meeting of the Chair of Bulgarian Literature, which was then published in early September in the journal *Literary Forum* (*Literaturen Forum*). On 5 September 2001, news of the imminent withdrawal of the title spread through Bulgarian radio and television channels and was reflected in the comments released at high institutional levels. On this occasion, all scholars and experts in Bulgarian studies saw first and foremost the political side of the question (Alipieva 2013: 260), and Kronsteiner's proposal was criticized in emotional discourses, which originated in reaction to the perception of a sort of "Western" paternalism towards an "underdeveloped" Balkan country (ibid.).

As a consequence, Kronsteiner became an "ex-doctor honoris causa," although he actually renounced the title before it was officially revoked by the University of Veliko Tarnovo. In his letter of protest, written in Salzburg and dated 11 September, dismissing the discussion that had erupted in the media as "unworthy and childish," Kronsteiner declared that it was no longer a point of pride for him to be honored as "doctor" by a university that, as in the Stalinist era, used awards in the field of Bulgarian Studies as a disciplinary measure against diversity of viewpoints (Kronsteiner 2001a). At the meeting held at the University of Veliko Tarnovo, with the exception of Professor Kazimir Popkonstantinov, all members of the Council agreed to the removal of the title (Radev, Kenanov & Vasilev 2002: 48). The decision was expressed a few days later (on 14 September) in a message addressed to Kronsteiner:

> The Chair of Bulgarian Literature at the University of Saints Cyril and Methodius in Veliko Tarnovo regards with great anxiety and concern (...) the idea

of replacing the Bulgarian alphabet (the "Cyrillic") in Bulgaria with the Latin alphabet. (Katedra BL 2001; my translation)

It was stated that Professor Kronsteiner played a very active role in this campaign, expressing his opinion in a series of concrete initiatives and in a number of articles published both in Bulgaria and Austria:

> Professor Kronsteiner's interpretations and views seem to have substantially changed over the last two or three years. These have evidently led him to yield to ideas diametrically opposed to his former views. And these are incompatible with the traditions, the essence and substance of what governs the activity of the Bulgarian University which bears the name of the creators of the Slavonic script—Saints Cyril and Methodius. (Katedra BL 2001; my translation)

On 17 September 2001, the withdrawal of Kronsteiner's title was formalized and several copies of the official justification statement were sent to President Petar Stoyanov; Prime Minister Simeon Saxe-Coburg-Gotha and the Ministry of Education; the philological faculties of the Universities of Sofia, Plovdiv, Shumen and Blagoevgrad; the Institutes of Literature, Bulgarian and Balkan Languages at the Bulgarian Academy of Sciences; and to the newspapers *Literaturen Forum*, *Literaturen Vestnik* and *Kultura*, with a request for publication. The text was then made available to the public on 24 September with another explanatory letter from the University of Veliko Tarnovo, which denounced the negative attitude towards the Cyrillic alphabet and the idea of introducing the Latin script in Bulgaria. Again, it was not specified in any way that the Kronsteiner had referred to a hoped-for situation of "biscriptality" or a "graphic compromise" in the country.

In their letter, the academics of the University of Veliko Tarnovo also referred to the situation in neighboring Greece. Kronsteiner was accused of having neglected the Greek case, that is, a Southeast European a country which continued to use its own, unique writing system, and remained a full member of the European Union (Katedra BL 2001). The content of the letter is indicative of the academics' unwillingness to deal with the issue of biscriptality from a "rational" and "technical" standpoint, excluding the evaluation of the possible advantages of a partly "Latinizing" position. The discourse is framed according to "ethnopsychological" tropes: "Do we need to explain to you that when we talk about 'national identity,' one of the most important and essential indicators is precisely the language and traditions of a nation's past?" (Katedra BL 2001; my translation).

The active preservation of the tradition of the Cyrillic script in the face of new modernization challenges emerged once again, intertwined with the crucial issue of the "ethical" meaning of being Bulgarian. The anxiety regarding the spread of the Latin alphabet in the country coincided with some other cultural, political and economic concerns that had arisen since the democratic transition. In this sensitive period, any discussion about the possibility of Cyrillic's "removal" from the sacred space it occupied was condemned as "blasphemous," or "anti-Bulgarian," as we read again in the letter:

> It would be sacrilegious for the question of substituting the Cyrillic alphabet with the Latin to become the subject of debate [...]. This would deal a destructive blow to the construction of the Bulgarian national system of values initiated, and would lead to the complete de-historicization of the thinking and the imaginary of the young and future generations. (Katedra BL 2001; my translation)

As regards the technical issues, they were downplayed in a few lines (Radev, Kenanov & Vasilev 2002: 32) with the remark that questions of computerization and the internet, and the possibility of arousing foreign interest in Bulgaria, constituted "improvised" and "speculative" arguments. However old-fashioned and orthodox it sounded, the text concluded, the University still firmly believed in the validity of the formula: "if the Bulgarian alphabet that accompanied our millennial development is still there, so will the Bulgarian nation be!" (Katedra BL 2001; my translation). These were the arguments that convinced the Chair of Bulgarian Literature at the University of Veliko Tarnovo to withdraw Kronsteiner's honorary doctorate in September 2001.

In 2002, three professors from the University of Veliko Tarnovo — Ivan Radev, Dimitar Kenanov and Sava Vasilev —

disappointed by the limited space given to their institution in the media during the debate, decided to publish a book about the affair. The introduction justified the book as an "act of truth," born of a desire to reconstruct as best as possible all the positions taken during the development of the "Kronsteiner affair," and to affirm the authority and legitimacy of the decision: "[o]ur proposals were entirely in the spirit of preserving a living tradition, in the name of our national identification with the Slavic script and the literature and culture it created" (Radev, Kenanov & Vasilev 2002: 13; my translation).

Ivan Radev went so far as to compare Kronsteiner's effort to an earlier case of Cyrillic's substitution by Latin, a little-known episode in European history: in June 1941, senior Reich officials asked Tsar Boris III to adopt the Latin alphabet and eliminate Cyrillic. Kronsteiner, according to Radev, was well aware of this event but avoided mentioning it because it was associated with the memory of Hitler and Goebbels (ibid., 42).

9.8 Further reactions in the periodical and scientific press

As early as 2000, Bulgarian newspapers such as *Demokracija*, *Sega*, *24 Chasa*, *Duma*, as well as the nationalist-oriented publications *Monitor* and *Nova Zora* started devoting space to Kronsteiner and his proposal on biscriptality. In some of these texts, reference was made to the difficulties involved in creating a Latin-based writing system that would meet the needs of the Bulgarian language: a special combination of characters was in fact needed in order to reproduce certain language-specific sounds in an effective and unambiguous way. As in the debate held seventy years earlier, the question was raised regarding the fate of the entire bibliographic heritage written in Bulgarian Cyrillic, which would be adversely affected by the implementation of any alphabet reform.

A number of newspapers proposed debates "for" or "against" the Latin alphabet, often addressing the issue of the impact of globalization on the national culture, a sensitive and highly topical subject; however, the media largely exploited the debate for political purposes, and the country's president, Petar Stoyanov, was forced to publicly distance himself from Kronsteiner's ideas, stating that such a proposal would not find support in the country's institutions (Spasov 2012a). When Stoyanov later failed to win a second term as president, this was interpreted by some as resulting from the loss of authority due to his initial, seemingly "concessionary" attitude towards Kronsteiner's proposal (ibid.).

On 24 and 25 September 2001, the newspapers *Demokracija* and *24 Chasa* published two interviews with Kronsteiner, in which the Austrian academic made further controversial statements. The articles bore the (probably deliberately provocative) headlines "There are still Bulgarianists who live in the Middle Ages" ("При вас все още има българисти, които живеят в средновековието") (Kronsteiner 2001b) and "Write one day in Cyrillic, one day in Latin" ("Пишете един ден на кирилица, един на латиница") (Kronsteiner 2001c). Kronsteiner noted, among other things, that a "new Middle Ages and a new fundamentalism" were emerging in the field of Bulgarian studies, according to which national identity was exclusively based on the use of the Cyrillic alphabet. In his column on language issues in the newspaper *Labor* (*Trud*), the professor and linguist Stefan Brezinski declared that for 90% of the country, the Cyrillic alphabet was the most obvious and visible proof of their "Bulgarianness":

> This percentage was stunned by the possibility that the last remaining Bulgarian element, the alphabet of Cyril and Methodius, would be taken away from them [...]. For it is precisely the visible form of the language, the alphabet, that is the most sensitive chord in every Bulgarian. (cit. in Panayotov 2014: 20; my translation)

As in the 1930s, opponents of the introduction of the Latin alphabet defended their positions using rhetoric linked to the danger of losing the national culture. This has emerged as a constant in all the cases of proposed script change in the twentieth century analyzed in this book: those rejecting Latinization in Bulgaria in the 1920s, those fearing the loss of the Arabic tradition in Turkey or Bosnia, the defenders of the Greek alphabet, and those who today safeguard the Cyrillic alphabet in Serbia against the risks of "Croatianization." In this context, strategies of stimulating collective consciousness are employed, based on the re-enactment of myths and symbols (cf. Smith 2009: 90ff) linked to a writing tradition originating in a "golden age."

The Cyrillic alphabet remained in use in Bulgaria despite various proposals to replace it with the Latin. In this context, it should not be overlooked that Turkey adopted the Latin alphabet in the same years similar proposals arose in Bulgaria, but also in Greece and the Soviet Union. The fact that this script reform did not prevail in Bulgaria can be explained not only by the will to keep a specific identity intact but perhaps also by refusing to adapt to the writing practices of a still significantly "disturbing" neighbor, one that embodied a past of domination also on the cultural level.[99] It is worth asking what would have happened in Bulgaria if Atatürk's reform had not taken place, although clearly the most decisive element in the interwar period was constituted by the alphabet ideologies and practices in the Soviet Union—and the failure to adopt the Latin script for the Russian language (see chapter 3).

In this respect, it can be argued that the sense of "intimacy" created by the linguistic bond corresponds to the ability of language to erect a "symbolic barrier" against outsiders (Barth 1969: 34), a fact that is reinforced when the language is represented by means of a unique and distinctive graphic system. If the identity of a community is determined more by its relations to neighboring groups than by its intrinsic properties, then it is clear that much importance is attached not only to physical boundaries, but above all to symbolic ones, which are conceived as distinguishing features between "us" as a community of speakers (and "writers") and "others" who speak (or write) differently. For this reason, we can claim that the linguistic and "alphabetic" identity in this part of the world depends, at least in part, on the boundaries it has erected vis-à-vis another group with a different linguistic (and often alphabetic) system.

---

99 It is also important to consider the role of the other "Latin" neighbor, that is, Romania.

At the beginning of 2000, the Kronsteiner's proposal provoked the incensed reaction of Bulgarian right-wing extremists, who rejected his "crazy idea" (cf. Spasov 2012a): the case was exploited by the more conservative and xenophobic elites in many ways to reaffirm old fears and paranoia. For example, an article appeared in the newspaper *Monitor*, a nationalist, xenophobic and anti-Semitic publication, written by Tamara Shishmanova (later a major supporter of the nationalist party *Ataka*). The title was "The Kronsteiner − P. Stoyanov Intrigue is a Stage in the Turkification of Bulgaria" ("Интригата Кронщайнер − П. Стоянов е етап от турцизацията на България"), already very illustrative in itself.

Kronsteiner's proposal, however, did not only provoke negative reactions. Many were positive, and included some by academics. For example, Svetlozar Igov, the main editor of the journal *Language and Literature* (*Ezik i Literatura*), commented on the topic in the journal *Literaturen Forum* already in the autumn of 2000, proposing the organization of a meeting between local and foreign Bulgarianists to discuss the sensitive issue raised by Kronsteiner. Several other moderate opinions were expressed in publications such as *Literaturen Forum* and *Culture* (*Kultura*), as well as in newspapers such as *Capital* (*Kapital*), by scholars, linguists, journalists and ordinary readers.

In the following months, those who opposed the transition to the Latin alphabet came to include also foreign intellectuals. As an example of an opinion refuting the effectiveness of the Latin alphabet in bringing Bulgaria closer to Europe, we find the Polish literary critic and semiologist Jerzy Faryno's article "European Alphabet! Is it possible?" ("Европейска азбука! Възможна ли е?"), published in the magazine *Literaturen Forum* in February 2002. Faryno claimed that, with its Cyrillic alphabet, Bulgaria was much more interesting to Western Europe than it would be were it to adopt the Latin alphabet. Cyrillic was indeed the special sign of a multicultural history, a valuable element and distinguishing feature of a particular "semiosphere." Faryna problematized the possible switch to the Latin alphabet, arguing that such a situation prove an ideal breeding ground for divisions, schisms, and nationalism: the Bulgarian

Church would not go so far as to abandon the Cyrillic alphabet altogether, since this would exacerbate the contradictions in the country.

Faryno also dwelled on the economic aspect of the matter, pointing out that, regardless of progress in the field of information technology, a script reform would entail enormous costs due to the need to reprint the entire corpus of national texts; furthermore, future generations would need to train specialists capable of reading in the Cyrillic alphabet. He also expressed doubts in relation to the variant of the Latin alphabet that Bulgarians might adopt, which in any case would not have brought them automatically closer to Europe in terms of writing, since the sound expressed by the Cyrillic letter <ш> corresponded in the different languages to various graphic representations, such as <sz> (Polish), <sh> (English), <sch> (German), <ch> (French), <s> (Hungarian).

At this point, Faryna provocatively noted, the simplest solution to be found was to create a common alphabet for all, at least for the European languages, without diacritics, by carrying out reforms of all alphabets and introducing a single keyboard for all. He also pointed out that, in Poland, despite the use of the Latin alphabet, similar obstacles to a rapprochement with Europe were encountered, since the mere fact of possessing a Latin-based writing system did not enable the two regions of the Old Continent to communicate with each other effectively. Faryna claimed ironically that the most effective writing system for communication purposes was the ideographic, and cited the example of China, where proposals had also been made in the middle of the twentieth century to replace the writing system with the Latin alphabet. Its failed adoption was not due to ideological reasons, but on the contrary to very practical considerations, since a common writing system united the different languages and populations of the country, but distinct pronunciations separated them. Even today, all the different ethnic groups in China understand one and the same meaning by means of the same character, but read and pronounce it differently. According to Faryna, alphabet reform did not constitute an effective way to unite the Old Continent, but was rather an ideology that had experienced temporary popularity in the past, corresponding to the more or less successful attempts at Latinization in the 1920s.

9.9 Moderate positions on opening to the Latin alphabet

In a 2001 article published in *Literaturen Forum*, the historian Vera Boneva compared the debate on script change taking place at that time with the one held in the 1930s (chapter 3). She pointed out that, while the discussions in the interwar period were held in a peaceful and productive atmosphere, at the beginning of the new century, emotion and extremism were driving the debates into irrationality. Many of the actors involved, according to Boneva, had in fact exaggerated Kronsteiner's opinion regarding the need for a parallel Latin alphabet to such an extent that the impression of an "imminent danger of the erosion of Bulgarian national identity" had been created among the population (Boneva 2001). Boneva pointed out the contradictions in Bulgarian society, which on the one hand reaffirmed the inviolable stability of the country's millennial writing tradition by vigorously defending its national myths, and on the other hand exchanged emails in "that fanciful and impossible Latin-script variant" of the modern Bulgarian literary language. Boneva concluded by stating:

> Bulgarian ethno-cultural identity [...] appears to be more destabilized in the present conditions by the hystericization of the debate concerning the fate of the Cyrillic alphabet than by the fact that we have been sending electronic bouquets of flowers to our pen-pals lately with the following greeting: "Chestit 24-mai—den na slavjanskata pismenost i na balgarskata kultura!"[100] (Boneva 2001; my translation)

A similar opinion was expressed by Borislav Georgiev, a linguist and semiologist in the Institute for Bulgarian Language at the Bulgarian Academy of Sciences, in a 2000 article that appeared in *Literaturen Forum*, and which preceded the actual "scandal." He noted that Bulgarian and Slavic philology in the 19th and 20th centuries

---

100 "Happy 24 May—day of Slavonic writing and Bulgarian culture!" (written in Latin script).

proceeded from the basic assumption that the distinguishing feature of Orthodox Slavs was the Cyrillic alphabet. This attitude went so far as to create a kind of antithesis between the Cyrillic and Greek alphabets that made it impossible for philologists to notice that out of the thirty graphic characters of the Cyrillic alphabet, sixteen were identical to those of the Greek alphabet, and fourteen of them had the same phonetic value in both languages. This antithesis was then applied to the relation between Cyrillic and Latin, which fitted very conveniently into the opposition between Orthodox and Catholic Christianity.

Even though the use of the Latin alphabet was to some extent already a reality in Bulgaria, the problem with Kronsteiner, according to Georgiev, was that he had targeted one of the most important Bulgarian "philological myths," that related to the nature and symbolism of the Cyrillic alphabet (Georgiev 2000: 14). The negative reactions showed the extent to which the issue had been quasi-mythologized in the collective national consciousness, demonstrating the widespread belief that one was "more Bulgarian" when using the Cyrillic alphabet. This notion originated from a time before the Bulgarian Revival Period, when a strong contrast existed between the Cyrillic alphabet and the dominant Ottoman Turkish Arabic alphabet used for transcription at the state level, as well as with the Greek alphabet and language.

According to Georgiev, the parallel drawn by Bulgarian academia to Greece, which had no intention of changing its alphabet to Latin, made little sense, since in the Hellenic territories all public signs, including road signs, already appeared in a bialphabetic way, by virtue of a well-established Latin transliteration tradition. Georgiev concluded by noting that "neither in Otto Kronsteiner's interview, nor anywhere else, was the question of a 'Latinization' of Bulgarian literature raised" (Georgiev 2000: 14). In short, it was clear that the situation had been overstated, and gone beyond the control of the actors involved.

In an article that appeared in the magazine *Kapital* in June 2001, a few days after the May 24 celebrations, the journalist Svilen Ivanov referred to the statement by President Stoyanov on the "Kronsteiner affair," promising to deepen the debate on the introduction of the Latin alphabet in parallel with the Cyrillic in the country. In the author's opinion, there was nothing very "scandalous" in this statement: it was certainly not the first time Bulgarian society was faced with the choice of which alphabet to use for transcribing its language. While at the time of Chernorizets Hrabar's defense of the Glagolitic alphabet (between the 9th and 10th centuries) arguments were based on the advantage of having one's "own" alphabet over a "foreign" one, the situation today was rather different: for example, the word "river" (in Bulgarian Cyrillic, "ръка") was transliterated as "raka," "ruka," "rqka" or in other ways, as the phoneme <ъ> could be indicated by various substitutes, including inverted question marks and commas. There was no single, coherent system of transliteration, and the proponents of the introduction of a parallel Latin alphabet into Bulgarian were actually insisting on something very simple, namely the establishment of precise and homogeneous rules for the use of the Latin alphabet. This was certainly not intended as a first step towards replacing the Cyrillic alphabet with the Latin (Ivanov 2001).

Not surprisingly, Ivanov also pointed to the category of "myth" in Bulgarian popular consciousness, noting that the debate on technical issues had shifted to another level, resulting in one of the most important Bulgarian "mythologies" being transformed once again into a national model, a kind of unquestionable dogma. Indeed, language in Bulgaria continued to be defined by the category of "sacredness," to such an extent that any debate regarding possible change to any aspect of the language, especially the graphic one, was inevitably thwarted by the representatives of the more conservative mentality (Ivanov 2001). According to Ivanov, the ensuing polemic was further evidence of the crisis in the value system of Bulgarian society: "[o]r otherwise stated — the fear of pronouncing 'Nothing sacred remains to us' or of writing 'Ni6to sve6teno ne ni ostana'" (written in *Shljokavitsa*) (ibid.).

The consideration of the "atavistic fear" of undermining one of the inviolable pillars of national identity was therefore a necessary element in the interpretation of the content of the "Cyrillic and/or Latin" debate. Ivanov also noted that Kronsteiner had perhaps not been very scrupulous in formulating some of his thoughts;

far more troubling, however, were the reactions of Bulgarian institutions and intellectuals who had reached "unimagined heights of denial" and accused Kronsteiner of interfering in the affairs of a sovereign state.

Also relevant in this context is the commentary by the academic Galin Tihanov published in *Literaturen Vestnik* (Tihanov 2001) in October 2001, shortly after Kronsteiner was stripped of his title. This professor of comparative literature, in an article entitled "Repression and Autonomy" ("Репресия и Автономия"), while expressing his disagreement with Kronsteiner's views, highlighted the disproportionate reaction of the Bulgarian academic institutions, claiming that his awards could not be revoked "retroactively." The removal of a title was academically unjustifiable and appeared more like a form of retaliation, as well as a return to the darkest days of persecution in the country (Tihanov 2001). The proposals made by Otto Kronsteiner had to be discussed critically and constructively in the press, in parliament and, of course, in the universities and other scientific institutions, avoiding any "tabooization" of the question.

In the view of many, it was appropriate for Bulgaria to develop precise rules leading to the creation of a uniform transcription system, so that no problems would be encountered in transliterating Bulgarian names into the Latin alphabet in the EU. In the context of opening up to European cultural values, Tihanov argued, no threat was posed to the country's historical and identity values, represented by the Cyrillic alphabet. This script was part of a relationship with the Russian and Balkan worlds, and Bulgaria could continue to perform its cultural function in this area even after joining Europe, strengthening its role as a mediator.

In this respect, the opinion of Bulgarians living abroad was also interesting. One example is an article by Ivan Zhekov, a young engineer resident in Germany for twenty years, published in *Literaturen Forum* in late May and early June 2001. Zhekov noted that Bulgarian culture was little known in Germany, one of the main reasons for this being the former communist regime and its proximity to the Soviet world. However, it was not only communism that separated the country from Western Europe. Another barrier preceded it: "For more than a thousand years, Europe has been divided into two parts, Catholic Western Europe and Orthodox Eastern Europe. This corresponds precisely to a border [...] of letters" (my translation).

Zhekov ventured the speculation that this "striving for distinction" had motivated the Orthodox Church to introduce its own alphabet, Cyrillic, which still managed to divide the peoples of the Old Continent in the third millennium. He believed that one of the first conditions for a successful unification was the introduction of the Latin alphabet in all European countries and contemplated the possibility of Bulgaria abandoning Cyrillic. This, according to him, contrary to the opinion of the majority of Bulgarians, would not mean the disappearance of the native language; quite the contrary. He himself, he said, had worked for years on a German-Bulgarian dictionary written entirely in the Latin alphabet (Zhekov 2001).

9.10 Conclusions: open issues of transliteration

In Bulgaria, the "Kronsteiner affair" triggered important discussions on the question of the relationship between the "small" Bulgarian language written in Cyrillic and the European majority languages, especially English. Undoubtedly, in the years following the controversy, also by virtue of the climate of "Europeanization," the Latin alphabet gained further ground in the context of urban public spaces and interpersonal means of communication, a fact that, as already mentioned, was often problematically received:

> Huge signs in the Latin alphabet shine in the squares and streets. Every day, television intensely "Latinizes" viewers with advertisements for Bulgarian brands and companies. The Latin alphabet can be found everywhere, sometimes appropriately and legitimately, but more often unjustifiably. (Bojadžiev 2008: 18; my translation)

Significantly, some city administrations tried to restrict the use of Latin characters by adopting special measures, enforcing the constitutional principle that, since Bulgarian was the official language, any writing in a foreign language had to be preceded by a transliteration in Bulgarian Cyrillic (Bojadžiev 2008: 20). Certainly, the massive presence of the Latin alphabet has stimulated and continues to stimulate debates about the value of Cyrillic, with its defenders producing conservative discourses that reduce the possibility of a more relaxed and rational attitude towards the Latin alphabet. Moreover, this situation also demonstrates that the technical recommendations for transliteration into the Latin alphabet suggested by Kronsteiner at the turn of the century were unfairly denigrated, and should have been evaluated with greater foresight.

In fact, as early as 2002, the Public Council of the Parliamentary Committee for Civil Society recommended that the Ministry of Education and Science include some basic notions of a simplified transliteration system in the national curriculum, but this proposal was never implemented. Consequently, it is possible to affirm that neglecting the question of adopting a uniform and official transliteration system in the country facilitated the later spread of the so-called *Shljokavitsa*, that is, the script used by the younger generations for communicating on the internet, in which transliteration into Latin adopts "creative" solutions that include numerical digits in place of alphabetic characters (cf. Mladenov 2005: 17).

10. THE POPULAR DIMENSION OF THE CYRILLIC ALPHABET AND THE REDISCOVERY OF GLAGOLITIC

10.1 The "Kronsteiner effect"

If we consider the impact of the debate on the Latin alphabet in Bulgaria, we can observe that the so-called "Kronsteiner effect" (cf. Spasov 2012a) led Bulgarian society to rigidly defend its national myths in the short and long term and stimulated discussions on restrictive laws concerning the language. An example of the latter is the so-called "Draft Law on the Bulgarian Language," submitted to the National Assembly in 2004 but never adopted (Proekt Zakon 2004), where we can read:

> Art. 2 (1) The official language in the Bulgarian Republic is the Bulgarian literary language. (2) The writing system of the Bulgarian language is Cyrillic.
> Art. 3 The intention of this law is to defend the language as the basis of Bulgarian national identity by ensuring the conditions for the preservation and enrichment of the Bulgarian literary language […].

The conditions which made the preservation of the language possible corresponded to a great extent to general educational questions, the improvement of which could lead to a more favorable climate for the Cyrillic script in common writing practices. Some of the politicians who initiated this proposed legislation lamented the sparse presence of the Cyrillic alphabet in some of the country's tourist landmarks, including Vitosha Avenue in Sofia and Sunny Beach on the Black Sea.

Although the law was abandoned in the course of the decision-making process, the proposal was symptomatic of a kind of anxiety emerging in the aftermath of the "Kronsteiner affair" regarding Bulgaria's position as a "minority" element in relation to a larger and more complex whole, namely the European Union. The sensitivity to issues of writing practices in the country can be interpreted also as dependent on a pronounced identitarian uncertainty characteristic of the post-socialist transition phase. In a sense, the years leading to the accession to the EU reawakened ghosts and fears which had never really subsided over the years, especially as regards questions of national history. Despite the undeniable influence of the Soviet Union during the communist years, the country had not confronted a larger state structure in which a different writing system dominated since the time of Ottoman rule.

As in the interwar period, this moment embodied a so-called epochal "caesura," providing the opportunity to reaffirm the historical continuity essential to the national discourse; as a result of the so-called "Kronsteiner affair," the Cyrillic alphabet was further "re-signified," emerging as the "winner." The debates about Cyrillic in Bulgaria echo the romantic ideal of the correspondence between language and nation: this has proved more than resistant, even in the face of the processes of globalization and European integration. In contrast to what happened in Turkey with Atatürk's alphabet reform of 1928, which entailed the adoption of a new and "foreign" writing system, in the Balkans the focus on the alphabet corresponds to an attempt to draw a line of continuity between the nation's past and present, to show that a particular identity has always existed thanks to the irrefutable evidence of its written heritage.

The principles of linguistic (and "alphabetic") diversity appear as elements of great importance in the policy of the European Union, which aims at defending them from processes of cultural levelling, and includes them in an ideal vision of mutual understanding, tolerance and stability. Significantly, in the Bulgaria-EU accession agreement we find the "Declaration of the Bulgarian Republic on the use of Cyrillic in the European Union" ("Декларация на Република България относно използването на кирилицата в Европейския съюз"), which states that, with the recognition of the Bulgarian language as a legitimate language of the Treaties and as an official working language, Cyrillic has become one of the three official alphabets of the European Union: "This essential part of Europe's cultural heritage represents the specific Bulgarian contribution to the linguistic and cultural diversity of the Union" (Dogovor 2005; my translation).

The national Cyrillic script was given a place and recognition as an added value to the new cultural and political path of European history (cf. Raynov, Mircheva & Kostadinova 2008). The use of three official scripts—Cyrillic, Greek and Latin—constitutes a new opportunity for the European Union itself: "if its actions follow its words and it admits some or all of these states to membership, it stands a good chance of reviving the tradition of European multiscripturality, alongside its legally enshrined commitment to multilingualism" (Kamusella 2012: 10).

10.2 Cyrillic and modern technologies

As previously mentioned, since the advent of the internet in the late 1990s in Bulgaria, the Latin alphabet's presence became ever more evident, used mainly by the younger generations for surfing (cf. Ivanov 2003: 115), who produced a type of online Latin-based written communication that became increasingly inconsistent. The responsibility for the spelling chaos related to the context of modern technologies in the country was partly due to the shortcomings of the educational system, which did not encourage the use of a specific transliteration system for Bulgarian Cyrillic characters. Apparently, the transliteration of Cyrillic into Latin letters is cause of great confusion among young Bulgarian people, as evidenced by the results of the 2009 Bulgarian language entrance exams for prospective students at Paisii Hilendarski University in Plovdiv. These provoked quite a stir, since some of the candidates made a series of mistakes, replacing some letters of the Cyrillic alphabet with Latin ones, for example by writing "uтpe" instead of "утре," a phenomenon occurring for the first time.[101]

It is important to point out that the increasing use of the Latin alphabet in contemporary electronic communication is not due to purely technical reasons, but also to its relative prestige as a symbol of the Western world: this association has had important consequences for the fate of the Cyrillic alphabet in many parts of Eastern

---

101 https://www.24chasa.bg/Article/183484 (last access: 3/11/21).

Europe and the former Soviet territories since the decline of Russian political domination (cf. Coulmas 2000: 48-49). The Bulgarian authorities have long maintained a relationship with the Latin alphabet characterized by rigidity and taboos: to some extent, this attitude manifests itself even when it comes to transliteration practices, as if the introduction of an official transcription scheme in school curricula constituted a kind of threat to the integrity of the Cyrillic alphabet, legitimizing in some way the use of an alternative writing system.

In terms of the virtual space of the web, interestingly, a number of initiatives have emphatically called for the promotion of the Cyrillic script and supported initiatives to restrict the use of the Latin alphabet. As an example, for some years now, a number of website moderators force users to write in Cyrillic letters exclusively. In many cases, the campaigns take on an inflammatory tone, emphasizing the unpatriotic behavior of the "Latinophiles" (Spasov 2012a). Furthermore, a fact of great significance for the fate of the Cyrillic script on the web has been the introduction of the Cyrillic web domain, an initiative first launched by the Bulgarian government, followed by Russia. This proposal was adopted by the European Commission in 2009 and has become a reality since 1 June 2016.

The advent of domains in Cyrillic and other non-Latin writing systems represents indeed an epochal change in the world of the internet, perhaps one of the most significant since its creation. It implies the existence of websites accessible only to people who know how to type their web address in Cyrillic, as opposed to previous practices that required knowledge of the Latin alphabet. This is also true for Chinese, Japanese, and Arabic websites: in short, for users of all the world's languages not written in Latin characters. The appearance of online domains in alphabets other than Latin will therefore enable people not familiar with this writing system to carry on alternative writing practices on the internet. Furthermore, European institutions will also be obliged to write in the Cyrillic alphabet and to create parallel content in this alphabet through the specific domain.[102]

10.3 The link between Cyrillic and capitalism and the Bulgarian typefaces

In analyzing the advance of the Cyrillic script into areas that hitherto seemed completely excluded from everyday practice, one should not overlook another significant level of interpretation. Indeed, initiatives in favor of the spread of the Cyrillic alphabet in areas of modern communication can be interpreted not only as the recognition granted by the "great powers" to smaller languages and non-dominant scripts, but also as a deeper penetration by liberalizing ideologies, and thus as a "facilitation of capitalism." In addition to its important emotional, national, rhetorical, and ideological implications, the impact of the logic of global capitalism on cultural elements such as writing systems should not be underestimated.

A consideration of the relationship between capitalism and nationalism in the context of the use of Cyrillic could therefore prove very fruitful. According to Spasov (2012a), the global economic logic has a vested interest in supporting smaller national languages and minor, traditional writing systems. For big companies it is not a question of "goodness" but of the profit motive, of "language policy" in the financial sense, since it is a way of opening new markets by reaching consumers who cannot use the dominant Latin alphabet. The "national" element serves as a good commercial product for large globalized businesses: "Hence, surprisingly, those responsible for the problem of the Latin script find themselves at the center of the Cyrillic renaissance, and the debate about the 'best' alphabetic character finds an unexpected finale in the language of business" (ibid.; my translation).

In relation to this aspect of the question, it is interesting to note that such dynamics were also active in the past, revealing an

---

[102] http://www.balkaninsight.com/en/article/eu-domain-in-cyrillic-to-kick-off-in-june-03-20-2016-2 (last access: 3/11/21).

already existing relationship with capitalism: a little-known and unique fact, for example, is the adaptation of the global brand Coca Cola to the writing needs of the Bulgarian population when creating its logo. Indeed, starting in the 1960s, in the midst of the Cold War, when Bulgaria was under the full influence of Soviet power, Coca Cola decided to introduce Cyrillic characters for the lettering of its famous drink, a device that was implemented and maintained throughout the communist period. In Bulgaria, the production of the drink began in 1965, and for this country the brand changed its logo, "transliterating" it into Cyrillic characters. Only in Bulgaria did the brand name of the drink appear in Cyrillic letters on the distinctive glass bottle containing the product.

Since even such minor signs as the seemingly insignificant lettering on the labels of popular consumer goods are in fact a measure of the ideological climate of the times, the logo was transliterated back into Latin characters with the onset of democratic changes in Bulgaria. Nevertheless, more than twenty years later, on 24 May 2013, a group of young fans of the drink launched a campaign called "Let's restore the Coca Cola Logo in Cyrillic" ("Да върнем логото на Кока-Кола на кирилица"). The initiators of the petition, Petya Lozanova and Radomir Ivanov, were aware of the contribution that the logo, written in Cyrillic script, could make in terms of visual and symbolic impact:

> We believe that, at a time when young people are increasingly writing in the Latin alphabet, the return to the Cyrillic logo of one of their most popular drinks will encourage them to rediscover the beauty and richness of the Bulgarian language. Our alphabet deserves such an act of respect from the brand that, although global, has a very special history with Bulgaria.[103]

Over the course of the last few years, further initiatives have emerged supporting the use of the Bulgarian Cyrillic alphabet. In particular, we can recall one calling for a Bulgarian graphic standard Cyrillic font, launched before Bulgaria's entry into the EU by Vladko Murdarov, president of the Scientific Council of the Institute of the Bulgarian Language at the Bulgarian Academy of

---

103 http://bgbarman.bg/Логото-на-Кока-Кола-на-Кирилица.html (last access: 3/11/21). My translation.

Sciences, and journalist Kin Stoyanov, and called "Appeal in the Name of Bulgarian Cyrillic." ("Призив в името на българската кирилица"). In 2004, in view of the country's accession to the EU, which would entail the use of this alphabet also at an official European level, Murdarov and Stoyanov advocated for an effective promotion of the specific Bulgarian form of the Cyrillic typefaces in graphics both inside and outside the country. The typographical issue was not insignificant, and evidence of this is the fact that it had arisen earlier in the late and post-imperial era of nation-building:

> During the Renaissance, when Bulgarian books, newspapers and magazines were printed in different printing houses and under different conditions, the present variant of our Cyrillic script, of which we are proud and in which we preserve the beauty of each Bulgarian letter, gradually came into being. In recent years, Bulgarian artists have employed this traditional beauty to create original Bulgarian letters, which meet all the requirements of modern technology. We believe that Bulgarian Cyrillic should be enforced as a European standard! (cit. in Raynov 2005: 10; my translation)

A few years later, the first issue of the graphic magazine *Pro-GRAFICA* dealt with the typographic implications of the Cyrillic alphabet in a European context. The magazine's editor, Desislava Brajkova, polemically recalled that the printing of official documents in Bulgarian within the European Union was realized through characters developed and produced outside Bulgaria, in what she defined as a completely "paradoxical" process (Brajkova 2007: 1). The magazine devoted several pages to an interview with Kin Stoyanov and the appeal he supported, defined by him as "a matter of moral defense of the whole of Bulgarian society" (in: Stoyanov 2007: 12; my translation). Stoyanov invoked the recognition of the Bulgarian Cyrillic font as the official standard for the redaction of EU documents in Bulgarian, in contrast to the use of fonts produced by large companies on the market, which created them according to the standards of Russian Cyrillic.

The issue lay in the need to develop special software that would make it easier to adopt Bulgarian Cyrillic characters in general writing and printing practices. This was of great importance at the national level and triggered a reaction from both public opinion and the Bulgarian authorities active at the relevant EU institutions.

Stoyanov contributed to the popularization of this cause by organizing an exhibition that toured Bulgaria and reached abroad, entitled "The Alphabet from A to Z and Я" ("Азбуката от А до Z и Я"), in which drawings of letters of the Cyrillic and Latin alphabets by leading Bulgarian artists were exhibited. The truth is that, even today, few of the many Bulgarian publications adhere to the use of Bulgarian fonts: an exception is the magazine *Culture*, which uses exclusively Bulgarian Cyrillic typefaces for its articles. In addition, more and more initiatives are being launched to promote and "update" the Bulgarian typographic tradition, such as the festival *Typofest*, "A Feast of Type, Calligraphy and Typography" ("Празник на шрифта, калиграфията и типографията"), held in conjunction with the 24 May holiday in the country, whose webpage reads:

> In recent years, interest in typeface and typography has grown in a variety of ways. The mass emergence of computers and mobile devices in our lives has made the ability to work with text and type a necessity [...] The Bulgarian font is an unknown phenomenon to many people. Few know that Bulgaria has given the world the contemporary Bulgarian form of Cyrillic alongside the Church Slavonic script.[104]

For many representatives of Bulgarian society, the development of electronic communications did not necessarily entail a decline in the use of the Bulgarian Cyrillic alphabet, but rather a significant opportunity for its typefaces to be valorized in new and modern ways: capitalism, globalization and the process of European integration were three intertwined elements that could be linked in a similarly effective way to the preservation of a part of the country's writing tradition.

10.4 The popularization of Cyrillic and the May 24 celebration

As emerged from the debates over the Cyrillic/Latin alphabets both in the interwar period and in recent times, the Bulgarian language and its alphabet are viewed in Bulgarian national rhetoric as

---

104 https://kultura.bg/web/за-празника-на-шрифта/

the privileged link that people have with their past, their ancestors and the historical sites of their national memory.

> The Cyrillic script is of emblematic importance to Bulgaria. By continuing its use, we keep alive a sacred part of our history and heritage. Like the Bulgarian word, our ancient Cyrillic script preserves Bulgarianness and creates in us a sense of belonging to a culture that played its part in the European one. (Bojadžiev 2008: 20; my translation)

At the level of national representation, the Cyrillic alphabet appears indissolubly connected with the Cyrillo-Methodian mission, viewed as the most prestigious cultural event of the nation's past: in the dominant narrative, the myth of a Bulgarian "civilizing mission" is continuously re-actualized with reference to the invention of the Cyrillic alphabet (cf. Sygkelos 2011: 189), even though the script Constantine-Cyril invented was the Glagolitic. The discourse of a nation that has written and continues to write with its own letters, perpetuating its "graphic image," thus plays an extremely important role. Pride in the cultural past, cleverly linked to the present, is particularly evident in the focus on language and the alphabet as invaluable markers of the historical heritage: "Ever since its birth in the 19th century, the national ideology has invariably listed the Slavic alphabet and writing, created by the Byzantine missionaries Constantine-Cyril and Methodius in the 9th century, among the 'Bulgarian' cultural achievements" (Marinov 2011: 6).

In contrast to the attitude prevailing in Western European countries, more concerned with the glorification of the Renaissance and, consequently, "post-medieval" history, in Bulgaria and the Balkans in general it is precisely the period of the early Middle Ages that epitomizes the privileged object of research and "rediscovery." In the national historiography, this indeed represents the true "golden age," which was followed by a "dark age" under foreign domination (Ottoman, etc.) (cf. Daskalov & Vezenkov 2015: 6). Therefore, it is not surprising that the moment of "graphopoietic" work that took place in the 9th century is relentlessly presented to the collective imagination as the golden epoch of Bulgarian culture, when the importance of Bulgarian writing began to be consecrated, as a means of approaching the Word of God in the first instance.

As Cardona affirmed, "[i]n the traditions where writing has a creator, it is rare that the invention is not sanctioned by the seal of a divine apparition that establishes its direct supernatural descent: the signs are created so that they too can communicate to men" (Cardona 1986: 59; my translation). In the national discourse, the May 24 celebration serves as a reminder that Bulgarians exist primarily thanks to the work of Cyril and Methodius, hailed as Bulgarian Enlighteners who "'originated from the Bulgarian people' and fulfilled an apostolic mission on its behalf" (Mishkova 2015: 165).[105]

In this context, it is interesting to note that the dominant national rhetoric is also reflected in literary production addressed to a wider public. An example in this regard is the case of the novel *The War of the Letters* ("Войната на буквите") by Lyudmila Filipova, published in 2014. The events narrated in this book take place in the 10th century, after the invention of the Glagolitic alphabet, when Cyrillic had already emerged.[106] Filipova decided to set the historical novel in a period when "the survival of the Bulgarian people was at stake": the point of the book was to celebrate the majesty of "one of the most unique and perfect alphabets in the world—the Bulgarian one" (my translation).

According to the writer, the Bulgarian people were one of the few nations who dared to fight to protect their writing system, to preserve themselves as a nation at a time when "the alphabet gave power and control" and when the great empires "killed anyone who did not use the Greek or Latin alphabets." The situation faced

---

[105] Mishkova also affirms: "Byzantium's two major cultural legacies to the Bulgarians—religion and the Cyrillic alphabet—were thus fully alienated from it and consigned to the national patrimony. The logic of nationality, in which religion and language played the key role, largely predetermined this outcome" (Mishkova 2015: 165).

[106] Among the reader reviews of this book, we find that of Hristo Pimpirev, head of the Bulgarian Arctic Institute: "Az, Buki, Vedi—sacred letters, which made us a nation, which survived through the dark centuries of the Middle Ages and Ottoman rule. Hate, blood, intrigue and love are part of the great battle for the alphabet to give us strength, so that Bulgaria survives through the centuries. Reading this book, you will feel proud to be Bulgarian" (my translation). https://enthusiast.bg/bg/enthusiast-books/voinata-na-bukvite (last access: 3/11/2021).

THE ALPHABET OF DISCORD   259

by her country in the 2000s, she maintains, was very similar to the one of that distant past: doubts about the meaning of "being Bulgarian" also plagued the population, and threats of assimilation made society vulnerable, giving rise to "a great need for national unity."[107] The Bulgarian alphabet constituted, from the moment of its creation, "a powerful weapon in the hands of the people in their struggle for a glorious future," one that remained valid even in the modern era of globalization.

The importance of May 24 as a holiday of national culture fits well into this discourse. After all, the Day of the Slavonic Alphabet, Bulgarian Enlightenment and Culture is itself a tradition that dates back to the mid-19th century. It is not surprising that it was maintained even during the years of communism (cf. Sygkelos 2010: 62): an Orthodox feast day for Saints Cyril and Methodius, which the communists, belittling the religious element, interpreted in terms of a celebration of Slavic culture, literacy, and solidarity, emphasizing Bulgaria's role in the fate of the Slavic East and thus its close links with the Soviet Union. Moreover, in the 1970s, statues and monuments dedicated to the two saints were erected in the capital city.[108] The veneration of Cyril and Methodius was no longer associated with a purely ecclesiastical meaning; from a socialist perspective, the importance of the holiday was emphasized by referring to the context of national liberation from foreign domination and to the democratic value intrinsic to the acquisition of literacy by "all the people."

Following the democratic changes, the May 24 holiday took on the function of an identity ritual and became part of the official practices of cultural memory (cf. Assman 2011: 6). Through this celebration, the "imaginative" meaning of the alphabet is both handed down and realized in contemporary social practices. In this way, the alphabet becomes a symbol that transcends the boundaries of

---

107 The writer refers to the Cyrillic alphabet as Българицата, echoing the expression used by the politician Solomon Passi, who initiated an effort to name the Cyrillic alphabet according to an "ethnic category."
108 The statue at the entrance of the National Library in Sofia, created by the sculptor Ginovski in 1975, and, around the same time, the monumental column *Za buvkite* in the park close to the NDK building, also in the capital.

the memory object and makes explicit the connection between time and identity (ibid.). Practices of cultural memory and processes of collective remembrance that focus on these "symbolic figures" (ibid., 37) of the past make history a living reality: a religious, cultural and political one.

It can be argued that the main characteristic of writing is its leaving ubiquitous traces: despite the absence of its authors, it continues to be accessible in time and, in many cases, in space. Cardona adds that its direct contact with thought implies that it can take on something of the force that characterizes thought itself: a propositional, active, creative force, depending on the ideologies behind it (Cardona 1982: 5). In the Bulgarian case, the strongest ideology is that of "remembering" the national past. By exercising a certain "cultural memory," one could say that the main function attributed to writing is that of evoking a "distinctive culture."

Tradition, here, also corresponds to a certain kind of writing: it is a matter of national pride, combined with the conviction that these signs can also draw a continuous line through the history of the country. Such rhetoric of "national survival," in reference to the "anti-assimilatory" value of the alphabet, is thus crucial to understanding the reason for its age-old celebration and probable survival for a long time to come.

10.5 Conclusions: the revitalization of Glagolitic and "ethnogenetic" questions

In the discourse on the glorification of the Cyrillic alphabet as the Bulgarian element par excellence, the question of Glagolitic deserves separate treatment. Because of its connection with the Western (Catholic) tradition, it was, in a sense, ignored in Bulgaria for a long time, to the point that the Cyrillic alphabet is still sometimes considered the writing system invented by Cyril. The downplaying of the historical role of Glagolitic is also evident in iconographic representations, where the Slavic alphabet appearing next to the figures of the two Holy Brothers is almost always the Cyrillic one (cf. Daiber 2015: 141). Since the post-socialist transition period, however, the role of Glagolitic seems to have undergone a kind of rediscovery, albeit in a strictly pseudo-scientific context, and in relation to "ethnogenetic" issues. Indeed, in Bulgaria, attempts to legitimize the nation's distinctiveness and its "ancient" and "prestigious" history are sometimes accompanied by the appropriation of Glagolitic as a symbol, claiming its exclusive Bulgarian origin.

In recent years, in addition to the proliferation of art works dedicated to this alphabet (by artists such as Antonia Duende, Angel Geshev, Pavlin Petrov), we find a noteworthy example of its practical application at the level of propaganda in the logo of the nationalist party *Ataka*, founded in 2005 and characterized by strongly xenophobic rhetoric. Its leader, Volen Siderov, chose the Glagolitic letter A3 (A) for its logo, created by artist and writer Hristo Tanev, who had previously collaborated with the poet Petko Kanevski on the publication of the book *The Az of the Bulgarians and National Symbols* ("АЗ-ът на българите и националните символи"). This was a sort of political, esoteric and "cultural" manifesto that identified Glagolitic as the most authentic symbol of the Bulgarian collective spirit. The book's irrational assertions characterized by the "pseudo-historical" style that was fashionable in the country in the 1990s, contained many references to ancient symbols and emblems of the Bulgarian past.

In his 2011 book *Fundamentals of Bulgarianism* ("Основи на Българизма"), Siderov himself referred to the Glagolitic alphabet as the most important symbol of Bulgarian national identity and justified its inclusion in the party logo by pseudohistorical considerations similar to those made by Tanev (Siderov 2011: 66ff). Ethnogenetic theories using this cultural element to claim an "autochthonous" origin of the Bulgarian people are very popular in the country. These include those supported by the Bulgarian Horde Association ("Българска Орда"), a far-right racist organization that was active during the period 1938-1944 and was re-established in 1995. One of its founders in 1938 was the historian Gancho Tsenov, an ambiguous figure (cf. Nikolov 2013) whose remarks about the Glagolitic alphabet appear somewhat fanciful. In his book *The Origin of Bulgarians and the Beginning of the Bulgarian State and the Bulgarian Church* ("Произходът на българите и начало на българската държава и българската църква") (1910), among other things, Tsenov affirmed the autochthonous origin of Cyril and Methodius, but above all the theory of a Bulgarian and Thracian origin[109] of the Glagolitic alphabet, long before the mission of the two Holy Brothers, who were instead credited with having invented the Cyrillic alphabet. Gancho Tsenov is especially remembered and praised by *Ataka*: in a text written in support of the 2014 reprint of his work, Siderov claimed that Tsenov aimed to prove "that the Bulgarians are the direct descendants of the Thracians who lived long before Christ in the present territories, that they were Christianized long before other European peoples, and transmitted the alphabet and the faith to all of Europe" (in: Tsenov 2014: 3; my translation).

Statements such as those of Tanev, Siderov, and others, though expressing the political orientation of a minority, nevertheless attract a certain amount of public interest. Together with works of a similar character published by questionable editors or tabloids, dealing with "pseudo-historical" topics often linked to an ethnogenetic obsession, a form of identity discourse has indeed succeeded in penetrating part of the Bulgarian audience, potentially influencing their attitudes on issues linked not only to events of the distant past but also to the immediate present. This, in turn, also has implications for their opinions on the much more topical issues of immigration, multilingualism, minority rights, etc.

In light of this, it is important not to neglect this "popular" level in the analysis of the ideologization of writing systems, as it is on this level that certain discourses about Glagolitic and Bulgarian identity are most effectively disseminated. Also, in this case, the construction of national rhetoric is based on the use of certain

---

109 Since about the mid-1990s in Bulgaria, questions of "ethnogenesis" have been intensely linked to the "pseudoscientific" and popular rediscovery of the heritage of the ancient Thracians, who were attributed great cultural merit in a perspective that excluded any contribution from neighboring civilizations, such as the Greek and Roman. In fact, the first impulse towards the valorization of the cultural and "genetic" heritage of the Thracians occurred in the 1970s, in the so-called period of "nationalist communism," in the context of the cultural policy advocated by Todor Zhivkov's daughter, Lyudmila.

"unique," "ancient" elements that stand in contrast to others and legitimize a particular ideology of defending the native writing heritage. Once again, the alphabetic element exercises its role as an identity marker that concretizes difference and legitimizes borders and divisions, be they geographical, political, historiographical, ethnic, etc.

Recently, some modern sculptures dedicated to the Glagolitic alphabet have been erected in the capital, and as in the Croatian case, this writing system appears on many tourist gadgets as well as in graffiti, demonstrating its transformation into a popular and mass element. This is also a manifestation of the "commodification" of the national idea that has increasingly developed in recent years, in another interesting combination of nationalism and capitalism. As we have seen, it is precisely the collective symbols and myths with which Bulgarian identity builds its narrative that are privileged for material dissemination; moreover, the same cultural elements are often propagated in parallel ways throughout the Balkans, i.e. by asserting an "exclusive" past that goes back many centuries.

There are significant similarities between the valorization of the Glagolitic element in Bulgaria and Croatia: in both countries, radical socio-political and cultural changes have triggered an intense process of restructuring cultural values and redefining national historiographies. National identity is therefore established both through juxtaposition with that of the "Other" (or "Others") in the region and through assertion of the more important primacy of "authenticity."

11. FINAL NOTES

11.1 The relevance of the post-imperial and post-socialist factors

In the countries of the Balkan region, issues of national identity have gained additional complexity as a result of the political changes of the 1990s. This corresponds to a transitional process that has also had a significant impact on culture and which, in many respects, can be considered not yet completed. In this book, I have compared the post-imperial and post-socialist moments in the region, highlighting possible similarities between these two critical turning points of political transition and change. One of the most salient reasons that justify a comparison between these two historical phases is that they are both characterized by an important shift from a context of "commonality" within a larger political structure to the creation of a more "individual" narrative of identity.

The similarity between the post-imperial and post-socialist moments also corresponds to the intense differentiation and institutionalization of languages and writing systems, phenomena that are perhaps even more evident now than in the previous historical phase. The current trend of language rediscovery taking place in the Balkans could be interpreted as comparable to the period of Romanticism, inspired by Herder's ideas on the role of language, understood as an emblem of the spirit of the nation.

The principle of the existence of an ethnic group as a culturally distinct community (Barth 1969) has undoubtedly found wide application in the Balkans, where the glorification of certain cultural elements as markers of separateness stands in stark contrast to a past of sharing and coexistence (cf. Barkey & Von Hagen 1997). This tendency has found a useful element in the alphabet, a fact that is evident in many controversies over the status of Cyrillic in the former Yugoslavia, where this script has become a symbol of Serbian national identity. A paradigmatic case is that of Montenegro, where the decision to receive official documents in Latin or Cyrillic (both official writing systems in the country) depends strictly on the willingness to declare one's national identity: to choose Cyrillic is to assert the Serbian one.

A similar situation occurs in Bosnia and Herzegovina: here, the boundaries of the Republika Srpska are drawn through the affirmation of the physical and symbolic presence of the Cyrillic script, which marks "Serbianness" in the country's space. In addition, it is important to remember also the disputes between Bulgaria and North Macedonia over the heritage of Cyril and Methodius and Saint Clement Ohridski, and their work of alphabet creation. Indeed, these historical symbols are often claimed as "exclusive" in the dominant narratives of both countries, which ascribe a "national" or "ethnic" character to the phenomena of the 9th-10th centuries (see Frusetta 2006: 114).[110]

In the conception of the nation-state, communities that are "on the margins" are associated with a defined and "monolithic" identity that rarely corresponds to reality: one of the central problems of nation-states therefore corresponds to the denial of identities expressing forms of "multiple belonging" (Selvelli 2017: 82). These are certainly still experienced by many people, but represent an "inconvenient" fact that contradicts the exclusive notion of identity. In this respect, it is undeniable that the element of language, and with it the alphabetic aspect, are subjected to ideological pressure to become the main symbols of the nation. If the political manipulations in this sense are undeniable, it remains that the idea of a correspondence between the state and a national language/alphabet is a strictly "European" idea that originated in the Old Continent and then spread to the countries that adopted the Western model: basically, we do not find this kind of linguistic conception of identity in other parts of the world.

---

[110] In this context, we can also recall the ongoing dispute between these two countries regarding the Macedonian language, which is not recognized by Bulgaria as an independent language, but is considered a "Bulgarian dialect."

In the Balkans, borders have proved to be a key issue in the last century: reified and constructed as an "ontological" boundary, they assumed the role of a dividing line between the successor states of imperial (now socialist) systems, and at the same time contained an internal dimension that excluded the "Others" from the dominant collective imagination. In the process of constructing a national narrative, historians from neighboring countries argued and fought over a common heritage, claimed exclusivity of certain cultural elements, and often denied or ignored some "undesirable" aspects of their own history. Through this, the past was cleverly selected and re-signified in order to define rigid ethnic boundaries that came with a sense of territorial and historical continuity (Daskalov & Vezenkov 2015: 6, Zerubavel 2005: 67ff). In the Yugoslav case, ethnic boundaries and borders were "absolutized" as something sacred, along with their markers and protectors, that is, the symbols of national unity and distinction such as language and the alphabet.

The process of "alphabetic revival" taking place in the Balkans can be compared to some extent to another post-socialist reality characterized by complex ethnic interactions and great cultural and linguistic diversity, namely the Caucasus. Both areas represent not only geographically, but also politically, culturally and economically two important crossroads that have been subject to different rulers and a variety of influences over the centuries. For this reason, issues of linguistic, religious, and ethnocultural diversity in the two regions are an important focus for comparative research (Kahl 2012: 172-173). What makes them analogous is not only the imperial legacy, but also the past of socialism and the present of post-socialism. In countries such as Georgia and Armenia, there is a similar focus on the alphabet, which is often the object of different forms of celebration: indeed, it is viewed as an autochthonous writing system (linked to the scriptural tradition) that has preserved national culture over the centuries, despite the various foreign dominations. After the collapse of the USSR and the proclamation of an independent Georgia and Armenia, new borders were and are being drawn, as in the Balkans after the collapse of Yugoslavia and other communist regimes, and "diversity" is also affirmed by national symbols, in a process that does not yet seem to have reached its end.

11.2 The symbolic dimension of the alphabet in the Balkans

The Balkans represent one of the most appropriate contexts to study the relevance and weight of script ideologies and disputes.[111] In this part of the world, the affirmation and "rediscovery" of writing systems are accompanied by the emergence of processes of nation-building based on the assumption of a "homogeneous" and "prestigious" cultural identity. The alphabetic element is employed to distinguish the country from the history of its neighbors, and it also proves useful in the identification of precise historical periods of society itself, reflecting clear "graphocentric" ideologies.

In the case studies examined in this book, the graphic form of the language proves capable of establishing and legitimizing collective relations on two fronts, corresponding to the communicative and the symbolic dimensions (cf. Edwards, 1985: 17). If the first dimension guarantees the possibility of mutual understanding and exchange of messages and information, the latter, on the other hand, embodies an even more direct instrument of collective identification that can involve also those who do not know the language. In an ideal projection, there would be a total correspondence between the communicative and the symbolic space of a language (Škiljan 2004: 17). However, since the symbolic function has the power to separate different ethnic groups by highlighting their specificities, it is not surprising that this dimension may become the preferred one in the context of nation-building processes and post-conflict contexts. Societies based on the principle of national identification, striving to strengthen their identity in a homogeneous sense, tend in fact to emphasize this aspect of the language (cf.

---

111 Other "ideal" places to investigate it are some of the countries of the former Soviet Union, similarly characterized by a post-socialist present and a multicultural past, such as the above-mentioned Caucasus, the Central Asian republics of Uzbekistan, Kyrgyzstan, Turkmenistan and Tajikistan, Tatarstan and Moldova (cf. Garzaniti 2009).

Garzaniti 2009) in order to reinforce demarcations through notions of exclusivity and distinction (Barth 1969).

The symbolic function of language, especially in its graphic aspect, needs to be mentioned also with regard to issues of collective self-representation in relation to the question of the "Other," together with its effect in defining a public space, and recognizing certain identities as official. There are indeed symbolic demands that are put forward whenever the space of a city or a significant public place is "re-inscribed" for identity purposes. The public and symbolic representation of certain identities can legitimize them, while a change in those same representations can deny and challenge them, reducing and marginalizing their presence and rights in a way that is visible to all. The destruction in many Balkan countries of the Islamic and Ottoman cultural (written) heritage is a paradigmatic demonstration of this, together with some more recent examples highlighted in this book, revealing the extent to which processes of national construction can be implemented in terms of (writing) negation.

The concept of the nation-state corresponding to a unified linguistic community has proved to be very influential in the post-socialist context, as it did in the period following the dissolution of the previous empires, Habsburg and Ottoman. It is not surprising, therefore, that within the new state structures, attempts at "homogenization" are the norm, consisting in language policies aimed at affirming the "naturalness" of a monolingual and monoalphabetic situation, while multilingualism and multigraphism are perceived as a problematic and "disturbing" condition. Yet, in most cases, the "biunivocal correspondence" between alphabet and culture is relatively recent, having been refuted on numerous occasions in the past, especially in the Balkans, by important practices of cultural synthesis and syncretism characteristic of multiethnic societies, where contacts between different communities were the order of the day.

There were indeed Armenian communities using the Turkish language (with the Armenian alphabet), Sephardic Jewish communities using the Greek language, Turkish-speaking Slavs, as well as Pomak (Muslim) Bulgarians writing in the Greek alphabet, and many other examples (cf. Zakhos-Papazahariou 1972: 154, Parmeggiani Dri 2005: 12). The disruption of practices of exchange between communities due to the emergence of the "exclusionary" idea of the nation-state has undoubtedly had a detrimental effect on cultural diversity and heterogeneous identities, contributing to the submersion of valuable examples of long-standing cultures that did not fit into the canonical category of the nation. As a consequence, "the cultural centralism of nation-states has succeeded in removing most of the particularism of ethnic groups, especially when they bear some linguistic resemblance to the ethnic groups of the neighboring country" (Zakhos-Papazahariou 1972: 178; my translation).[112]

In the cases I have analyzed, I have not only placed alphabets in the appropriate context of socio-political and cultural signification, but also demonstrated how writing systems can achieve a kind of emancipation from the linguistic dimension of which they are the bearers, by taking on non-alphabetic and non-phonemic properties that sometimes make them more similar to complex systems such as ideographs. If the classical Augustinian definition of letters according to phonological criteria (Todorov 2008 [1977]: 65) is based on the concept of written language as dependent on the orality of pronunciation, some of the examples discussed demonstrate that, in the case of the use of writing systems for national identity purposes, this fundamental basis of correspondence between sound and sign is undermined by the emergence of another level of interpretation of writing, namely the symbolic one. In practice, it looks

---

[112] In his article, Zakhos-Papazahariou made a prediction that would turn out to be resoundingly mistaken: "In the new phase of the struggle of cultures in the Balkans, more than one ethnic peculiarity risks being distanced from the official cultures of the nation states that lock it up between their borders. But this time, while religions may still play some role, alphabets will no longer play the central role they had in the struggle of cultures on Balkan soil over the past five centuries" (179; my translation). As demonstrated in the parts of this book devoted to the post-socialist moment in Croatia and Serbia, history proved him wrong.

as if an ideographic aspect was recovered: ideographic scripts transcribe thoughts (ideas), not language, and therefore they reveal themselves to some extent (especially in the case of the Glagolitic alphabet) as precise notions of identity to be preserved, rather than sounds to be pronounced.

This symbolic and ideological aspect of the alphabet in the process of identity construction emerges clearly in all the cases of "alphabetic controversies" I have considered, involving different writing systems, countries and actors in the Balkans. It formed an essential component in the discussion surrounding the publication of the school primer *Abecedar* for the Slavic population of Aegean Macedonia in Latin letters, as well as in the positions of Bulgarian intellectuals in the early 1930s who opposed the abandonment of the Cyrillic alphabet, and in those of the Bulgarian government that obstructed the adoption of the Latin alphabet by the Turkish community within its borders. The same is true when considering the alphabet debates in the Kingdom of Yugoslavia, which, although oriented on different fronts, demonstrated the importance of the element of the alphabet in the construction of a new collective identity, while recognizing its value in maintaining the different cultural traditions of the peoples that formed the new political identity.

The emblematic case of the Independent State of Croatia, examined in relation to its "purist" policies in the linguistic and alphabetic spheres, confirms the role of writing systems as catalysts of the "mania for control" within totalitarian regimes, which, by virtue of their power, use them to visually and symbolically represent an exclusionary and "monovalent" idea of the nation. The treatment of the issue of the Glagolitic alphabet in Croatia since the 1970s has only marginally included the related linguistic dimension, focusing almost exclusively on its symbolic component, which conveys both historiographical and aesthetic, or rather "iconic" messages. However, this theme was related to the alphabetic developments that the country experienced since the collapse of Yugoslavia, showing that, in this situation of the "rediscovery" of its national heritage, this alphabet took on a quite different role from the one attributed to it by intellectuals such as Zvane Črnja during the Yugoslav period. The post-socialist situation of symmetrical "rivalry" with the Serbian neighbor has led to new manifestations of intolerance towards the Cyrillic alphabet in Croatia, substantiating the power of the alphabet in creating and representing cultural divisions as well as political boundaries.

Finally, Bulgaria's post-socialist transition was marked by a kind of "identity crisis" which in many ways also affected the Cyrillic alphabet, engaging it in new debates about its suitability for modern and "modernizing" purposes, particularly in relation to the process of integration and convergence with the European Union and its use in modern communication technologies. Cyrillic seems to have emerged fortified from this phase of "rewriting the nation," participating in the dynamics of repositioning the country in the new global order and in the renewed rhetoric about the legacy of the Cyrillo-Methodian mission in Bulgaria. Cyrillic, adopted by the European institutions as the third writing system at the official level, has been validated as an inalienable element of "cultural diversity" that continues to play a fundamental role in the practices of internal and external representation of Bulgarian identity, while keeping its symbolic meaning intact.

Cardona maintained that neglecting or ignoring for too long the fundamental symbolic function of writing contributed to creating significant gaps in our knowledge of the practices and meanings related to the cultural worlds in which it is embedded: "We still know too little, even simply about the different traditions, the different ideological systems, the [...] ethno-graphia" (Cardona 1982: 4; my translation). The subject appears undoubtedly thorny and complex, and this book, while not claiming to provide "absolute" or "definitive" interpretations, has endeavored to answer the question raised by the great pioneer of the anthropology of writing as comprehensively as possible in relation to the Balkan region, and to highlight the currency and relevance of alphabet questions in this fascinating area of the world.

12. LIST OF REFERENCES

Primary Sources

Aranđelović, D. 1934. "Dva mišljenja o jugoslovenskoj azbuci". *Život i rad* VII (118): 861-862.

Belić, A. 1923. *Pravopis srpskohrvatskog književnog jezika*. Beograd: Skerlić.

Belić, A. 1935. "Nova azbuka". *Naš Jezik* III (1) 1935: 1- 3

Belić, A. 1949. *Borba oko našeg književnog jezika i pravopisa: predavanje održano na Kolarčevom narodnom univerzitetu*. Beograd: Kolarčev narodni univerzitet.

Belić, A. & Žeželj A. 1940. *Gramatika srpskohrvatskog jezika za I razred srednjih škola*. Beograd: Kreditna i pripomoćna zadruga Profesorskog društva.

Brajkova, D. 2007. "'Върви народе възродени... Или празникът на буквите". *ProGRAFICA* 1: 1-2.

Bratulić, J., Čačić, B., Janeš, Ž., Jendričko, S. & Paro, F. 1987. *Svečanost glagoljice*. Sisak: Centar za kulturu Vladimir Nazor.

Bratulić, J. 2009. "Kultura je dio politike". *Vijenac* 393, 23 March 2009 (online version) https://www.matica.hr/vijenac/393/kultura-je-dio-politike-3551/

Bratulić, J. 2014. "Hrvatska cirilica kao poslovno pismo". *Filologija* 63: 17-32.

Tsenov, G. 2014. *Произходът на българите и начало на българската държава и българската църква*. Sofia: Heliopol.

Črnja, Z. 1962. *Cultural history of Croatia*. Zagreb: Office of Information.

Črnja, Z. 1966. *Žminjski libar*. Rijeka: Matica hrvatska.

Črnja, Z. 1971. *Hrvatski Don Kihoti*. Rijeka: Otokar Keršovani.

Črnja, Z. 1978a. *Pogled iz provincije*. Pula: Impresum.

Črnja, Z. 1978b. *Kulturna povijest Hrvatske* I-III. Opatija: Otokar Keršovani.

Črnja, Z. and Bertoša M. 1968. *Knjiga o Istri*. Zagreb: Školska knjiga.

Čunčić, M. 1995. "Kulturna baština i hrvastki identitet". *Hrvatsko slovo. Tjednik za kulturu* XX (1005): 3-4.

Đorđević, M. 1931. "Анкета о буквицама: две словенске буквице". *Letopis Matice Srpske* CV (327): 150-153.

Faryno, J. 2002. "Европейска азбука! Възможна ли е?". In *Literaturen Forum*, 6 (490): 1-12. Electronic version: https://www.slovo.bg/old/litforum/206/yefarino.htm (last access: 3/11/2021).

Filipova, L. 2014. *Войната на буквите*. Sofia: Egmont, 2014.

Gaj, L. 1830. *Kratka osnova horvatsko-slavenskoga pravopisa – Kurzer Entwurf einer kroatisch- slavischen Ortographie.* Budim.

Georgiev B. 2000 "Националните езикови митове днес", in: *Literaturen Forum* 9 (432), (electronic version) http://www.slovo.bg/old/litforum/009/bgeorgiev.htm (last access: 3/11/2021).

Goshev, I., 1985 [1930]. "Латиница или кирилица". In: Popstefanov Smilov, B. and Živkova Pavova, C. (eds.), *И на вси словене книга да четат. Сборник материали за Кирил и Методий.* Sofia: Sinodalno Izdatelstvo: 152-155.

Guberina, P., & Krstić, K. 1940. *Razlike između hrvatskoga i srpskoga književnog jezika.* Zagreb: Matica hrvatska.

Horvat, J. 2009. *Az.* Zagreb: Ljevak.

Hrvatski narod II (50), 19 January 1940.

Hrvatski narod (posebno izdanje) III, 10 April 1941.

Hrvatski narod III (96), 19 May 1941.

Hrvatski narod III (135), 29 June 1941.

Isaković, V. 1931. "За једно писмо". *Letopis Matice Srpske* CV (328): 141-142.

Ivanov, S. 2001. "За буквите: кирилица vs latinica". *Капитал*, 2/6/2000 (electronic version). https://www.capital.bg/politika_i_ikonomika/obshtestvo/2001/06/02/209103_za_bukvite_kirilica_vs_latinitca/ (last access: 3/11/2021).

Yakovlev N. F. 1930. "За латинизацию русского алфавита". In *Культура и письменность востока* 6: 27- 43.

Jendričko, S. 2014. "Ironični demistifikator globalnih (i lokalnih) mitova", *Kolo* 2. (online version). Available at: https://www.matica.hr/kolo/424/Ironi%C4%8Dni%20demistifikator%20globalnih%20(i%20lokalnih)%20mitova/ (last access: 3/11/2021).

Jergović, M. 2013. "Ako je kad i bila, ćirilica odavno nije hrvatsko pismo". (online) https://www.jergovic.com/sumnjivo-lice/ako-je-kad-i-bila-cirilica-odavno-nije-hrvatsko-pismo/ (last access: 3/11/2021).

Jespersen, O. 1934. "Introduction". In: Société des Nations. *L'adoption universelle des caractères latins. Institut international de coopération intellectuelle.* Paris: Librairie Stock: 13-26

Jespersen, O. 2010 [1928]. "Introduction, an international language". In *Selected Writings of Otto Jespersen.* London: Routledge: 400-410.

Katedra Balgarska Literatura. 2001. "Открито писмо до Професор Ото Кронщайнер—Залцбург". *Literaturen Forum* 29 (470) (electronic version). https://www.slovo.bg/old/litforum/129/vtu.htm (last access: 3/11/2021)

Kronsteiner, O. 2000a. "Latinica *und* Kirilica? Gedanken zu einer entscheidenden kulturellen Herausforderung Bulgariens". *Die Slavischen Sprachen* 65: 7-20.

Kronsteiner, O. 2000b. "*Аз съм за кирилица, Az săm za Latinica*. За двете азбуки трябва да има място в ЕС". *Die Slavischen Sprachen* 65: 32-43.

Kronsteiner, O. 2001a. "Чуждестранна Българистика". *Literaturen Forum* 29 (470). (electronic Version) https://www.slovo.bg/old/litforum/129/otok.htm (last access: 3/11/2021)

Kronsteiner, O. 2001b "При вас все още има българисти които живеят в средновековието", Interview appeared on the Bulgarian Daily *Demokracija* on September 24, 2001.

Kronsteiner, O. 2001c. "Пишете един ден на кирилица, един на латиница". Interview appeared on the Bulgarian Daily *24 Chasa* on September 25, 2001: 10-11.

Krstić, K. 1942a. "Pitanje srbizama". *Alma Mater Croatica* V: 296-298.

Krstić, K. 1942b. "Povijesni put hrvatskoga knjizevnog jezika". *Hrvatska revija* XV (8): 412-420.

Kutinchev, S. 1930. "Кирилица или латиница. Българският шрифт". *Balgarska Kniga* I (2): 173-174.

Kujundžić, V. 1934. "Jugoslovenska latinica". *Život i rad* VII (118): 862-864.

Makedonski, A. 1930. "Кирилица или латиница. Българският шрифт". *Balgarska Kniga* I (2): 166-168.

Malin, F. 1930. "Za jedno pismo". *Letopis Matice Srpske* CIV (326): 181-187.

Miletich, L. 1925. "Нова латинска писменост за македонските българи под Гърция. Abecedar". *Makedonski Pregled* I (5-6): 229-232.

Mircheva, E. 1998. "За българския език — maytapsiz". *Култура* 22 (2296) (electronic Version elettronica) www.kultura.bg/bg/print_article/view/920 (last access: 3/11/2021)

Mladenov, S. 1930. "Кирилица или латиница. Българският шрифт". *Balgarska Kniga* I (2): 177-178.

Mladenov, S. 1931. "Кирлица или латиница". *Rodna Reč* IV: 3-6

Mladenov, S. 1934. "Bulgarie". In: Société des Nations. *L'adoption universelle des caractères latins. Institut international de coopération intellectuelle.* Paris: Librairie Stock: 178-179.

Mlaednov, I. 2005. "Наука и срам. Предговор". In *Истината за Професор Кронщайнер*, edited by Kronsteiner, O., et al. Sofia: Rabotilnica za knizhnina Vasil Stanilov: 8-19.

Omarchevski, S. 1930. "Кирилица или латиница. Българският шрифт". *Balgarska Kniga* I (2): 178.

Pelin, E. 1930. "Кирилица или латиница. Българският шрифт". In *Balgarska Kniga* I (2): 178.

Peregud Pogoreljski, T.K. 1924. *Album šrifta: ćirilica i latinica*. Zemun.

Plochev, T. J. 1930. "Кирилица или латиница. Българският шрифт". In *Balgarska Kniga* I (2): 172-173.

Popova, D. 1998. "Латински български—bez maytap". In *Kultura* 20 (2294) (electronic version) http://www.online.bg/kultura/my_html/2029/diana.htm (last access: 3/11/2021)

Radev, I., Kenanov, D. & Vasilev, S. 2002. *'Случаят' Ото Кронщайнер и кирилицата българистика, малките филологии*. Veliko Tarnovo: Universitetsko Izdatelstvo Sv. Sv. Kiril i Metodiji.

Radivojević, P. Ž. 1934. *Ћирилица—Латиница? Или Ћирилица у Латиници*. Beograd: Privrednik.

Sagiaksis, G., Lazarou, I. & Papazahariou. 1925. *Abecedar*. Athens: Typois P. D. Sakellariou.

Siderov, V. 2011. *Основи на Българизма*. Sofia: PP Ataka.

Shishmanov, I. 1926. *L'Abécédaire à l'usage des minorités bulgares en Grèce*. Sofia: Imprimerie de la Cour.

Skerlic´, J. 1913. Источно или јужно наречје?. *Српски књижевни гласник*, XXXI (11): 862-873.

Skerlic´, J. 1914, "Анкета о јужном или источном наречју у српско хрватској књижевности". *Српски књижевни гласник*, Књ. XXXII, (2): 114-125.

Skitnik, S. 1930. "Кирилица или латиница. Българският шрифт". *Balgarska Kniga* I (2): 176.

Société des Nations. 1934. *L'adoption universelle des caractères latins. Institut international de coopération intellectuelle*. Paris: Librairie Stock.

Stainov, P. 1930. "Кирилица или латиница. Българският шрифт". *Balgarska Kniga* I (2): 175-176.

Starčević, A. 1852. "Odgovor Srbskome Dnevniku i beogradskim novinam". *Narodne Novine* 221.

Stojanov, K. 2007. "голготата на българските кирилски шрифтове". *ProGRAFICA* (1): 12-15.

Stojanović, B. 1934. "Jugoslovenska Azbuka". *Život i Rad* VII (116): 724-733.

Stošić, P. 1931. "Неколико речи о потреби једног писма". *Letopis Matice Srpske* CV (327): 154-158.

Tanev, H. 1997. *АЗ-ът на българите и националните символи*. Sofia: Heliopol.

Tihanov, G. 2001. "Репресия и автономия". *Literaturen Vestnik* 11 (32) (electronic version) http://eprints.nbu.bg/1983/1/lv0132002.htm (last access: 3/11/2021)

Trivunac, M. 1931. *Ćirilica ili Latinica?* Beograd: Rajković i Ćuković.

Udicki, J. 1931. *Način učenje latinice posle ćirilice i ćirilice posle latinice.* Novi Sad: Štamparija učiteljskog d. Natoševic ́.

Vogrinec, M. 2013. "Politikantska kvadratura ćiriličnog kruga" (online version) http://www.zarez.hr/clanci/politikantska-kvadratura-cirilicnog-kruga (last access: 3/11/2021)

Vaillant, A. 1934. "Yugoslavie". In Société des Nations. *L'adoption universelle des caractères latins. Institut international de coopération intellectuelle.* Paris: Librairie Stock: 184.

Žagar, M. 2012. "Hrvatska ćirilica dio je bogatstva hrvatske povijesne raznolikosti". *Vijenac* XX (488) (online version) https://www.matica.hr/vijenac/488/Hrvatska%20%C4%87irilica%20dio%20je%20bogatstva%20hrvatske%20povijesne%20raznolikosti/ (last access: 3/11/2021)

Zahariev, V. 1930. "Кирилица или латиница. Българският шрифт". In *Balgarska Kniga* I (2): 169-171.

Zhekov, I. 2001. "От азбука към alphabet". In *Literaturen Forum* 21 (462) (electronic version). https://www.slovo.bg/old/litforum/121/izhekov.htm (last access: 3/11/2021)

Živaljević, D., A. 1935. *Ćirilica i Latinica.* Beograd: Privrednik.

Official Legislative Sources

BAN. 2001. Информационен бюлетин на БАН VI (50): 6-7.

Dogovor. 2005. Договор относно присъединяването на България и Румъния към Европейския съюз, Декларация на Република България относно използването на кирилицата в Европейския съюз. In Официален Вестник на Европейския съюз, 21/6/2005, p. 392.

European Charter for Regional or Minority Languages, Strasbourg, 1992.

Kanun. 1928. Yeni Türk harflerinin kabul ve tatbiki hakkında kanun. Kanun Numurası: 1353. Ankara. 3 November 1928.

Krfska deklaracija. 1917. In Srpske Novine 83, Beograd, 13 July 1917.

Memorandum SANU. 1986. Memorandum Srpske Akademije Nauke i Umetnosti, appeared in the Belgrade daily *Večernje novosti* on September 24th and 25th, 1986.

Mermagen N. 2012. Report: Local elections in Serbia, The Congress of Local and Regional Authorities of the Council of Europe, 6 May 2012.

Novosadski dogovor. 1954. "Zaključci novosadskog sastanka o hrvatskom ili srpskom jeziku i pravopisu". *Jezik* 3 (5), Zagreb: 65-68.

Pravopisno upustvo: za sve osnovne, srednje i stručne škole u Kraljevini S.H.S., Ministarstvo Prosvete kraljevine SHS. Beograd: Državna štamparija, 1929.

Proekt Zakon za Balgarski Ezik no.454-01-40, included in the register XXXIX of the Narodno Sabranie in Sofia on 26.05.2004.

Minorities in Croatia. Report. Minority Rights Group International, London, 2003. Available online: http://www.refworld.org/pdfid/469cbf8f0.pdf (last access: 3/11/2021)

Recommendation CM/RecChL (2015)2 of the Committee of Ministers on the application of the European Charter for Regional or Minority Languages by Croatia, adopted by the Committee of Minister April 15, 2015. Available online: https://www.coe.int/t/dg4/education/minlang/Report/Recommendations/CroatiaCMRec5_en.pdf (last access: 3/11/2021)

Rješenje. Republika Hrvatska Ministarstvo kulture. Uprava za zaštitu kulturne baštine. Ur. broj 532-04-01-02-02/2-14/1, Zagreb, 7 Feburary 2014.

"Statut grada Vukovar". *Službeni Vjesnik. Službeno glasilo grada Vukovara* X (4). July 16, 2009.

Stenografski Dnevnici. 1928. Стенографски Дневници на XXII-то обикновено народно събрание. Редовна сесия 47, 1 March 1928, Sofia: 871-886.

Treaty Series n. 11, 1920. London: His Majesty's Stationery Office.

Treaty of Friendship. 1926. Treaty of Friendship between Bulgaria and Turkey. In League of Nations. Treaty Series 54: 127-133.

Progress of literacy in various countries. A preliminary statistical study on available census data since 1900, UNESCO, Paris, 1953.

Ustav Socialističke Republike Hrvatske. *Narodne Novine* 8. 24 Feburary 1974: 110-161.

Ustav Republike Hrvatske. In *Narodne Novine* 56, nr 1092. 22 December 1990.

Ustavni zakon o pravima nacionalnih manjina Republike Hrvatske. In *Narodne Novine*, n.155, 2002.

Secondary Sources

Aleksandrov, V. 2000. *Европейската идея*. Sofia: Voen. Izd.

Alipieva, A. 2013. "Literature and Nationalism in Bulgaria in the Last 25 Years. A Look from Inside". In Proceedings from the 1st Human and Social Sciences at the Common Conference, Žilina: 256-264

Allcock, J. 2000. *Explaining Yugoslavia*. New York: Columbia University Press.

Alpatov, V. M. 2001. "Un projet peu connu de latinisation de l'alphabet russe". *Slavica Occitania* XII: 13-28.

Alpatov, V. M. 2002. "Alphabet reform: Cyrillic or Latin?". *Central Asia and the Caucasus* 2 (14): 116-25.

Alpatov, V. M. 2015. "A Latin alphabet for the Russian language". In *Slavic Alphabets in Contact*, edited by Tomelleri Springfield, V. & Kempgen S. Bamberg: University of Bamberg Press: 1-12.

Andreev Georgov, I. 1926. "Fouques Duparc, La protection des minorités de race, de langue et de religion". *Makedonski Pregled* 2 (1): 132-139.

Arnheim, R. 1974. *Il pensiero visivo. La percezione visiva come attività conoscitiva*. Torino: Einaudi. (*Visual Thinking*, Berkeley: Rudolf Books [1969]).

Arutyunov, S. 2001. "Всеобщий переход на латиницу неизбежен". (online version) https://echo.msk.ru/programs/beseda/15310/ (last access: 3/11/2021)

Ashbrook, J. 2011 "Politicization of identity in a European borderland: Istria, Croatia, and authenticity, 1990-2003". *Nationalities Papers. The Journal of Nationalism and Ethnicity* XXXIX (6): 871-897.

Assman, J. 2011. *Cultural memory and early civilization. Writing, remembrance and political imagination*. Cambridge: Cambridge University Press.

Augustinović, Đ. 1846. *Misli o ilirskom pravopisu: s tablicom glagolski i ćirilski slovah*. Vienna: Šmidova štamparija.

Babić, G. 2000. *Ustaški zakoni*. Beograd: Adeona—Stručna knjiga.

Baglioni D., & Tribulato, O. 2015. "Introduzione". In *Contatti di lingue—contatti di scritture. Multilinguismo e multigrafismo dal Vicino Oriente Antico alla Cina contemporanea*, edited by Baglioni D., & Tribulato O. Venezia: Edizioni Ca' Foscari: 9-38.

Balım, Ç. 1996. "Turkish as a symbol of survival and identity in Bulgaria and Turkey". In *Language and Identity* in the *Middle East and North Africa*, edited by Suleiman, Y. London: Curzon Press: 101-115.

Bakić-Hayden, M. 1995. "Nesting Orientalisms: The Case of Former Yugoslavia". *Slavic Review* LIV (4): 917-931.

Banac, I. 1984. "Main Trends in the Croat Language Question". In *Aspects of the Slavic language question, vol. I, Church Slavonic—South Slavic—West Slavic*, edited by Picchio, R., Goldblatt, H. New Haven: Yale Concilium on International and Area Studies: 189-259.

Bardos, N. G. 2013. *Ethnoconfessional nationalism in the Balkans: analysis manifestation and management*. Doctoral Thesis. New York: Columbia University.

Barkey, K. 1997. "Thinking about consequences of Empire". In *After Empire. Multiethnic societies and nation-building. The Soviet Union and the Russian, Ottoman and Habsburg Empires*, edited by Barkey K. & Von Hagen. Boulder—Oxford: Westview: 99-114.

Barth F., 1969. *Ethnic groups and boundaries. The social organization of culture difference*. Oslo: Universitetsforlaget.

Barton, D. 1994. *Literacy: An Introduction to the Ecology of Written Language*. Oxford: Blackwell.

Barton, D. & Papen, U. 2010. "What is the anthropology of writing?". In *The anthropology of writing*, edited by D. Barton & U. Papen. London: Continuum, London: 3-26.

Bartulin, N. 2006. *The ideology of nation and race: the Croatian Ustasha regime and its policies towards minorities in the independent state of Croatia, 1941-1945*, Doctoral Thesis. University of New South Wales.

Bateson, G. 1977. *Verso un'ecologia della mente*. Milano: Adelphi (Steps to an Ecology of the Mind. University of Chicago, 1972).

Batovic, A. 2009. "The Balkans in Turmoil—Croatian Spring and the Yugoslav position Between the Cold War Blocs 1965-1971" Cold War Studies Programme Paper, London School of Economics, 2009.

Bekerie, A. 1997. *Ethiopic. An African Writing System: Its History and Principles*. Lawrenceville: RSP.

Bellamy, A. J. 2003. *The Formation of Croatian National Identity: A Centuries-Old Dream?* Manchester: Manchester University Press.

Bernal, J. M. 2007. "Spelling and script debates in interwar Greece". *Byzantine and Modern Greek Studies* 31 (2): 170-190.

Berry, J. 1977. "'The making of alphabets' revisited". In *Advances in the Creation and Revision of Writing Systems*, edited by Fishman, J. The Hague, Mouton: 3-16.

Biletić, B. 2001. *Bartuljska Jabuka: Ogledi o književnom djelu Zvane Črnje*. Buzet: Reprezent.

Billig, M. 1995. *Banal nationalism*. London: Sage.

Biscaldi, A. & Matera, V. 2016. *Antropologia della comunicazione. Interazioni, linguaggi, narrazioni*. Bologna: Carocci.

Bjelić, D. I. 2011. *Normalizing the Balkans. Geopolitics of Psychanalisis and Psychiatry*. Farnham: Ashgate.

Bogdanović, B. 1995. "The City and Death". In *Balkan Blues. Writing out of Yugoslavia*, edited by Labon J. Illinois: Northwestern University Press: 36-73.

Bojadžiev T. 2008. "Езиковата ситуация у нас в исторически и съвременен план и европейската езикова политика". *Balgarski Ezik* 3: 5-28.

Bojić, V. 1977. *Jacob Grimm und Vuk Karadžić, Ein Vergleich ihrer Sprachauffassungen und ihre Zusammenarbeit auf dem Gebiet der serbischen Grammatik*. München: Verlag Otto Sagner.

Boneva V. 2001. "Идеологии и букви или Букви за идеологиите", in: *Literaturen Forum*, n. 38 (479) (electronic version). https://www.slovo.bg/old/litforum/138/vboneva.htm (last access: 3/11/2021).

Bourdieu, P. 1989. "Social Space and Symbolic Power". *Sociological Theory* 7(1): 14-25.

Bourdieu, P. 1990. In *Other Words: Essays Towards a Reflexive Sociology*. Stanford: Stanford University Press.

Bratulić, J. 1983. *Aleja glagoljaša: Roč – Hum*. Roč: Katedra Čakavskog sabora.

Brehmer, B. 2015. "The Cyrillic Script as a Boundary Marker between 'Insiders' and 'Outsiders': Metalinguistic Discourse about Script Choices in Slavic-German Bilingual Computer-Mediated Communication". In *Linguistic Construction of Ethnic Borders*, edited by Rosenberg, P., Jungbluth, K. & Zinkhahn Rhobodes, D. Frankfurt am Main: Peter Lang: 55-80.

Brooks, T. 2010. *Endangered alphabets. An essay on writing*. Burlington: The Champlain College Publishing Initiative.

Bugajski, J. 2000. "Nationalist Majority Parties: The anatomy of ethnic domination in Central and Eastern Europe". In *The Politics of National Minority Participation in Post-communist Societies: State-building, Democracy and Ethnic Mobilization*, edited by Stein, J. P. London: Routledge: 65-100.

Bugarski, R. 1997. *Jezik od mira do rata*. Beograd: Slovograf.

Bugarski, R. 2004a. "Language and Boundaries in the Yugoslav Context". In *Language, Discourse and Borders in the Yugoslav Successor States*, edited by Busch, B., & Holmes K. Clevedon – Buffalo – Toronto: Multilingual Matters Ltd: 21-37.

Bugarski, R. et al. 2004b. "Debate. Codification, Borders and Linguists as Political Actors". In *Language, Discourse and Borders in the Yugoslav Successor States*, edited by Busch, B., & Holmes K. Clevedon – Buffalo – Toronto: Multilingual Matters Ltd: 50-66.

Bugarski, R. 2009a *Nova lica jezika*. Beograd: Biblioteka XX Vek.

Bugarski, R. 2009b. *Pismo*. Beograd: Cigoja.

Bunčić, D. 2016. "Introduction". In: *Biscriptality: A Sociolinguistic Typology*, edited by Bunčić, D., Lippert, S., L. & Rabus, A. Heidelberg: Universitätsverlag Winter: 15-25.

Bunčić, D. 2016. "A heuristic model for typology", In: *Biscriptality: A Sociolinguistic Typology*, edited by Bunčić, D., Lippert, S., L. & Rabus, A. Heidelberg: Universitätsverlag Winter: 51-72.

Bunčić, D. 2017. "Factors Influencing the Success and Failure of Writing Reforms". *Studi Slavistici* XIV: 21-46.

Caferoğlu, A. 1934. "Turquie". In: Société des Nations. *L'adoption universelle des caractères latins. Institut international de coopération intellectuelle*. Paris: Librairie Stock: 121-131.

Canakis, C. 2018. "Contesting Identity in the Linguistic Landscape of Belgrade: An Ethnographic Approach". *Belgrade English Language and Literature Studies (BELLS)* 10: 229-258.

Cardona, G. R. 1982. "Introduzione". *La Ricerca Folklorica* 5: *La scrittura: funzioni e ideologie*: 3-7.

Cardona, G. R. 1986. *Storia universale della scrittura*. Milano: Mondadori.

Cardona, G. R. 2009a. *Antropologia della scrittura*. Torino: Utet [1981].

Cardona, G. R. 2009b. *Introduzione alla sociolinguistica*. Torino: Utet [1987].

Chartier, R. 1992. "Laborers and Voyagers: From the Text to the Reader". *Diacritics* 22 (2): 49-61.

Clayer, N. 2004. "Le premier journal de langue turque en caractères latins : Esas (Manastır/Bitola, 1911)". *Turcica*, 36: 253-264.

Clement, V. 2008. "Emblems of independence: script choice in post-Soviet Turkmenistan in the 1990s". In *International Journal on the Sociology of Language* 192: 171-185.

Cohen, L., J. 1995. *Broken Bonds: Yugoslavia's Disintegration and Balkan Politics in Transition*. Boulder: Westview Press.

Collin, R. O. 2011. "Revolutionary scripts". In *Culture and language. Multidisciplinary case studies*, edited by Morris, M. Frankfurt am Main: Peter Lang: 29-67.

Coulmas, F. 1989. *The Writing Systems of the World*. London: Basil Blackwell.

Coulmas, F. 2000. "The nationalizing of Writing". In *Studies in the Linguistic Sciences* 30 (1): 47-59.

Crampton, R., J. 1997. *A Concise History of Bulgaria*. Cambridge: Cambridge University Press.

Crampton, R. J. 2002. *The Balkans since the Second World War*. London: Routledge.

Crisp, S. 1990. "Soviet Language Planning since 1917-53". In *Language planning in the Soviet Union*, edited by Kirkwood, M. London: Palgrave Macmillian: 23-45.

Cubberley, P. 2003. "Alphabets and transliteration". In *The Slavonic Languages*, edited by Comrie, B. London: Taylor & Francis: 20-60.

Čunčić, M. 2003. *Izvori hrvatske pisane rijeci*. Zagreb: Školska Knjiga.

Daiber, T. 2015. "Bemerkungen zum Alphabet auf Ikonen von Konstantin-Kyrill". In *Slavic Alphabets in Contact*, edited by Springfield Tomellieri, V. & Kempgen, S. Bamberg: Bamberg University Press: 131-158.

Dale, I. R. H. 1980. "Digraphia". *International Journal of the Sociology of Language* 26: 5–13.

Daskalov, R. 2011. *Debating the Past: Modern Bulgarian History from Stambolov to Zhivkov*. Budapest—New York: Central European University Press.

Daskalov, R., & Vezenkov, A. 2015. "Introduction". In *Entangled Histories of the Balkans, Vol. 3. Shared Pasts, Disputed Legacies*, edited by Daskalov R., Vezenkov A. Leiden—Boston: Brill: 1-9.

Dayıoğlu, A. 2005. "Toplama Kampından Meclise; Bulgaristan'da Türk Azınlığı ve Müslüman Azınlığı". İstanbul: İletişim Yayınları.

De Certeau, M. 2005. *La scrittura dell'altro*. Milano: Raffaello Cortina Editore (*L'Écriture de l'histoire*. Paris: Gallimard [1975])

Дечев, Z. 2014. *Устност-Писменост във възрожденската култура*. Sofia: Zhanet 45.

Denich, B. 1993. "Unmaking multiethnicity in Yugoslavia: Metamorphosis observed". In *Anthropology of East Europe Review* 11 (1-2): 48-60.

Đerić, G. 2005. *Pr(a)vo lice mnozine. Kolektivno samopoimanje i predstavljanje: mitovi, karakteri, mentalne mape i stereotipi*. Beograd: Institut za filozofiju i društvenu teoriju Filip Višnjić.

Dermendžieva, M. 2015. "Убива ли се вик на свобода". In *Kultura* (electronic version) http://kultura.bg/web/убива-ли-се-вик-за-свобода (last access: 3/11/2021).

Dogo, M. 1999. *Storie balcaniche. Popoli e stati nella transizione alla modernità*. Gorizia: Libreria editrice goriziana.

Đorđević, V. 2012. "Da li je Vuk tvorac srpske latinice". In *Nova srpska politička misao* (online version) http://www.nspm.rs/kulturna-politika/da-li-je-vuk-tvorac-srpske-latinice.html?alphabet=c> (last access: 3/11/2021).

Đorđević, V. 2014. "Problemi sa dvoazbučnošću. In *Ćirilococid*, edited by Zbiljić, D., & Ivanović, D. J. Novi Sad: Ćirilica: 354-369.

Drücker, J. 1995. *The Alphabetic Labyrinth: The Letters in History and Imagination*. New York: Thamesand Hudson.

Druckman, D. 1994. "Nationalism, Patriotism, and Group Loyalty: A Social Psychological Perspective". *Mershon International Studies Review* 38 (1): 43-68

Duličenko, A 2001. "Changements d'alphabets et doubles alphabets dans les langues slaves orientales: histoire et pratique". *Slavica Occitania* XII: 171-189.

Durand, O. 2014. "L'uso politico-ideologico della scrittura". In *Etnografia della scrittura*, edited by Mancini M. & Turchetta, B. Roma: Carocci: 205-227.

Đurđević, D. F., Milin P., & Feldman, L. B. "Bi-alphabetism: A window on phonological processing". *Psihologija* 46 (4): 421-438.

Edroiu, N. 2015. "La questione alfabetica nelle terre rumene dal XVII al XIX secolo". In *Studi cirillometodiani. Nel 1150° anniversario della missione tra gli Slavi dei santi Cirillo e Metodio*, edited by Stantchev, K. & Ziffer, G. Milano–Roma: Biblioteca Ambrosiana–Bulzoni Editore: 225-242.

Edwards, J. 1985. *Language, Society and Identity*. London: Blackwell & Deutsch.

Edwards, J. 2009. *Language and identity: an introduction*. Cambridge: Cambridge University Press.

Eglitis, D. S. 2002. *Imagining the Nation: History, Modernity, and Revolution in Latvia*. Pennsylvania State University Press.

Ekl, V. & Fučić, B. 1968. *Glagoljica, izložba: vodič*. Rijeka: Naučna biblioteka.

Elsie, R. 2017. *Albanian Alphabets. Borrowed and Invented*. CreateSpace Independent Publishing Platform.

Eminov, A. 1997. *Turkish and other Muslim minorities of Bulgaria*. London: Hurst & Co.

Fabietti, U. 2014. "Ideologie della scrittura riguardo ai popoli 'senza scrittura'". In *Etnografia della scrittura*, edited by Mancini M. & Turchetta, B. Roma: Carocci: 229-261.

Feldman L. & Barac-Cikoja D. 2006. "Serbo-Croatian: A Biscriptal Language," In *The World's Writing Systems*, edited by Daniels P. & Wright W. New York: Oxford University Press: 769-772.

Fishman, J. 1972. *Language in Sociocultural Change*. Stanford: Stanford University Press.

Fishman J. 1977. "Introduction". In *Advances in the Creation and Revision of Writing Systems*, edited by Fishman, J. The Hague: Mouton: XI-XXVII.

Fishman, J. 1988. *Language and ethnicity in minority sociolinguistic perspective*. Clevedon: Multilingual matters.

Fouques-Duparc, J. 1922. *La protection des minorités de race, de langue et de religion. Ètude des droits des gens.* Paris: Dalloz.

Freud, S. 1919. "Das Unheimliche". In *Imago. Zeitschrift für Anwendung der Psychoanalyse auf die Geisteswissenschaften* V: 297-324.

Frusetta, G. 2006. "Common Heroes, Divided Claims: IMRO Between Macedonia and Bulgaria". In Ideologies and National Identities. The Case of Twentieth-Century Southeastern Europe, edited by J. Lampe & M. Mazower, Budapest: Central European University Press: 110-130.

Galanti, A. 1995. *Arabi Harflar Tarakkimize mani değildir.* İstanbul: Kitabevi Yayınları [1927].

Gamkrelidze, T. V. 1994. *Alphabetic writing and the old Georgian script. A typology and provenience of Alphabetic writing systems.* Delmar—New York: Caravan Books.

Garde, P. 2004. "Unity and Plurality in the Serbo-Croatian Linguistic Sphere". In *Language, Nation, and State: Identity Politics in a Multilingual Age*, edited by Judt, T. & Lacorne, D. New York: Palgrave Macmillan: 215-230.

Garzaniti, M. 2007. "Slavia latina e Slavia ortodossa. Per un'interpretazione della civiltà slava nell'Europa medievale". *Studi Slavistici* IV: 29-64.

Garzaniti, M. 2009. "Le lingue dai Balcani all'Asia centrale". In *XXI secolo. Comunicare e rappresentare.* Roma: Istituto della Enciclopedia italiana: 319-334.

Gažáková, Z. 2014. "Some Remarks on Aljamiado Literature and the Usage of Arebica in Bosnia and Herzegovina". In: *Script Beyond Borders: a survey of allographic traditions in the Euro-Mediterranean world.* edited by den Heijer, J., Schmidt, A. & Pataridze, T. Leuven: Peeters: 453-471.

Geertz, C. 1988. *Interpretazione di culture.* Bologna: Il mulino (*The interpretation of cultures*, New York: Basic Books [1973])

Gelb I. J. 1983. *A study of writing.* Chicago: University of Chicago Press.

Getliher, A. 1994. "Glagoljski natpis u Zagrebačkoj katedrali". *Baščina. Glasilo Društva prijatelja glagoljice* 4: 3-5.

Ghata, Y. 2006. *The Calligrapher's Night.* London: Hesperus Press.

Giatzidis, E. 2002. *An Introduction to Postcommunist Bulgaria: Political, Economic and Social Transformation.* Manchester: Manchester University Press.

Glavašević, S. 1992. *Priče iz Vukovara.* Zagreb: Matica Hrvatska.

Greenberg, R. 2004. *Language and Identity in the Balkans.* New York: Oxford University Press.

Guentcheva, R. 1999. "Symbolic Geography of Language: Orthographic Debates in Bulgaria (1880s-today)". *Language and Communication* XIX (4): 355-371.

Gundersen, D. 1977. "Successes and failures in the modernization of Norwegian spelling". In *Advances in the Creation and Revision of Writing Systems*, edited by Fishman, J. The Hague: Mouton: 247-265.

Guzina, D. 2000. "The Self-Destruction of Yugoslavia". *Canadian Review of Studies in Nationalism* 22: 21-30.

Haksöz, C. 2007. *Linguistic Rights of the Turkish Minority in Bulgaria* [Unpublished Master Thesis]. Ankara: Middle East Technical University.

Hacıoğlu, S. 2020. "1920'lerin Sovyetlerinde Latin Alfabesine Geçme Sebepleri". *Ege Üniversitesi İletişim Fakültesi Yeni Düşünceler Hakemli E-Dergisi*, (13): 4-22.

Hammel, E. A. 2000. "Lessons from the Yugoslav Labyrinth". In *Neighbors at War: Anthropological Perspectives on Yugoslav Ethnicity, Culture, and History*, edited by Halpern, Joel M. & Kideckel David A. Penn State University Press: 19-38.

Hayden, R. M. 1992. "Constitutional Nationalism in the Formerly Yugoslav Republics". *Slavic Review* 51: 654-673.

Heimer Ž. "National identity in the political flags of Croatia". In *Proceedings of the 24th International Congress of Vexillology*, Washington: 437-498.

Henze, P. B. 1997. "Politics and Alphabets in inner Asia". In *Advances in the Creation and Revision of Writing Systems*, edited by Fishman, J. The Hague: Mouton: 371-420.

Hobsbawm, E. J. 1997. "The end of empires". In *After Empire. Multiethnic societies and nation-building. The Soviet Union and the Russian, Ottoman and Habsburg Empires*, edited by Barkey K. & Von Hagen, M. Boulder—Oxford: Westview: 12-16.

Höpken, W. 1997. "From Religious Identity to Ethnic Mobilization: The Turks of Bulgaria Before, Under and Since Communism". In *Muslim Identity and the Balkan State*, edited by Poulton H. & Taji-Farouki, S. London: Hurst & Company: 54-81.

Huković, M. 1986. *Alhamijado Književnosti i njeni stvaraoci*. Sarajevo: Svjetlost.

Ivanišević, F. 1929. *Pobjeda glagoljice kroz tisućuljetnu borbu*. Split: Jugoslovenska Matica.

Ivanov, L. 2003. "On the Romanization of Bulgarian and English". *Contrastive Linguistics* XXVIII (2): 109-118.

Ivanov, A. 2007. "Minority nationalism in the Balkans: the Bulgarian case". Online version. https://ime.bg/en/articles/minority-nationalism-in-the-balkans-the-bulgarian-case/ (last access: 03/11/2021).

Janjatović, Đ (ed.). 2011. *Borba za Ćirilicu*. Novi Sad: Prometej.

Jensen, H. 1969. *Sign, Symbol and Script. An account of man's efforts to write*. New York: G. P. Putnam's Sons.

Jezernik, B (ed.). 2010. *Imaginarni turčin*. Beograd: Biblioteka XX Vek.

Johnson, S. R. 2005. *Spelling Trouble: Language, Ideology, and the Reform of German Orthography*. Clevedon: Multilingual Matters.

Jovanović, S. M. 2018. "Assertive discourse and folk linguistics: Serbian nationalist discourse about the Cyrillic script in the 21st century". *Language Policy* 17 (4): 611-631.

Kahl, T. 2012. "Ethno-cultural Diversity in the Balkans and the Caucasus as an Objective for Comparative Research". In *The Balkans and the Caucasus. Parallel Processes on the Opposite Sides of the Black Sea*, edited by Biliyarski I., Cristea O., & Oroveany A. Newcastle upon Tyne: Cambridge Scholar Publishing: 172-187.

Kamusella, T. D. 2012. "Scripts and politics in modern Central Europe". *Mitteilungen der Österreichischen Geographischen Gesellschaft* 154 (1): 9-42.

Karpat, K. 2004. *Studies on Turkish politics and society*. Leiden – Boston: Brill.

Kemplerer, V. 2011. *La lingua del terzo impero. Taccuino di un filologo*. Firenze: Giuntina (*Lingua Tertii Imperii: Notizbuch eines Philologen*. Berlin: Aufbau Verlag [1947]).

Keyder, C. 2011. "The Ottoman Empire". In *After Empire. Multiethnic societies and nation-building. The Soviet Union and the Russian, Ottoman and Habsburg Empires*, edited by Barkey K. & Von Hagen, M. Boulder – Oxford: Westview: 30-44.

King, C. 1994. "Moldovan Identity and the Politics of Pan-Romanianism". [*Slavic Review* 53 (2): 345-368.

Klajn, I. 2006. "Odumiranje ćirilice". Interview appeared on the daily *Politika*, 6 August 2006, Beograd. (Online version) http://www.politika.rs/sr/clanak/825/Tema-nedelje/Odumiranje-cirilice/IVAN-KLAJN#! (last access: 3/11/2021).

Köksal Y. 2006. "Minority Policies in Bulgaria and Turkey: The Struggle to Define a Nation". *Southeast European and Black Sea Studies* 6 (4): 501-521.

Koneva, P. 2011. *Иван Шишманов и Обединена Европа*. Sofia: IK Gutenberg.

Kordić, S. 2010. *Jezik i nacionalizam*. Zagreb: Durieux.

Kramer C., Ivković D. & Friedman V. "Seeing Double: Latin and Cyrillic in Linguistic Landscape". In Зборник на трудови од меѓународната конференција за применета лингвистика, edited by Mitkovska, L. Skopje: Fon University: 14-20.

Krstitch, Dragolioub. 1924. *Les minorités, l'État et la communauté internationale*. Paris: Librairie Arthur Rousseau.

Kumnova M. & Shabani, F., 2009. "Obljetnica albanske zajedničke grafije". In *Hrvatski* VII (1): 69-84.

Kuševski V. D. 1983. "За појавата на Абецедарот". *Istorija* XIX (2): 179-191.

Kymlicka, W. 2002. "Multiculturalism and Minority Rights: West and East". In *Journal on ethnopolitics and minority issues in Europe* 4: 1-27.

Landry, R. & Bourhis R. Y. 1997. "Linguistic Landscape and Ethnolinguistic Vitality. An Empirical Study". In *Journal of language and Social Psychology* 16 (1): 23-49.

Langston, K. & Peti-Stantić, A. P. 2014. *Language Planning and National identity in Croatia*. New York: Palgrave Macmillan.

Latcheva, R. 2010. "Nationalism versus Patriotism, or the Floating Border? National Identification and Ethnic Exclusion in Post-communist Bulgaria". *Journal of Comparative Research in Anthropology and Sociology* 1 (2): 187-216.

Lazić, D. 2019. "Obilježavanje Dana hrvatske glagoljice i glagoljaštva u školama". *Hrvatski Jezik. Znanstveno-popularni časopis za kulturu hrvatskoga jezika* 6 (2): 14-17.

Lehfeldt, W. 2001. "L'écriture arabe chez les Slaves". *Slavica Occitania* XII: 267-282.

Lepsius. K. R. 1863. *Standard alphabet for reducing unwritten languages*. London: Williams & Norgate.

Lešaja, A. 2012. *Knjigocid. Uništavanje knjiga u Hrvatskoj 1990-ih*. Zagreb: Srpsko narodno vijeće.

Lewis, G. 1999. *The Turkish Language Reform: A Catastrophic Success*. New York: Oxford University Press.

Lomagistro, B. 2004. "Paleografia ed ideologia". In *Studi Slavistici* I: 127-138.

Lörinczi M. 1982. "Coscienza nazionale romanza e ortografia: il romeno tra alfabeto cirillico e alfabeto latino". *La Ricerca Folklorica* 5. *La scrittura: funzioni e ideologie*: 75-85.

Lory, B. 1985. *Le Sort de L'Heritage Ottoman en Bulgarie, L'Example des Villes Bulgares, 1878–1900*. Istanbul: Isis Press.

Lotman, J. M. 1985. *La Semiosfera*. Venezia: Marsilio ("О семиосфере". In *Труды по знаковым системам*, Tartu [1984]).

Lucien-Brun, J. 1923. *Le problème des minorités devant le droit international.* Paris: Editions Spes.

Lunacharski. A. "Латинизация русской письменности". *Культура и письменность Востока* 6: 20-26.

Mac Giolla Chriost, D. 2003. *Language, identity and conflict. A comparative study of language in ethnic conflict in Europe and Eurasia.* London and New York: Routledge.

Magner, T. F. 2001. "Digraphia in the territories of the Croats and Serbs". *International Journal of the Sociology of Language* 150: 11-26.

Maksoudian, F. K. 2006. *The Origins of the Armenian Alphabet and Literature.* New York: St.Vartan Press.

Malešević S. 2002. *Ideology, legitimacy and the new state: Yugoslavia, Serbia and Croatia.* London—New York: Routledge.

Malešević, S. 2004. *The sociology of ethnicity.* London: Sage.

Malešević S. 2013. *Nation-states and Nationalisms.* Cambridge—Malden: Polity.

Mancini M. & Turchetta, B. 2014. *Etnografia della scrittura.* Roma: Carocci.

Marinov, T. 2011. "National myths in post-communist Bulgaria and their criticism". In *Euxeinos* 2: 5-12.

Marinov, T. 2013. "Introduction to section one. Nations and national ideologies in the Balkans". In *Entangled Histories of the Balkans, Volume 1: National Ideologies and Language Policies*, edited by Daskalov R. & Marinov. Leiden—Boston: Brill: 3-12.

Martin, H-J. 1988. *Histoire et pouvoirs de l'écrit.* Paris: Librairie académique Perrin.

May, S. 2013. *Language and minority rights.* London: Routledge.

McLuhan M. 1976. *Galassia Gutenberg, nascita dell'uomo tipografico.* Roma: Armando Editore, (*The Gutenberg Galaxy. The Making of Typographic Man.* Toronto: Toronto University Press [1962]).

Michailidis, I. D. 1996. "Minority Rights and Educational Problems in Greek Interwar Macedonia: The Case of the Primer 'Abecedar'". *Journal of Modern Greek Studies* 14 (2): 329-343.

Michailidis, I. D. 2005. "National Identity versus Minority Language. The Greek and Bulgarian Experience in the 20th century". In *Language and identities in historical perspective*, edited by Isaacs, A. K. Pisa: Edizioni Plus Pisa University Press: 91-97.

Mishkova, D. 2015. "The Afterlife of a Commonwealth: Narratives of Byzantium in the National Historiographies of Greece, Bulgaria, Serbia and Romania". In *Entangled Histories of the Balkans, Vol. 3. Shared Pasts, Disputed Legacies*, edited by Daskalov R. & Vezenkov A. Leiden—Boston: Brill: 118-273.

Moguš M. & Vončina J. 1969. "Latinica u Hrvata". *Radovi Zavoda za slavensku filologiju* 11: 61-81.

Muyhtar, F. 2003. *The Human Rights of Muslims in Bulgaria in Law and Politics since 1878*. Sofia: Bulgarian Helsinki Committee.

Mutlu, E. & Kavanoz, S. 2010. "Mother Tongue Education of Turkish Minority in Bulgaria". In *Uluslararası Sosyal Ara tırmalar Dergisi* 3 (14): 363-384.

Nahapetyan, H. 2007. "The Turks of Bulgaria, the 5th column of Ankara". *21st Century* 1: 33-49.

Naumow, A. "Gli alfabeti slavi nelle polemiche ottocentesche—appunti". In *Studi cirillometodiani. Nel 1150° anniversario della missione tra gli Slavi dei santi Cirillo e Metodio*, edited by Stantchev, K., & Ziffer, G. Milano—Roma: Biblioteca Ambrosiana—Bulzoni Editore: 243-255

Nazor, A. 2008. *Knjiga o hrvatskoj glagoljici. 'Ja slovo znajući govorim...'*. Zagreb: Erasmus.

Neuburger, M. 2004. *The Orient Within: Muslim Minorities and the Negotiation of Nationhood in Modern Bulgaria*. London: Cornell University Press.

Nikčević, M. 2008. "Fonemi, Ś, Ź, 3, Ć, Đ u crnogorskom standardom jeziku". *Lingua Montengrina* 2: 25-40.

Nikolov, A. 2013. "'Параисторията' като феномен на прехода: преоткриването на древните българи". In *Историческият хабитус: опредметената история*, edited by Todorov, J. & Lunin, A. Sofia: Kooperacija IF-94: 24-63.

Njegovan, D. 2008. "Jedna bibliografija periodike Nezavisne države Hrvatske (1941-1945)". In *Zbornik Matice srpske za društvene nauke* 124: 127-137.

Nurmakov N. 1934. "Латинизация алфавита—орудие пролетарской революции". In *Алфавит Октября. Итоги введения нового алфавита среди народов РСФСР*, edited by Nurmakov N. Moskva—Leningrad: 3-8.

Ong, Walter J. 2009. *Oralità e Scrittura. Le tecnologie della parola*. Bologna: Mulino. (*Orality and Literacy. The Technologizing of the Word*. New York: Methuen [1982]).

Opačić, T. 2014. *Nasilje i nesnošljivost prema Srbima u 2014*. Zagreb: Srpsko narodno vijeće i Vijeće srpske nacionalne manjine Grada Zagreba.

Palmieri, A. 1913. "L'antagonismo greco-bulgaro nel campo politico e religioso". *Rivista Internazionale di Scienze Sociali e Discipline Ausiliarie* 61 (242): 145-165.

Panayotov, R. V. 2014. Опитът да бъде заменена кирилицата с латиницата: езикът и писмеността като обект и средство за психотронно въздействие: невежество, престъпно съглашателство и продажност подпомагат противниците на българския дух. Sofia: Simolini 94.

Parmeggiani Dri, A. 2005. *Scritti Sulla Pietra. Voci ed Immagini dalla Bosnia ed Erzegovina fra Medioevo ed Età Moderna*. Udine: Forum.

Peeva, P. 2015. "Bulgarian-Russian relations in the context of global powers' geopolitical strategies in the Balkans". *International Journal of Arts & Sciences* 8(4): 537-546.

Pentzopoulos, D. 2002. *The Balkan exchange of minorities and its impact on Greece*. London: Hurst & Co. [1962].

Petrucci, A. 2002. *Prima lezione di Paleografia*. Roma: Laterza.

Peyró, M. 2016. "The world of writing". In *Escriptures, simbols, paraules, poders*, edited by Peyró, M. Barcelona: Museu de cultures del Mon: 192-204.

Picchio, R. 1991. "Slavia ortodossa e Slavia romana". In *Letteratura della Slavia ortodossa (IX-XVIII sec.)*, edited by Picchio, R. Bari: Dedalo: 7-83.

Raynov V. 2005. "Изображението като нажало на нова изказност в езика". In *Balgarski Ezik* 3: 5-11.

Raynov V., Mircheva E. & Kostadinova P. 2008: Съвременният български книжовен език и българската държава. In *Balgarski ezik i Literatura* 1 (electronic version) https://liternet.bg/publish22/v_rajnov/syvremenniiat.htm (last access: 3/11/2021).

Rallo, M. 2004. *Bulgaria e Macedonia (1919-1945)*. Roma: Europa Libreria editrice.

Rechel, B. 2009. "Bulgaria. Minority rights 'light'". In *Minority Rights in Central and Eastern Europe*, edited by Rechel, B. London -New York: Routledge: 77-89.

Reinkowski, L. 2019. "Zwischen Philologie und Ideologie: Die kyrillische Schrift im heutigen Kroatien". In *Slavic Alphabets und Identities*, edited by Kempgen, S. & Tomelleri, V. Bamberg: Bamberg University Press: 195-220.

Cultural survival report. 1995. "Nationalism in Eastern Europe Ethnic Identities in the Making: The Case of Bulgaria". In *Cultural Survival* 19 (2) (electronic version) https://www.culturalsurvival.org/publications/cultural-survival-quarterly/bulgaria/ethnic-identities-making-case-bulgaria (last access: 3/11/2021).

Richter Malabotta, M. 2004. "Semantics of War in former Yugoslavia: a response to the papers and debate". In *Language, Discourse and Borders in the Yugoslav Successor States*, edited by Busch, B., & Holmes K. Clevedon—Buffalo—Toronto: Multilingual Matters Ltd: 78-87.

Riedlmayer, A. 2007. "Crimes of War, Crimes of Peace: Destruction of Libraries during and after the Balkan Wars of the 1990s". *Library trends* 56 (1): 107-132.

Rivlina, A. 2016. "Global English-related digraphia and Roman-Cyrillic biscriptal practices". *Procedia – Social and Behavioral Sciences* 236: 207-212.

Roe, P. 2005. *Ethnic Violence and the Societal Security Dilemma.* London—New York: Routledge.

Rossi, E. 1934. "Turquie. II". In: Société des Nations. *L'adoption universelle des caractères latins. Institut international de coopération intellectuelle.* Paris: Librairie Stock: 131-140.

Rossos, A. 2008. *Macedonia and the Macedonians. A history.* Standford: Hoover.

Roudometof, V. 2002. *Nationalism, Globalization, and Orthodoxy: The Social Origins of Ethnic Conflict in the Balkans.* London: Praeger.

Safran, W. 1999. "Nationalism". In *Handbook of Language & ethnic identity*, edited by Fishman, A. J. & Garcia, O. New York: Oxford University Press: 77-93.

Said, E. 1978. *Orientalism.* London: Penguin.

Samardžija, M. 1993. *Hrvatski Jezik u Nezavisnoj Drzavi Hrcatskoj.* Zagreb: Hrvatska sveučilišna naklada.

Samardžija, M. 2008. *Hrvatski jezik, pravopis i jezična politika u Nezavisnoj Državi Hrvatskoj.* Zagreb: Hrvatska sveučilišna naklada.

Šarić & Radanović Felberg 2017. "»Cyrillic does not kill«: Symbols, identity, and memory in Croatian public discourse". *Družboslovne razprave* 33 (85): 51-71

Scarcia, G. 1999. "Da federati a protettorati (e percorsi inversi)". *Letterature di Frontiera– Littératures Frontalières* 9 (1): 179-186

Sebba, M. 2006. "Ideology and Alphabets in the former USSR". *Language Problems & Language Planning* 30 (2): 99-125.

Sebba, M. 2009. "Sociolinguistic approaches to writing systems research". *Writing Systems Research.* 1: 35-49.

Selvelli, G. 2015a. "Alphabet and Writing in the Armenian Diaspora of Plovdiv. Anthropological and Sociolinguistic Perspectives". *Mediterranean Language Review* 22: 157-188.

Selvelli, G. 2015b. "Caratteri arabi per la lingua bosniaca. Caratteri arabi per la lingua bosniaca. Esempi di scrittura fra influssi ottomani e riappropriazioni locali". In *Contatti di lingue – contatti di scritture. Multilinguismo e multigrafismo dal Vicino Oriente. Antico alla Cina contemporanea*, edited by Baglioni, D. & Tribulato, O. Venezia: Edizioni Ca' Foscari: 197-218.

Selvelli, G. 2015c. "Sistemi di scrittura, confini e identità nazionali. Uno sguardo su alcune ideologie alfabetiche in ex-Jugoslavia". In *Atti del Convegno Ca' Foscari, Venezia e i Balcani*, edited by Bellingeri, G. & Turano G. Venezia: Edizioni Ca' Foscari: 93-108.

Selvelli, G. 2015d, "Su alcuni aspetti ideologici dei sistemi di traslitterazione degli alfabeti cirillici nei Balcani". *Studi Slavistici* XII: 159-180.

Selvelli, G. 2017. "Identity and Multiplicity in Canetti's and Wagenstein's Birthplaces: Exploring the Rhizomatic Roots of Europe. *Bulgarian Studies* 1: 60-85.

Sen, S. 2009. "Cyrillization of Republika Srpska". In *The Nation in the Global Era: Conflict and Transformation*, edited by Harris, J. Boston – Leiden: Brill: 399-419.

Shivarov, S. 2008. "Bulgaristan'da Muhafıza Edilen Osmanlıca Gazeteler. Durumu, Katalog ve Dijital Çalışmaları" In *Balkan Ülkeleri Kütüphaneler Arası Bilgi-Belge Yönetim ve İşbirliği – Sempozyum Bildirileri*. Edirne: Trakya Üniversitesi Rektörlüğü: 133-139.

Silić, J. 2009. "Nikčevića crnogorksa gramatika". *Lingua Montengrina* 2: 5-13.

Simmel, G. 1904. "The Sociology of Conflict". *The American Journal of Sociology* 9 (4): 490-525.

Şimşir, B. N. 1988. *The Turks of Bulgaria. 1878-1985*. London: K. Rustem and Brother.

Şimşir, B. N. 1992. *Türk Yazı Devrimi*. Ankara: Türk Tarih Kurumu Yayınları.

Škiljan, D. 2004. "A Linguist on the Train to Vienna". In *Language, Discourse and Borders in the Yugoslav Successor States*, edited by Busch, B., & Holmes K. Clevedon – Buffalo – Toronto: Multilingual Matters Ltd: 13-20.

Smith, A. D. 2009. *Ethno-symbolism and Nationalism. A Cultural Approach*. London – New York: Routledge.

Spasov, O. 2012a "Латиница, кирилица, политика: спорът за миналото и новите медии". In *Liberalen Pregled* (online version) http://www.librev.com/index.php/discussion-culture-publisher/1628-2012-06-05-10-18-06 (last access: 3/11/2021).

Spasov, O. 2012b. "Contesting Bulgaria's Past Through *New Media*: Latin, Cyrillic and Politics". *Europe-Asia Studies* 64 (8): 1486-1504.

Stančić, N. 2005. "Grafija i ideologija: hrvatski narod, hrvatski jezik i hrvatska latinica Ljudevita Gaja 1830. i 1835. godine". *Rad Hrvatske akademije znanosti i umjetnosti/ Razred za društvene znanosti*. 492 (43): 261-296.

Stantchev, K. 2014. "La questione dell'alfabeto e la questione dell'identità etno-linguistica, confessionale e politico-culturale nel mondo slavo. Lineamenti per un progetto di ricerca". In *Studi cirillometodiani. Nel 1150° anniversario della missione tra gli Slavi dei santi Cirillo e Metodio*, edited by Stantchev, K., & Ziffer, G. Milano—Roma: Biblioteca Ambrosiana—Bulzoni Editore: 123-138.

Starshenov S. G. 1933. *Ръководство за изучаване турски език с новата турска азбука: Пълна граматика с турско-български речник*. Sofia: Rahvira.

Stefanović, S. 2015. "О јавној употреби језика и писма". In *Odjeljenje za Istoriju*, edited by Emir Kusturica. Andrićev Institut: Višegrad: 109-138.

Stojanović, J. 2020. *The Development Path of the Serbian Language and Script*. Podgorica: Matica Srpska.

Strezov, G. 1926. "S. Frangoudis, l'Hellenisme en lutte contre l'Orient et l'Occident". *Makedonski Pregled* 2 (1): 140-148.

Suleiman, Y. 2004. *A War of Words: Language and Conflict in the Middle East*. Cambridge: Cambridge University Press.

Sygkelos, Y. 2011. *Nationalism from the left. The Bulgarian communist party during the Second World War and the early post-war years*. Leiden—Boston: Brill.

Tanayeva, L. 2007. "The politics of the Latin alphabet in Kazakhstan". In *The Annual of Language & Politics and Politics of Identity* 1: 79-84.

Tandarić, J. 1985. "Branko Fučić. Glagoljski natpisi". *Slovo* 35: 172-178.

Tanner, M. 2001. *Croatia, a nation forged in war*. New Haven: Yale University Press.

Tyran, K. 2019. "Deutungen kroatischer Schriftkultur: Schreibsysteme als nationale und kulturelle Symbole". In *Slavic Alphabets und Identities*, edited by Kempgen, S. & Tomelleri, V. Bamberg: Bamberg University Press: 283-297.

Todorov, T. 2008. *Teorie del simbolo*. Milano: Garzanti (*Théories du symbol*. Paris: Le Seuil [1977]).

Todorova, M. 1996. "The Ottoman legacy in the Balkans". In *Imperial Legacy: The Ottoman imprint on the Balkans and the middle East*, edited by Brown, C. L. New York: Columbia University Press: 45-77.

Todorova, M. 1997. *Imagining the Balkans*. New York: Oxford University Press.

Todorova, M. 2009. "Language, Ethnicity and Nationalism: the Bulgarian case". In *Nationalisms Today*, edited by Kamusella, T. & Jaskulowski, K. Oxford — Bern: Peter Lang: 155-198.

Tomasevich J. 2002. *War and Revolution in Yugoslavia, 1941-1945: Occupation and Collaboration*. Stanford: Stanford University Press.

Tramontano, L. 1999. "Un esempio di politica linguistica: l'Abecedar del 1925 per la minoranza slavofona in Grecia". *Littératures Frontalières* 9 (2): 303-332.

Triandafyllidou, A. 2003. *Immigrants and National Identity in Europe*. London: Routledge.

Ugrešić, D. 2004. *Ministarstvo boli*. Zagreb: Faust Vrančić.

Uluhogian, G. 1999. "Lingua e cultura scritta". In *Gli Armeni*, edited by Alpago Novello, A., Ieni, G., Manoukian, A., Pensa, A., Uluhogian, G. & Levon Zekiyan, B. Milano: Jaca Book: 115-130.

Van der Hoeven, H. 1996. *Memory of the World: Lost Memory — Libraries and Archives destroyed in the Twentieth Century*. Paris: UNESCO.

Unseth, P. 2005. "Sociolinguistic parallels between choosing scripts and languages". *Written Language and Literacy* 8 (1): 19-42.

Venezky, R. L. 1977. "Principles for the Design of Practical Writing Systems". In *Advances in the Creation and Revision of Writing Systems*, edited by Fishman, J. The Hague: Mouton: 37-54.

Vezenkov, A. 2013. "Introduction to section two: language and language policies in the Balkans". In *Entangled Histories of the Balkans, Volume One. National Ideologies and Language Policies*, edited by Daskalov R. & Marinov, T. Boston — Leiden: Brill: 333-9.

Vishniak, M.V. 1920. *La protection des droits des minorités dans les traités internationaux de 1919-1920*. Paris: J. Povolozky.

Vjolgi, B-B. 2012. "Етнонационализмът по време на демократичния преход в България- част 1. Политическият плурализъм като ефективно лечение на етническите конфликти". *Liberalen Pregled* (online version) http://librev.com/index.php/discussion-bulgaria-publisher/1839-2012-11-12-23-32-05 (last access: 3/11/2021).

Filipov Voskopoulos P. 2006. "Куса историја на Абецедарот" In *Abecedar*. Thessaloniki: Batavia: 45-56.

Wachtel, A. 1998. *Making a Nation, Breaking a Nation: Literature and Cultural Politics in Yugoslavia*. Stanford: Stanford University Press.

Wellish, H. 1978. *The Conversion of Scripts. Its Nature, History, and Utilization*. New York — Chichester — Brisbane — Toronto: John Wiley & Sons.

Wertheim, S. 2012. "Reclamation, Revalorization, and Re-Tatarization Via. Changing Tatar Orthographies". In *Orthography as Social Action: Scripts, Spelling, Identity and Power*, edited by Jaffe, A., Androutsopoulos, J., Sebba, M. & Johnson, S. Berlin: Walter de Gruyter, Berlin: 65-101.

Yeomans, R. 2013. *Visions of annihilation. The Ustasha regime and the cultural politics of fascism, 1941-1945*. Pittsburgh: University of Pittsburgh Press.

Žagar, M. 2008. *The Glagolitic Heritage of Croatian Culture*. Zagreb: Erasmus Publisher.

Zakhos-Papazahariou E. 1972. "Babel balkanique. Histoire politique des alphabets utilisés dans les Balkans". *Cahiers du monde russe et soviétique* 13 (2): 145-179.

Zbiljić, D. 2002. "Ćirilica treba da bude naša briga". In *Jezik danas. Glasilo Matice srpske za kulturu usmene i pisane reči* 6 (15): 20-23.

Zbiljić, D., & Ivanović, D. J. 2014. *Ćirilococid*. Novi Sad: Ćirilica.

Zerubavel, E. 2005. *Mappe del tempo. Memoria collettiva e costruzione sociale del passato*. Bologna: Il mulino. (*Time Maps: Collective Memory and the Social Shape of the Past*. Chicago: University of Chicago Press [2003]).

Zima, P. 1974. "Digraphia: The case of Hausa". *Linguistics* 124: 57-69.

Zürcher, E. J. 2004. *Turkey: a modern history*. London – New York: I.B.Tauris.

1. The Abecedar (1925) primer in Latin characters for the Slavic population of Aegean Macedonia, Greece.

2. Biliteracy practices in the Kingdom of Serbs, Croats and Slovenes: the 1924 book by T.K. Pogoreljski Peregud published in Zemun.

БРОД СРЕМ БЕЧ ZEMUN ORMOŽ
КОЧАНЕ ПРИЛЕП NEGOTIN VRBAS
СКОПЉЕ УЖИЦЕ BANAT PRIZREN
БЕОГРАД ШТИП ZAGREB DRINA
ПИРОТ ВУКОВАР POŽEGA RUMA
КИКИНДА НИШ TUZLA VARDAR

3. The monument to Saint Cyril and Methodius in Sofia, Bulgaria (source: author).

4. One of the few surviving examples of Ottoman Arabic public writing in Bulgaria, here in Plovdiv (source: author).

5. Commemorative marble plaque in Latin and Glagolitic in the town of Vrbnik, on the Croatian island of Krk (source: author).

6. Graffiti appeared in Zagreb against the erection of official plaques in Cyrillic in the city of Vukovar (source: Wikimedia Commons. Licensed under CC BY-SA 3.0, https://creativecommons.org/licenses/by-sa/3.0/deed.en).

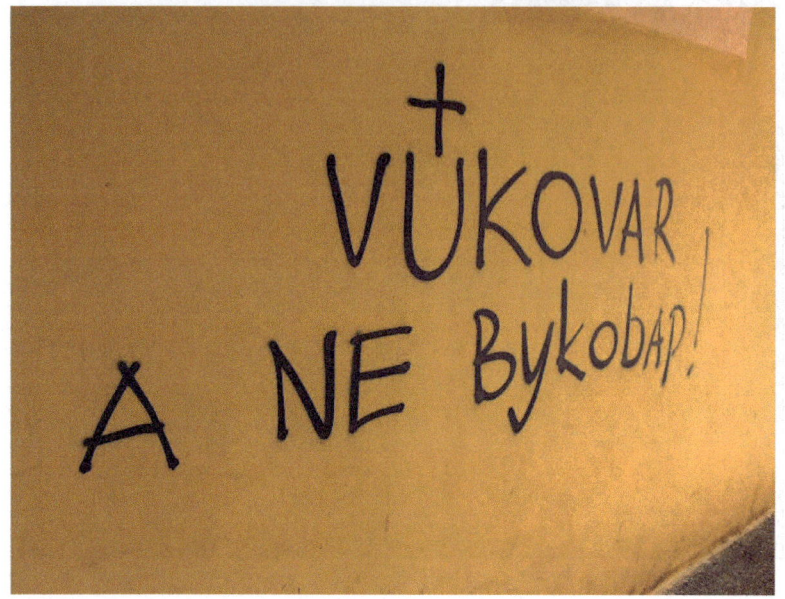

7. Cyrillic label on the Coca Cola in Bulgaria during communism (source: socbg.com).

8. Official celebrations of the May 24 festivity in Bulgaria, at Plovdiv University, 2013 (source: author).

ibidem.eu